8TH GRADE READING COMPREHENSION AND WRITING SKILLS

2nd Edition

LEARNING EXPRESS ®

NEW YORK

Library of Congress Cataloging-in-Publication Data:
8th grade reading comprehension and writing skills—Second edition.
    pages   cm
  ISBN 978-1-57685-948-3
  1. Language arts (Middle school)   I. LearningExpress (Organization)   II. Title: Eighth grade reading comprehension and writing skills.
  LB1631.A16 2013
  428.0071'2—dc23

2013037407

Printed in the United States of America

9 8 7 6 5 4 3

Second Edition

ISBN 978-1-57685-948-3

For information on LearningExpress, other LearningExpress products, or bulk sales, please write to us at:
  80 Broad Street
  Suite 400
  New York, NY 10004

Or visit us at:
  www.learningexpressllc.com

CONTENTS ▶

HOW TO USE THIS BOOK   vii

PRETEST   1

SECTION 1   **BUILDING A STRONG FOUNDATION**   19

LESSON 1   Becoming an Active Reader   21

LESSON 2   Finding the Main Idea   27

LESSON 3   Defining Vocabulary   33

LESSON 4   Distinguishing between Fact and Opinion   41

LESSON 5   Putting It All Together   49

SECTION 2   **STRUCTURE**   55

LESSON 6   The Parts of a Plot   57

LESSON 7   Organizing Principles   67

LESSON 8   Similarities and Differences: Comparison and Contrast   75

LESSON 9   Cause and Effect   83

CONTENTS

LESSON 10   Summaries and Outlines   91

LESSON 11   Putting It All Together   99

SECTION 3   **LANGUAGE AND STYLE**   **107**

LESSON 12   Point of View   109

LESSON 13   Word Choice   117

LESSON 14   Style   123

LESSON 15   Literary Devices   131

LESSON 16   Putting It All Together   139

SECTION 4   **READING BETWEEN THE LINES**   **147**

LESSON 17   Finding an Implied Main Idea   149

LESSON 18   Identifying an Author's Purpose   157

LESSON 19   Assuming Causes and Predicting Effects   163

LESSON 20   Analyzing Characters   169

LESSON 21   Putting It All Together   177

SECTION 5   **INTERPRETING NON-LITERARY SOURCES**   **185**

LESSON 22   Instructions   187

LESSON 23   Advertisements   195

LESSON 24   Graphs   205

LESSON 25   Visual Aids   213

LESSON 26   Putting It All Together   221

SECTION 6   **WRITING SKILLS**   **231**

LESSON 27   Prewriting   233

LESSON 28   Organizing Ideas   241

LESSON 29   Writing with Focus and Clarity   249

CONTENTS

LESSON 30   Reviewing and Revising   257

LESSON 31   Putting It All Together   265

POSTTEST   **273**

APPENDIX   Suggested Reading for 8th Graders   291

ADDITIONAL ONLINE PRACTICE   **295**

HOW TO USE THIS BOOK ▶

As an eighth grader, you'll be required to take tests that measure your reading, writing, and math skills. This year is also your last chance to brush up on your academic skills before you enter high school. Reading comprehension is perhaps the most important set of skills you'll need for success.

In eighth grade and beyond, you'll be asked to read, understand, and interpret a variety of texts, including stories, poems, reports, essays, and scientific and technical information. While a lot of your learning will still take place in the classroom, you'll be expected to read more outside of class. You'll need not only to understand what you read but also to respond to and assess it. And as the texts you read become more complex, you'll spend a lot more time "reading between the lines" and drawing your own conclusions from the text. As your reading skills improve, so will your writing. You'll learn to recognize and implement the techniques good writers use to communicate ideas to their readers. Fluent writers are most often frequent readers as well.

As you work through the lessons in this book you will build your critical reading, thinking, and writing skills. Each of the 31 short lessons should take about a half hour to complete. You'll start with the basics and move on to more complex reading and writing strategies. While each chapter can be an effective skill builder on its own, it is important that you proceed through this book in order, from Lesson 1 through Lesson 31. Each lesson builds on skills and ideas discussed in the previous chapters, and as your skills improve, the practice passages will become longer and more difficult.

The lessons are divided into six sections. Each section focuses on a different group of related reading comprehension strategies and skills. These strategies are outlined at the beginning of each section and reviewed at the end of the section in a special lesson, Putting It All Together.

Each lesson includes several exercises to practice the skills you have learned. At the end of each lesson you'll find answers and explanations for the practice questions so you can catch your mistakes and learn what to watch out for in the future. You'll also find a section called Skill Building until Next Time after each practice session, featuring helpful suggestions for practicing your new skills.

This book also includes a pretest and posttest. Take the pretest before you begin Lesson 1 to get a sense of your strengths and weaknesses; when those chapters come up, pay special attention to them. After you finish the lessons, take the posttest to see how much your reading comprehension has improved. You'll also find out whether there are areas in which you may still need practice.

PRETEST ▶

Before you begin, find out how developed your reading comprehension skills already are—and how much you need to improve. This pretest has 40 multiple-choice questions and one writing assignment that cover all the topics in this book. If your score is high, you may move through this book more quickly than you expected. If your score is low, you may need more than 30 minutes to get through each lesson. Either way, be thorough and go at your own pace. This book is about developing skills, not cramming for a test. Think of it like strengthening a muscle or learning to ride a bike—the more solid your foundation is, the stronger you'll be. On page 3 there is an answer sheet that you can tear out or photocopy, or you can just circle the correct answers on the page. If you don't own this book, write the numbers 1 to 40 on a sheet of paper, and write your answers next to the numbers. Then answer the writing assignment in the space given, on a sheet of lined paper, or on a computer. Take as much time as you need for this test. Use the answer key at the end of the test to check your answers. The answer explanations at the end of the test tell you which lesson covers the strategy in that question. Good luck!

1. ⓐ ⓑ ⓒ ⓓ
2. ⓐ ⓑ ⓒ ⓓ
3. ⓐ ⓑ ⓒ ⓓ
4. ⓐ ⓑ ⓒ ⓓ
5. ⓐ ⓑ ⓒ ⓓ
6. ⓐ ⓑ ⓒ ⓓ
7. ⓐ ⓑ ⓒ ⓓ
8. ⓐ ⓑ ⓒ ⓓ
9. ⓐ ⓑ ⓒ ⓓ
10. ⓐ ⓑ ⓒ ⓓ
11. ⓐ ⓑ ⓒ ⓓ
12. ⓐ ⓑ ⓒ ⓓ
13. ⓐ ⓑ ⓒ ⓓ
14. ⓐ ⓑ ⓒ ⓓ

15. ⓐ ⓑ ⓒ ⓓ
16. ⓐ ⓑ ⓒ ⓓ
17. ⓐ ⓑ ⓒ ⓓ
18. ⓐ ⓑ ⓒ ⓓ
19. ⓐ ⓑ ⓒ ⓓ
20. ⓐ ⓑ ⓒ ⓓ
21. ⓐ ⓑ ⓒ ⓓ
22. ⓐ ⓑ ⓒ ⓓ
23. ⓐ ⓑ ⓒ ⓓ
24. ⓐ ⓑ ⓒ ⓓ
25. ⓐ ⓑ ⓒ ⓓ
26. ⓐ ⓑ ⓒ ⓓ
27. ⓐ ⓑ ⓒ ⓓ
28. ⓐ ⓑ ⓒ ⓓ

29. ⓐ ⓑ ⓒ ⓓ
30. ⓐ ⓑ ⓒ ⓓ
31. ⓐ ⓑ ⓒ ⓓ
32. ⓐ ⓑ ⓒ ⓓ
33. ⓐ ⓑ ⓒ ⓓ
34. ⓐ ⓑ ⓒ ⓓ
35. ⓐ ⓑ ⓒ ⓓ
36. ⓐ ⓑ ⓒ ⓓ
37. ⓐ ⓑ ⓒ ⓓ
38. ⓐ ⓑ ⓒ ⓓ
39. ⓐ ⓑ ⓒ ⓓ
40. ⓐ ⓑ ⓒ ⓓ

Reading

Directions: Read each passage below carefully and actively. Answer the questions that follow each passage.

Ecosystems

(1) An ecosystem is a group of animals and plants living in a specific region and interacting with one another and with their physical environment. Ecosystems include physical and chemical components, such as soils, water, and nutrients. These components support the organisms living in the ecosystem. Ecosystems can also be thought of as the interactions among all organisms in a given habitat including humans. These organisms may range from large animals to microscopic bacteria and work together in various ways. For example, one species may serve as food for another. Human activities, such as housing developments and trash disposal, can greatly harm or even destroy local ecosystems. Proper ecosystem management is crucial for the overall health and diversity of our planet. We must find ways to protect local ecosystems without stifling economic development.

1. Which sentence best expresses the main idea of this passage?
    a. Our actions can have a great impact on our ecosystems.
    b. Ecosystems have been badly managed in the past.
    c. Humans must clean up their trash.
    d. Ecosystems interact with one another.

2. Which of the following best sums up the activities within an ecosystem?
    a. predator–prey relationships
    b. interactions among all members
    c. human–animal interactions
    d. human relationship with the environment

3. An ecosystem can most accurately be defined as
    a. a specific place.
    b. a community of plants and animals.
    c. a group of animals working together.
    d. a protected environment.

The Story of Dr. Mudd

(1) On the night of April 14, 1865—five days after the Civil War ended—President Abraham Lincoln was attending the theater in Washington, D.C. In the middle of the performance, an actor named John Wilkes Booth, seeking to avenge the defeat of the South, slipped into the presidential box and shot the president.

(2) Booth broke his leg when he leaped from the president's box seat to the stage. Before anybody could stop him, he limped out the back door, mounted a waiting horse, and disappeared into the night with a fellow conspirator.

(3) Five hours later, at four o'clock in the morning, Booth and his companion arrived at the home of Samuel Mudd, a doctor living in southern Maryland. Dr. Mudd knew nothing about the assassination of the president. Acting as any doctor would with a stranger in distress, he set the leg and persuaded the two travelers to stay in his house for the rest of the night. The next morning, Booth and his friend, using false names, paid the bill and departed.

(4) Because of this merciful act, Dr. Mudd was arrested, taken to Washington, and tried on the charge that he was a friend of Booth's and therefore helped plan the assassination. Dr. Mudd insisted that he knew nothing of the plot. But the military courts, angry at the president's death, sentenced the unfortunate doctor to life imprisonment.

(5) Dr. Mudd was imprisoned at Fort Jefferson, an island fortress about 120 miles west of the southern tip of Florida.

(6) As horrible and unjust as this punishment must have been, a greater plight lurked at Fort Jefferson. The warm, humid climate was a perfect breeding ground for mosquitoes. Again and again, these pests spread yellow fever germs to prisoners and guards alike.

(7) When the fever struck, Dr. Mudd volunteered his services, because he was the only doctor on the island. He had to fight the disease, even after he was infected himself. In spite of the fact that the guards and other inmates called him "that Lincoln murderer," and treated him very badly, he worked hard to fight the disease.

(8) Meanwhile, his wife was working heroically back in Washington for her husband's cause. After a four-year struggle, she secured a pardon for him—for a crime he never committed.

(9) Dr. Mudd returned to Maryland to pick up the pieces of his shattered life. Soon after Dr. Mudd's release, Fort Jefferson was abandoned. Today, the one-time prison is accessible to visitors as part of Dry Tortugas National Park.

4. What was the cause of Dr. Mudd's conviction?
   a. He helped Booth assassinate Lincoln.
   b. He helped Booth get away.
   c. The military courts wanted someone to pay for Lincoln's death.
   d. He lied to the military courts.

5. An alternative title for this passage might be
   a. Lincoln's Assassination.
   b. Good Doc Gone Bad.
   c. A Prison Abandoned.
   d. An Unfair Trial for a Fair Man.

6. What sort of doctor was Dr. Mudd?
   a. careless, sloppy
   b. generous, caring
   c. greedy, money-hungry
   d. cold-hearted, unfeeling

7. Dr. Mudd fought the yellow fever outbreak at Fort Jefferson because
   a. there was no one else to treat the sick prisoners.
   b. he thought it would help get him a pardon.
   c. he didn't want to get sick himself.
   d. he was forced to by the prison warden.

8. Read this sentence from the essay.

> As horrible and unjust as this punishment must have been, a greater plight lurked at Fort Jefferson.

As it is used in this passage, *plight* most nearly means

a. challenge.
b. difficulty.
c. scare.
d. sickness.

Year-Round School versus Regular School Schedule

Both year-round school and regular school schedules are found throughout the United States. With year-round school schedules, students attend classes for nine weeks and then have three weeks' vacation. This continues all year long. The regular school schedule requires that students attend classes from September to June, with a three-month summer vacation at the end of the year. This schedule began because farmers needed their children at home to help with crops during the summer. Today, most people work in businesses and offices. Year-round school is easier for parents who work in businesses and don't have the summer to be with their children. The regular school schedule is great for kids who like to have a long summer vacation. While some educational systems have changed their schedules to keep up with their population, others still use the old agrarian calendar. Both systems have disadvantages and advantages, which is why schools use different systems.

Comparison of U.S. School Schedules

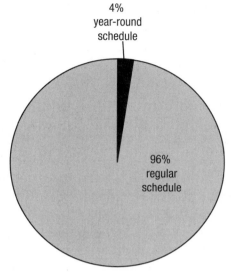

In the United States, only 4% of schools currently use a year-round schedule, but the number has risen steadily in the last 20 years.

9. What percentage of schools in the United States use a year-round schedule?
a. 96%
b. 4%
c. more than 20%
d. less than 4%

10. The author feels that
a. each school should decide what schedule to follow.
b. year-round school is better.
c. both year-round and regular school schedules have different advantages and disadvantages.
d. the regular school schedule is better.

11. The main organizing principle of this passage is
  a. chronology.
  b. order of importance.
  c. comparison and contrast.
  d. cause and effect.

A Sibling Rivalry
You will need to know the following words as you read the story:

tandem: working together
maneuver: make a series of changes in direction

(1) The man with the bullhorn encouraged the runners as they made their way up the hill. "Two hours, fifteen minutes, forty seconds." His deep, amplified voice boomed toward us.

(2) It was mile 17 of the marathon.

(3) "Hey, great stride!" a bearded spectator yelled to me. He clapped loudly. "You're looking strong. Keep going—go, go, go!"

(4) You betcha I'm looking strong, I thought, as I followed my younger sister, Laura. I had just gotten started. She had been diligently clocking eight-minute miles since the race had begun downtown. Initially in the middle of a pack, which was several thousand people, she had been steadily passing other runners for the past ten miles or so. We were now on the relatively steep rise to the St. Cecelia Bridge. Once we crossed, we would begin heading back into town, running along the east side of the Rincon River. Laura had asked me to run the most difficult section of the marathon with her. Not having trained for anything more challenging than a brisk walk and with no experience running in organized events, I figured I might be good for two or three miles.

(5) Despite our running in tandem, we were taking different approaches to the event. Laura was on an aggressive tack, maneuvering quickly through the slowing pack of runners.

She began calling out "On your left, sir" and "Excuse me" as she doggedly yet gracefully attacked the rising slope approaching the bridge. Keeping up with her was no small feat. On one hand, I felt like saying to her, Wait up! On the other hand, I knew that a timely finish would be a personal record for her.

(6) Up ahead, steel drums were playing. A group of percussionists was pounding out rhythms, chanting, and encouraging us with their music and smiles. Crossing the bridge, I recalled the advice in the Marathon Handbook to be sure to spit off of the steely span. During my preview of the route, it had seemed like a juvenile thing to do. But now it seemed like a fine idea, and I spat magnificently over the side of the bridge.

(7) "I read the handbook, too!" trumpeted a triumphant woman behind me, who also let loose over the side of the bridge. We had now initiated a chain reaction of subsequent bridge spitters. It was quite a sight, but I had other things to occupy my attention, namely the back of Laura's jersey.

(8) Easing off the bridge and heading south on Avila Boulevard, Laura and I found our pace together again. Here we could hang to the left of the group and enjoy some brief conversation. "You keeping up okay?" she asked. Being her older brother, and therefore unable to admit weakness, I nodded convincingly.

(9) "Hey, Lee!" yelled a waving man on the sidewalk. Immediately pleased that my marathon efforts had been recognized by someone I knew, I waved back and reflected on the importance of wearing tie-dyed clothing to a road race of this size. It made it a lot easier to be spotted!

(10) The town marathon is a "people's" marathon in that it tends to be a family affair, with the runners and spectators creating a festive atmosphere instead of a competitive

one. The crowds are demonstrably vocal and supportive all day, which means a lot to the participants. I managed to run six miles before bowing out, and Laura finished the entire race in under four hours.

(11) I now pride myself on telling people that I ran in a marathon. The distinction between having run a marathon and having run in a marathon seems unimportant. If pressed, however, I'll admit that I only ran one-fourth.

(12) Inspired by this year's experience, I plan to walk the entire course—really fast—next year. It's not because I'm jealous of my sister's accomplishment. This is not some silly sibling rivalry in which I must do whatever she does. But Laura got free cookies at the finish line, and the promise of that will lead me to any goal.

12. This story is told from the point of view of
   a. Laura.
   b. Lee.
   c. both Laura and Lee.
   d. an unidentified, third-person narrator.

13. Read these sentences from the story. Below them are four definitions of **tack**. Which one describes the meaning of the word as used in this section of the passage?

> Laura was on an aggressive tack, maneuvering quickly through the slowing pack of runners. She began calling out "On your left, sir" and "Excuse me" as she doggedly yet gracefully attacked the rising slope approaching the bridge.

   a. a sharp, pointed nail
   b. something that attaches
   c. a sticky or adhesive quality
   d. a zigzag movement

14. What happened immediately after Lee spit over the side of the bridge?
   a. Laura was embarrassed.
   b. A woman spat over the bridge.
   c. Lee apologized for his manners.
   d. Lee saw someone that he knew.

15. Why did the author write this story?
   a. to explain how marathons are won
   b. to tell about the history of marathons
   c. to tell a story about a marathon experience
   d. to show how difficult running in a marathon can be

16. Why was Lee glad he wore a tie-dyed shirt?
   a. It helped people locate him easily.
   b. The shirt brought him good luck.
   c. It added to the festival atmosphere.
   d. The shirt was a favorite of Laura's.

17. What part of the marathon did Laura ask Lee to run?
   a. the last six miles
   b. the downhill section
   c. the most difficult section
   d. the last two to three miles

18. At next year's marathon, Lee plans to
   a. run half of the course.
   b. beat his sister Laura.
   c. walk the race really fast.
   d. improve his time.

19. Which of the following words best describes Laura as she is presented in this passage?
   a. competitive
   b. foolish
   c. comical
   d. carefree

20. The author wants the reader to think that Lee
  a. is too aggressive.
  b. has little self-confidence.
  c. has a future as a runner.
  d. is a good-natured brother.

21. Lee tells Laura that he's keeping up okay because
  a. he doesn't want her to think he can't keep up with her.
  b. he is always lying to her.
  c. he really is doing okay.
  d. he wants to motivate her.

22. Which event is the *climax* of the passage?
  a. Laura finishes the race.
  b. Lee spits over the bridge.
  c. Lee gets recognition from the crowd as he runs.
  d. Laura and Lee begin the race.

Journey to a New Life

For hundreds of years, people have come to the United States from other countries seeking a better life. One of the first sights to greet many immigrants is the Statue of Liberty. This is the story of Tatiana and her journey to the United States.

(1) In 1909, when Tatiana was just 11 years old, her parents and older brother traveled to the United States. Because the family could not afford to buy her a ticket, she had to remain in Russia. She had lived with her uncle and cousins for almost a year in a small and crowded house before the special letter arrived from her father. "Dear Tatiana," he wrote. "At last we have earned enough money to pay for your ticket. After you join us in New York, we will travel by train to a place called South Dakota where we have bought a farm."

(2) A week later, Tatiana's uncle took her into the city of St. Petersburg and, using the money her father had sent, bought her a ticket for the *Louisa Jane*, a steamship that was leaving for America. Tatiana clutched her bag nervously and walked up the ramp onto the steamship that would be her home until she reached America. She listened to the ship's whistle give a piercing blast and then leaned over the railing to wave good-bye to her uncle.

(3) Although she was lonely and missed her family, Tatiana quickly made friends with the other children aboard the *Louisa Jane*. Together, they invented games that could be played on the ship, and they ran around the decks. One afternoon, tired of being pestered with questions, the ship's engineer gave them a tour of the engines.

(4) The next day, as Tatiana was walking along the deck, she heard some of the passengers talking about the Statue of Liberty. This conversation confused her because she knew that liberty was an idea; it was intangible. No one could see or touch it, so how could you make a statue of liberty? When she asked her friend's father, Mr. Dimitrivitch, he explained that the statue looked like a woman, but it represented freedom. This explanation just made Tatiana more curious to see the statue for herself.

(5) One morning, Tatiana woke up to the sound of wild shouting. Convinced that the ship must be sinking, she grabbed her lifejacket and ran upstairs. All the passengers were crowded onto the deck, but the ship wasn't sinking. The shouts were really cries of excitement because the *Louisa Jane* had finally reached the United States. When Tatiana realized that she would soon see her family again, she joined in with shouts of her own.

(6) As the *Louisa Jane* came closer to shore, the tall figure of a woman holding a torch became visible on the horizon. The cries died away and the passengers stared in awed silence at the Statue of Liberty. Tatiana gazed at the woman's solemn face as the ship steamed past. Mr. Dimitrivitch had told her that the statue represented freedom, and she finally understood what he meant. At that moment, Tatiana knew that she was free to start her new life.

23. For Tatiana, the Statue of Liberty was a symbol of
   a. a new beginning.
   b. interesting ideas.
   c. the excitement of traveling.
   d. the ability to earn money.

24. Which words in the story tell the reader that these events took place long ago?
   a. "stared in awed silence at the Statue of Liberty"
   b. "a steamship that was leaving for America"
   c. "she was lonely and missed her family"
   d. "Tatiana's uncle took her into the city"

25. The engineer showed the children the ship's engines because
   a. he was tired of answering their many questions.
   b. the parents asked him to amuse their children.
   c. Tatiana had asked him to do so.
   d. the tour was included in the price of the tickets.

26. The best way to learn more about the kind of ship described in this story would be to
   a. ask someone who builds sailboats.
   b. read a book about the immigrants in New York.
   c. visit a port where large ships dock.
   d. look in an encyclopedia under Steamships.

27. Which emotion did the passengers on the ship feel when they saw the statue?
   a. excitement
   b. awe
   c. loneliness
   d. regret

28. Which of the following statements best summarizes the story?
   a. Tatiana traveled to the United States.
   b. Tatiana, a Russian girl, had an amazing journey by steamship to America.
   c. Many Russian families moved to America in the 1900s.
   d. In 1909, a young Russian girl traveled to America to join her family.

Excerpt from "First," a Short Story

(1) First, you ought to know that I'm "only" fourteen. My mother points this out often. I can make my own decisions when I'm old enough to vote, she says. Second, I should tell you that she's right—I'm not always responsible. I sometimes take the prize for grade-A dork. Take last weekend, for instance. I was staying at Dad's, and I decided it was time I learned to drive. It was Sunday morning, 7 a.m., and I hadn't slept well. I'd been up thinking about an argument, which I'll tell you about in a minute. Well, nobody was up yet in the neighborhood, so I thought it couldn't hurt to back the car out of the garage and drive around the block. But Dad has a clutch car. The R on the shift handle was up on the left side, right next to first gear. I guess you can guess the rest.

(2) Dad's always been understanding. He didn't say, "Okay, little Miss Know-It-All, you can just spend the rest of the year paying this off," which is what Mom would have said. Instead, Dad worried about what might have happened to me. To me. And that made me feel more guilty than anything. I think he'd be a better number-one caregiver, but I can't say things like that to Mom. To her, I have to say, "But Mom, Dad's place is closer to school. I could ride my bike."

(3) To which she replies, "Amy Lynn, you don't own a bike. Remember? You left it in the yard, and it was stolen. And you haven't got the patience to earn the money to replace it."

29. How does the narrator show how she feels about her dad and mom?
   a. through specific detail
   b. by asking questions that make a point but don't invite a direct answer
   c. through similes and metaphors
   d. by contrasting her parents' typical reactions

30. The first-person point of view in this story
   a. hides the narrator's feelings.
   b. shows the thoughts and personality of the narrator.
   c. makes the narrator seem cold and distant.
   d. lets you hear the thoughts of all the characters.

31. The narrator feels guilty because she
   a. made her dad worry.
   b. ruined the car.
   c. broke the law.
   d. didn't tell her mom about the car incident.

32. The narrator says she "sometimes take[s] the prize for grade-A dork." This word choice means to show
   a. that she doesn't know proper English.
   b. that she can't judge her own actions.
   c. her age and culture.
   d. that she thinks she's better than other dorks.

33. The quotation marks around "only" suggest that the narrator
- **a.** is almost fifteen.
- **b.** thinks fourteen is old enough for some things.
- **c.** wishes she were older.
- **d.** thinks fourteen is a lousy age.

34. The narrator's tone is
- **a.** emotional and familiar.
- **b.** stuck-up and superior.
- **c.** angry and sad.
- **d.** pleasant and charming.

35. The main conflict between the narrator and her mother is about whether she
- **a.** can make her own decisions.
- **b.** should live with her mom or her dad.
- **c.** should be allowed to drive.
- **d.** should pay for things she loses or breaks.

36. The narrator's mom thinks the narrator is
- **a.** too attached to her dad.
- **b.** too emotional.
- **c.** too shy.
- **d.** irresponsible.

37. The narrator feels that her mom
- **a.** is too busy to care for her.
- **b.** should never have divorced her dad.
- **c.** makes too many rules.
- **d.** cares more about things than about people.

38. What most likely happened with the car?
- **a.** The narrator put the car in first gear instead of reverse. She ran into the garage wall.
- **b.** The narrator backed out of the driveway and into a neighbor's car.
- **c.** The narrator left the car in gear when she was finished. When her dad started the car, he ran into the garage wall.
- **d.** The narrator broke the clutch while trying to shift gears.

MIDLAND ADVENTURE GYM RATES		
	AGE 12 AND UNDER	ADULTS
Day Pass	$8	$12
Monthly Pass	$28	$36
Annual Pass	$125	$150

Midland Adventure Gym

If you like climbing, jumping on trampolines, or learning cool gymnastic tricks, you should call Midland Adventure Gym. With two giant trampolines, a foam pit, parallel bars, and two complete walls for rock climbing, we've got plenty of adventure for you. Professional instructors offer weekly classes or private lessons to build your skills. Or, consider Midland Adventure Gym for your next birthday party! Come explore the gym with a day pass, or become a privileged member with a monthly or annual pass. Stop by Midland Adventure Gym today!

39. What type of text is this?
- **a.** instructions
- **b.** informative
- **c.** an advertisement
- **d.** a narrative

40. How much does a monthly adult pass cost?
- **a.** $28
- **b.** $12
- **c.** $32
- **d.** $36

Composition

The four seasons of the year are characterized by different kinds of weather and activities. Which season is your favorite and why? Write a focused paragraph with a clear thesis and several supporting statements.

my favorite was. the "Midland Adventure Gym" well cause I love the gym and I do workout near the gym and doing activites with the gym is my favorite that is why I get A's in those subjects LOL, What I have plannig is In Agust I am going to workout every day to get stronger in th future hahaha cause you know I migh go up to tagl (top age group) next year that is why I am very thankful for the gym thehk you dear gym.

Answers

If you missed any of the questions, you can find help with that kind of question in the lesson(s) shown to the right of the answer.

QUESTION	ANSWER	LESSON	QUESTION	ANSWER	LESSON
1	a	2, 17	21	a	1, 19
2	b	1, 2	22	c	6
3	b	1, 2	23	a	17
4	c	9, 19	24	b	1, 13
5	d	2	25	a	19
6	b	20	26	d	1, 4
7	a	9, 20	27	b	13, 17
8	b	3	28	d	10
9	b	24	29	d	8, 17
10	c	2	30	b	12
11	c	8	31	a	17
12	b	12	32	c	13
13	d	3	33	b	13, 14
14	b	1, 7	34	a	15
15	c	17, 18	35	a	17, 19
16	a	1, 4	36	d	17
17	c	1, 4	37	d	17
18	c	20	38	a	19
19	a	13	39	c	22, 23
20	d	13, 17	40	d	25

Compositions will vary, but your paragraph should have a clear thesis and support. Here is one possible response:

> My favorite season of the year is autumn because it's nice outside, school starts, and I get to play soccer. I love the fall weather. It's not as hot as it is in summer, and the leaves turn colors. When it gets chilly at night we can have campfires! I also like autumn because school starts. Sometimes school is boring, but I really have fun seeing my friends every day. I also like learning new things, especially in art class. Soccer season is in the autumn, and soccer is my favorite sport. I play forward, and last year my team was really good. I enjoy the competition and teamwork that I get in soccer. I have fun in all the different seasons, but autumn is definitely my favorite.

✔ Can you identify your main idea?

✔ What evidence or information supports your main idea?

✔ Is there an organizing principle? How did you choose what information to put in what order?

✔ Ask a friend or adult to check for spelling or grammar errors.

1 ▶ BUILDING A STRONG FOUNDATION

1 ▶ BECOMING AN ACTIVE READER

LESSON SUMMARY

The most important thing you can do to improve your reading skills is to become an active reader. This lesson shows you how to read carefully and actively so that you can better understand and remember what you read.

f you want to earn a high score on a video game, you need to concentrate all of your attention on the game. You need to watch the whole screen carefully and look out for what's coming up ahead. You need to look for certain clues and be able to predict what will happen when you press a button or activate a lever. In other words to win, you need to be fully engaged with the game.

The formula for active reading sounds a lot like that.

To understand and remember what you read, you need to be involved with what you are reading. In other words, you need to be an active reader. People often think of reading as a passive activity. After all, you're just sitting there, looking at words on a page. But when you read, you should actually be *interacting with* the text.

Five specific strategies will help you become an active reader:

1. survey ahead and jumping back
2. highlighting or underlining key words and ideas
3. looking up unfamiliar vocabulary words
4. recording your questions and comments
5. looking for clues throughout the text

Survey Ahead and Jump Back

Surveying enables you to see what's coming up. Before you begin reading, scan the text to see what's ahead. Is the text broken up into sections? What are the main topics of those sections? In what order are they covered? What key words or ideas are boldfaced, bulleted, boxed, or otherwise highlighted?

> Reading quickly through a text before you read helps you prepare for your reading task. It's a lot like checking out a map before a cross-country road trip. If you know what's ahead, you know how to pace yourself. This head start will give you an idea of what's important in the passage you're about to read.

When you finish reading, **jump back**. Review the summaries, headings, and highlighted information. (This includes both what you and the author highlighted.) Jumping back helps you remember the information you just read. You can see how each idea fits into the whole and how ideas and information are connected.

Exercise 1

Just to test yourself, skim ahead through Lesson 2. Look at the summaries, headings, and other reading aids. Answers appear at the end of this chapter. Then answer the questions below.

1. What is the main thing you will learn in Lesson 2?

Review the summaries headings and
highlighted information

2. What are the main topics of Lesson 2?

Jumping back to read
and the key words.

3. What key words or phrases are defined in Lesson 2?

headings and highlights.

Finding Key Words and Ideas

In any text, some facts and ideas are more important than others. To be an active reader, you need to identify key ideas. Of course, to highlight key words and ideas, you must be able to determine which facts and ideas are most important. Ask yourself: What's the most important information to understand and remember? By highlighting or underlining the key words and ideas, you'll make important information stand out. You'll also make it easier to find that information when you want to write a summary or to study for an exam.

Here are two guidelines for highlighting or underlining a text (you'll learn a lot more about this in the next lesson when you learn how to determine the main idea):

1. Be selective. If you highlight four sentences in a five-sentence paragraph, you haven't helped yourself at all. The key is to identify what's most important in that passage. Ask yourself these questions:

   a. What is the author trying to say and what is the main idea of his or her passage?

   b. What information is emphasized or seems to stand out as important?

   c. What words or phrases will help you remember the larger concepts?

   You can also highlight information that you find particularly interesting.

2. **Watch for clues** that indicate an idea is important. Words and phrases like *most important, the key is,* and *significantly* signal that key information will follow. Watch for visual clues, too. Key words and ideas are often **boldfaced**, <u>underlined</u>, or *italicized*. They may be boxed in or repeated in a sidebar.

Exercise 2

Lesson 2 will show you how to identify topic sentences and main ideas. Meanwhile, you can do your best and practice looking for verbal and visual clues.

Read the paragraph below, twice, and highlight the most important information.

Wind Chill Factor

People have known for a long time that they feel colder when the wind is blowing. The reason for this is simple. The faster the wind blows, the faster your body will lose heat. To educate the public, scientists in Antarctica performed experiments and developed a table to give people a better idea of how cold they would feel outside when the wind was blowing. This is important because prolonged exposure to cold temperatures can be dangerous.

Look Up Unfamiliar Words

Looking up unfamiliar words is another very important active reading strategy. You need to know what the words mean to understand what someone is saying. After all, a key word or phrase can change the meaning of a whole passage.

Whenever possible, have a dictionary with you when you read. Circle and look up any unfamiliar words right away. (Circling them makes them easier to find if you lose your place.) Write the meaning in the margin. That way, you won't have to look up the meaning again if you forget it; it will always be there to refer to. (Of course, if you don't own the book, don't write in it! Instead, write down the vocabulary word and its definition in a notebook.)

If you don't have a dictionary with you, try to figure out what the word means. What clues does the author provide in that sentence and surrounding sentences? Mark the page number or write down the word somewhere so you can look it up later. See how closely you were able to guess its meaning. (You'll learn more about this in Lesson 3.)

Exercise 3

Read the paragraph below carefully. Circle any unfamiliar words, and then look them up in the dictionary. Write their meanings below or in the margins. Then reread the paragraph to fully understand its meaning.

We'd just moved to South Mountain, and I didn't know anyone in the neighborhood. On my first day at South Mountain High, I was petrified. I'm shy to begin with, you know, so you can imagine how I felt walking into that strange school. I wore my favorite outfit to bolster my confidence, but it didn't help much. It seemed like everyone was staring at me, but it was probably just my imagination running rampant, as usual. In fact, I thought I was imagining things when I walked into my new homeroom. I couldn't believe my eyes! There, sitting in the front row, was Maggie Rivers, my best friend from Oakwood Elementary School.

Record Your Questions and Comments

As you read, you're bound to have questions and comments. You're also likely to have reactions to the reading. You might wonder why the author used a certain example, or you might think a particular description is beautiful. Write your questions and comments in the margin (or on a separate piece of paper if the book is not yours) using a code like this one:

Place a **?** in the margin if you have a question about the text or if there is something that you don't understand.

Place a **✔** in the margin if you agree with what the author wrote.

Place an **X** in the margin if you disagree with what the author wrote.

Place a **+** if you see connections between the text and other texts you have read, or if you understand the experience being described. It may also help you to write additional notes to help you remember the connection.

Place an **!** in the margin if you are surprised by the text or the writer's style.

Place a **☺** in the margin if there is something you read that you like about the text or the style.

Place a box around something you read that you don't like about the text or the style.

This kind of note taking keeps you actively involved with your reading. It makes you think more carefully about what you read—and that means you will better understand and remember the material.

Here's an example of how you might respond to the Wind Chill Factor passage:

People have known for a long time that they
+ feel colder when the wind is blowing. The
reason for this is simple. The faster the wind
✔ blows, the faster your body will lose heat. To
educate the public, scientists in Antarctica
performed experiments and developed a table
to give people a better idea of how cold they
would feel outside when the wind was blowing.
? This is important because **prolonged** exposure
to cold temperatures can be dangerous.

As you used this shorthand, you would know that:

The **+** next to the second line means that you remember the cold temperatures on your school ski trip last February.

The **✔** next to the fourth line means that you know that cold winds make your body lose heat.

The box around "table" in the sixth line means that you wish the author had included the table to make the point more clear.

The **?** next to the ninth line means that you don't know how long is "prolonged."

Exercise 4

Reread the passage from Exercise 3, reprinted here. Record your own questions and comments.

We'd just moved to South Mountain, and I didn't know anyone in the neighborhood. On my first day at South Mountain High, I was petrified. I'm shy to begin with, you know, so you can imagine how I felt walking into that strange school. I wore my favorite outfit to bolster my confidence, but it didn't help much. It seemed like everyone was staring at me, but it was probably just my imagination running rampant, as usual. In fact, I thought I was imagining things when I walked into my new homeroom. I couldn't believe my eyes! There, sitting in the front row, was Maggie Rivers, my best friend from Oakwood Elementary School.

Looking for Clues

We've already mentioned the word *clues* a couple of times in this lesson. That's because good readers are a lot like detectives. They don't read just to get through a passage; they pay careful attention to words and details, much like Sherlock Holmes would do if he were solving a mystery. Detectives look for clues that will help them better understand the writer's ideas. These clues come in many forms:

- specific word choice and details
- repeated words or phrases
- the structure of sentences or paragraphs

The key to finding these clues is to *look carefully*. Be observant. As you read, keep your eyes open. Look at not just what the writer is saying, but also *how* he or she says it. *Notice* the words he or she uses. Consider how the ideas are organized, or how else they might have been presented.

Being observant is essential for reading success. People draw conclusions (make *inferences*) about what they read, and sometimes those conclusions are wrong. Usually this means that they just didn't read carefully enough. They didn't notice the clues the writer left for them, and they based their conclusions on their own ideas. But conclusions should be based on the ideas that are there in the text.

The rest of this book will give you specific strategies for recognizing these clues.

Summary

Active reading is the key to reading success. Active readers use the following strategies:

- skimming ahead and jumping back
- highlighting or underlining key words and ideas
- looking up unfamiliar vocabulary words
- recording their questions and comments
- looking for clues not just in what the writer says, but in how he or she says it

Answers

Exercise 1

1. The main thing you will learn in Lesson 2 is how to identify the main idea of a passage.
2. The main topics of Lesson 2 are the definitions of **main idea**, **topic sentence**, and **main ideas in paragraphs and essays**. You can tell because they are section headings.
3. The key words and phrases defined in Lesson 2 are **main idea**, **subject**, **assertion**, and **topic sentence**.

Exercise 2

You could have highlighted or underlined as follows:

People have known for a long time that they feel colder when the wind is blowing. The reason for this is simple. <u>The faster the wind blows, the faster your body will lose heat.</u> To educate the public, scientists in Antarctica performed experiments and developed a table to give people a better idea of how cold they would feel outside when the wind was blowing. This is important because <u>prolonged exposure to cold temperatures can be dangerous.</u>

The first underlined sentence is important because it explains the effect of the wind chill factor. Notice that the second underlined sentence begins with the signal phrase "This is important." This tells us that this fact, that exposure can be dangerous, is significant and should be highlighted.

Exercise 3

You circled the words *petrified*, *bolster*, and *rampant*.

- To *petrify* means to change or cause to change into a stony mass; to paralyze or stun with fear. The author of this paragraph is using the second meaning of the word.

- To *bolster* means to support or prop up; to strengthen.
- *Rampant* means unrestrained; going beyond normal limits; unchecked or excessive.

Now that you know the definitions, reread the paragraph. Does it take on a new meaning for you?

Exercise 4

Answers will vary. Here's one possibility:

<blockquote>
We'd just moved to South Mountain, and I didn't know anyone in the neighborhood. On my first day at South Mountain High, I was

+   petrified. I'm shy to begin with, you know, so you can imagine how I felt walking into that strange school. I wore my favorite outfit to

✔   bolster my confidence, but it didn't help much. It seemed like everyone was staring at me, but it

!   was probably just my imagination running
</blockquote>

rampant, as usual. In fact, I thought I was imagining things when I walked into my new homeroom. I couldn't believe my eyes! There, sitting in the front row, was Maggie Rivers, my best friend from Oakwood Elementary School.

If you use this shorthand, you would know that:

The + next to the fourth line means you understand what it means to be petrified. You may have been through a similar experience.

The ✔ next to the seventh line means that you recognize the feeling of wearing something special to feel better about things.

The ! next to the ninth line means that you are noticing that the narrator's imagination usually runs rampant.

SKILL BUILDING UNTIL NEXT TIME

Here are some ways to practice the skills you've learned in this lesson. Practice them today and for the rest of the week:

1. Write a quick note or e-mail to a friend and explain what "active reading" means. Describe the strategies that active readers use to better understand and remember what they read.
2. Develop a detective's eye. Notice the things around you. Look at the details on people's faces and clothing. Notice the names of the stores you pass on your way to school. Pay close attention to the things around you. You may be surprised at the interesting things you see that you hadn't noticed before. To test yourself, write down the names of all the stores on the block where you walk every day, or jot down the colors of all the houses on the street where you live.
3. Try your active reading strategies when you read for fun, in print or online.

2 ▶ FINDING THE MAIN IDEA

LESSON SUMMARY

Finding and understanding the main idea of a text is an essential reading skill. When you look past the facts and information and get to the heart of what the writer is trying to say, that's the main idea. This lesson will show you how to find the main idea of a passage. Then you'll learn how to distinguish the main idea from its supporting statements.

I magine that you are at a friend's home for the evening. "Here," he says, "let's watch this movie."

"Sure," you reply. "What's it about?" You'd like to know a little about what you'll be watching, but your question may not get you the answer you're looking for. That's because you've only asked about the *subject* of the film. The subject—what the movie is *about*—is only half the story. Think, for example, about all the alien invaders films that have been made. While these films may share the same general subject, what they have to say *about* the aliens (and about our response to invasion) may be very different. Each film has different ideas it wants to convey *about* the subject.

Similarly, writers write because they have something they want to write *about*, and they have something they want to say *about* that subject. They use different methods to illustrate or develop that idea. When you look beyond the facts and information to what the writer really wants to say *about* his or her subject, you're looking for the **main idea**.

Just What Is a Main Idea, Anyway?

One of the most common questions on reading comprehension exams is, "What is the main idea of this passage?" How would you answer this question for the paragraph below?

Wilma Rudolph, the child with disabilities who became an Olympic running champion, is an inspiration for us all. Born prematurely in 1940, Wilma spent her childhood battling illness, including measles, scarlet fever, chicken pox, pneumonia, and polio, a debilitating disease which at that time had no cure. At the age of four, she was told she would never walk again. But Wilma and her family refused to give up. After years of special treatment and physical therapy, 12-year-old Wilma was able to walk normally again. But walking wasn't enough for Wilma, who was determined to be an athlete. Before long, her talent earned her a spot in the 1956 Olympics, where she earned a bronze medal. In the 1960 Olympics, the height of her career, she won three gold medals.

What is the main idea of this paragraph? You might be tempted to answer "Wilma Rudolph" or "Wilma Rudolph's life." Yes, Wilma Rudolph's life is the **subject** of the passage—*who or what the passage is about*. But that's not the main idea. The **main idea** is what the writer wants to say about this subject. What is the main thing the writer says *about* Wilma's life?

Before we answer that question, let's review the definition of *main idea*:

> **Main idea:** The overall fact, feeling, or thought a writer wants to convey about his or her subject.

We call this the main idea because it is the idea that the passage *adds up to*; it's what holds all the ideas in the passage together. Now, reread the paragraph about Wilma Rudolph carefully. Which idea holds the paragraph together?

a. Wilma Rudolph was very sick as a child.
b. Wilma Rudolph was an Olympic champion.
c. Wilma Rudolph is someone to admire.

The best answer is choice **c**: Wilma Rudolph is someone to admire. This is the idea the paragraph adds up to; it's what holds all the information in the paragraph together.

This example also shows us three important characteristics of a main idea:

1. It is **general** enough to encompass all the ideas in the passage.
2. It is **specific** enough to be relevant in identifying the passage later.
3. It is an **assertion**. An assertion is a statement made by the writer.

Main Ideas Are General

The main idea of a passage must be general enough to encompass all the ideas in the passage. That is, it should be broad enough for all the other sentences in that passage to fit underneath it, like people under an umbrella. Notice that the first two options, "Wilma Rudolph was very sick as a child" and "Wilma Rudolph was an Olympic champion" are too specific to be the main idea. They aren't broad enough to cover all of the ideas in the passage, because the passage talks about both her illnesses and her Olympic achievements. Only the third answer is general enough to be the main idea of the paragraph. But it's not too general. The passage isn't about "athletes who overcame health issues," it's about Wilma Rudolph.

Exercise 1

In the group of sentences below, circle the sentence that is general enough to be a main idea.

    a. The Gold Rush began in 1849.
    b. Many people moved to California after gold was discovered.
    c. The history and population of California were shaped by the Gold Rush.
    d. The life of a gold miner was not an easy one.

Main Ideas Are Assertions

A main idea is also some kind of assertion about the subject. An assertion is a claim that something is true. An assertion, therefore, needs to be supported with specific details or evidence. Assertions can be facts (such as "Wind chills can be dangerous.") or opinions (such as "School uniforms for public school students are a bad idea."). In either case, an assertion should be supported by specific ideas, facts, and details. In other words, the main idea makes a general assertion that tells readers that something is true. The supporting sentences, on the other hand, demonstrate that it's true by providing specific facts and details.

For example, in the Wilma Rudolph paragraph, the writer makes a general assertion: "Wilma Rudolph, the child with disabilities who became an Olympic running champion, is an inspiration for us all." The rest of the sentences offer specific facts and details that prove that Wilma Rudolph is an inspirational person.

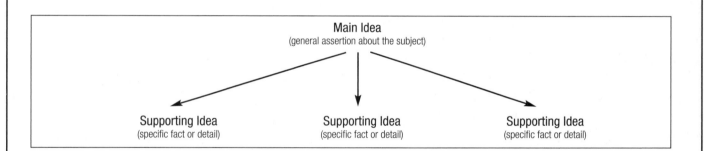

Exercise 2

Which of the following sentences are assertions that require specific evidence or support? Circle the letter of your answer choice (that's making an assertion!) and back it up by circling or writing down the specific words that convinced you it was correct (good practice for providing supporting details).

    a. Blue is a color.
    b. Blue is a calming color.
    c. Ray Bradbury is a fabulous science fiction writer.
    d. Ray Bradbury published *The Illustrated Man* in 1951.
    e. Ray Bradbury's best book is *The Illustrated Man*.

Topic Sentences

Writers often state their main ideas in one or two sentences so that readers can be very clear about the main point of the passage. A sentence that expresses the main idea of a paragraph is called a **topic sentence**. Notice, for example, how the first sentence in the Wilma Rudolph paragraph states the main idea:

> Wilma Rudolph, the child with disabilities who became an Olympic running champion, *is an inspiration for us all.*

That's why this sentence is the topic sentence for the paragraph.

Topic sentences are often found at the beginning of paragraphs, but not always. Sometimes writers begin with specific supporting ideas and lead up to the main idea. In this case, the topic sentence is often found at the end of the paragraph. Here's an example:

School is tough enough without having to worry about looking cool every single day. The less I have to decide first thing in the morning, the better. I can't tell you how many mornings I look into my closet and just stare, unable to decide what to wear. I also wouldn't mind not having to see guys wearing oversized jeans and shirts so huge they'd fit a sumo wrestler. And I certainly would welcome not seeing kids showing off designer-labeled clothes. To me, a dress code makes a lot of sense.

Notice how the last sentence in this paragraph is the only one that is general enough to cover the entire paragraph. It also tells you what the paragraph adds up to, why the details matter (they support the author's assertion). Each sentence in the paragraph provides specific support for the final assertion: A dress code is a good idea.

Sometimes the topic sentence is found somewhere in the middle. Other times there isn't a clear topic sentence at all. But that doesn't mean there isn't a main idea. It's there, but the author has chosen not to express it in a clear topic sentence. In that case, you'll have to look carefully at the paragraph for clues about the main idea. You'll learn more about this in Section 4.

Main Ideas in Paragraphs and Essays

We often talk about a text as having one main idea. But if the text has more than one paragraph, shouldn't it have as many main ideas as it has paragraphs? Yes and no. Each *paragraph* should have its own main idea. In fact, that's the definition of a paragraph: a group of sentences about the same idea. At the same time, however, each paragraph does something more: It works to support the main idea of the *entire passage*. Thus, there is an **overall main idea** (often called a **theme** or **thesis**) for the text. The main idea of *each paragraph* should work to support and develop the overall main idea of the entire text.

Here's another way to look at it. Think of a piece of writing as a table. The top of the table is the overall main idea—what the writer thinks, believes, or knows about the subject. But the table won't stand without legs to support it. In writing, those legs are the specific facts and ideas that support the overall main idea. If the text is just one paragraph, then we can think of the topic sentence as the table top and the supporting sentences as the table legs. If the text is several paragraphs (or pages) long, then each paragraph is actually its own leg. It has its own main idea and therefore needs supporting sentences of its own. The tabletop of a longer text is the overall main idea, or thesis.

Distinguishing Main Ideas from Supporting Ideas

If you're not sure whether something is a main idea or a supporting idea, ask yourself the following question: Is the sentence making a *general statement*, or is it providing *specific information*? In the school uniform paragraph, for example, all the sentences except the final one make specific statements. They are not general enough to serve as an umbrella or net for the whole paragraph.

Writers often provide clues that can help you distinguish between main ideas and their support. Here are some of the most common words and phrases used to introduce specific examples:

for example	in particular
in addition	specifically
some	furthermore
for instance	others

These signal words tell you that a su[p] fact or idea will follow. If you're having tro[uble find] ing the main idea of a paragraph, try elimi[nating sen] tences that begin with these phrases.

Exercise 3

Read the following passage carefully, using the active reading techniques from Lesson 1 and the detective skills taught in this lesson. After you read, answer the questions that follow. Keep in mind that you'll be asked to identify not only the overall main idea, but also the main ideas of individual paragraphs.

(1) At the age of six, Goran Kropp climbed his first mountain. Twenty-three years later, he tackled one of the highest mountains in the world, Mount Everest. His journey to the top shows just how independent, persistent, and determined this remarkable man is.

(2) While most people arrive at the foothills of Mount Everest by some sort of modern vehicle, Kropp bicycled 7,000 miles from his home in Sweden. Traveling by bike was not easy. Bumpy, rough roads caused mechanical problems for Kropp, and he stopped many times to repair his bike. In addition, he was chased by dogs, stung by hornets, and drenched by rain several times before he arrived at the base of the mountain.

(3) Kropp chose to climb Mount Everest the same way he traveled to the mountain: without the help of others and without modern conveniences. Unlike others, Kropp climbed not bring bottled oxygen to help him breathe at high altitudes, and he carried all his gear

ten stated in *topic sentences*. In lo[ng]
graph has a main idea (althou[gh]
[expl]itly stated), and each main i[dea]
overall main idea of the p[assage]

Exercise 1[...]

c. Choice c [...]
the main i[...]
and no[t...]
choice[...]
and [...]

1. What is the s[...]
the subjective
independent man (ra...)

2. What is the *main idea* of paragraph 2?
how driving a bike for
longer distance is not easy,

3. What is the *main idea* of paragraph 3?
That Kropp does not
need any help in life or a few

4. What is the *overall main idea* of the passage?
That soon after Kropp becam[e]
successful on his bike.

Summary

The **main idea** of a passage is the overall fact, feeling, or idea the author wants to convey about the subject. Main ideas are general enough to encompass all the ideas in the passage, but not so general you couldn't use them to identify the passage to a friend. They also make an assertion about the subject that the rest of the passage develops and supports. Main ideas are of-

...ger texts, each para-
...gh it may not be explic-
...dea works to support the
...ssage.

Answers

...s the only answer general enough to be
...dea. Choice **a** is a fact, which is too specific
...something to support with further details;
...**b** is too vague (how many people is "many"
...how long after gold was discovered did they
...ove?); choice **d** is a generality about miner life and
...is too vague to sum up the passage.

Exercise 2

b, c, e. Choices **a** and **d** are facts: they support themselves. In choice **b**, the adjective "calming" needs to be
supported with evidence; in choice **c**, calling Ray Brad-

bury "fabulous" requires some supporting evidence or
perhaps the citation of an authority; in choice **e**,
whether *The Illustrated Man* is Bradbury's "best" book
is debatable—how would you measure "best?"

Exercise 3

1. The subject is Kropp's journey to the top of
   Mount Everest.
2. The main idea of paragraph 2 is stated in the
   second sentence: "Traveling by bike was not
   easy."
3. The main idea of paragraph 2 is stated in the
   second sentence: "Traveling by bike was not
   easy." This is the only sentence in the
   paragraph that is an assertion; the others are
   all facts or details.
4. The overall main idea is stated in the topic
   sentence at the end of the first paragraph: "His
   journey to the top shows just how independent, persistent, and determined this remarkable
   man is."

SKILL BUILDING UNTIL NEXT TIME

1. As you read today and throughout the week, notice how texts are divided into paragraphs. Choose
   one paragraph from your social studies textbook and identify the topic sentence. What idea holds all
   the sentences in that paragraph together?
2. Create topic sentences about things that you come across in your day. Make general assertions
   about people, places, and things. For example, you might say, "Mrs. Elmore is a great teacher."
   Then, support your assertion. What does she do that makes her a great teacher? Provide several
   specific examples.

3 ▶ DEFINING VOCABULARY

LESSON

LESSON SUMMARY

Active readers look up unfamiliar words. But what if you don't have a dictionary? In a testing situation, for example, you almost certainly won't be able to look up words you don't know. But you can use context and word parts to help you determine meaning. This lesson shows you how.

O ften in your reading you will come across words or phrases that are unfamiliar to you. You might be lucky enough to have a dictionary handy to look up those words or phrases. But what if you don't? How can you understand what you're reading if you don't know what all the words mean? Fortunately, you can often use context to determine meaning. By looking carefully at the sentences and ideas surrounding an unfamiliar word, you can often figure out exactly what that word means. You can also examine the parts of the word, such as a prefix, suffix, or word root, for clues to the meaning.

How to Determine Meaning from Context

To demonstrate how you can use context to determine what a word means, let's begin with an example. Read the paragraph below carefully and actively.

Andy is the most unreasonable, pigheaded, subhuman life form in the entire galaxy, and he makes me so angry I could scream! Of course, I love him like a brother. I sort of have to, because he *is* my brother. More than that, he's my twin! That's right. Andy and Amy (that's me) have the same curly hair and dark eyes. Yet though we look alike, we have very different dispositions. You could say that we're opposites. While I'm often quiet and pensive, Andy is loud and doesn't seem to stop to think about anything. Oh, and did I mention that he's the most stubborn person on the planet?

As you read this passage, you may have come across at least two unfamiliar words: *dispositions* and *pensive*. While a dictionary would be helpful, you don't need to look up these words. The paragraph provides enough clues to help you figure out what these words mean.

Let's begin with *dispositions*. What is the context of this word? Let's take another look at the sentence and the two sentences that follow:

Yet though we look alike, we have very different *dispositions*. You could say that we're opposites. While I'm often quiet and *pensive*, Andy is loud and doesn't seem to stop to think about anything.

The context here offers several important clues. First, the sentence in which *dispositions* is used tells us something about what dispositions *are not*. The sentence sets up a contrast between the way that Amy and Andy look and their dispositions. This means that dispositions are *not* something physical.

Another clue is the general content of the paragraph. We can tell from the paragraph that *dispositions* have something to do with *who* Andy and Amy are, since the paragraph describes their personalities.

Yet another clue is where. Amy offers two specific examples of their dispositions: She's quiet and pensive; he's loud and doesn't seem to think much. These are specific examples of personality traits.

By now you should have a pretty good idea of what *dispositions* means. A *disposition* is

   a. a person's physical characteristics.
   b. a person's preferences.
   c. a person's natural qualities or tendencies.

The best answer, of course, is choice **c**, a person's natural qualities or tendencies. While a person's disposition often helps determine his or her preferences, this passage doesn't say anything about what Amy and Andy like to do (or not do). Nor are these characteristics physical. Amy is talking about their personalities.

Now, let's look at the second vocabulary word, *pensive*. Again, the context provides us with strong clues. Amy states that she and Andy "are opposites"—that although they look alike, she is quiet, and he is loud. Thus, we can expect that the next pair of descriptions will be opposites, too. So we simply have to look at her description of Andy and come up with its opposite. If Andy "doesn't seem to stop to think about anything," then we can assume that Amy spends a lot of time thinking. We can therefore conclude that *pensive* means

   a. intelligent, wise.
   b. deep in thought.
   c. considerate of others.

The best answer is choice **b**, deep in thought. If you spend a lot of time thinking, that may make you wise. But remember, we're looking for the opposite of Andy's characteristic, thoughtless, so neither choice **a** nor **c** can be the correct answer.

EXAM TIP

When you're trying to determine meaning from context on an exam, two strategies can help you find the best answer.

1. First, determine whether the vocabulary word is something positive or negative. If the word is something positive, then eliminate the answers that are negative, and vice versa.
2. Replace the vocabulary word with the remaining answers, one at a time. Does the answer make sense when you read the sentence? If not, you can eliminate that answer.

Exercise 1

Use context to determine the meaning of the italicized words in the sentences below. Circle the letter of the answer you think is correct.

1. He was so nervous that his voice was *quavering*.
   a. thundering, booming confidently
   b. trembling, shaking noticeably
   c. quiet, whispering softly
   d. undecided, unsure

2. By the end of eighth period, I was *famished*. I'd skipped breakfast and had eaten only a pear for lunch.
   a. famous
   b. exhausted
   c. starving
   d. impatient

3. The autographed picture of Tiger Woods turned out to be *bogus*. The man who sold it to me had signed it himself!
   a. fake, false
   b. believable
   c. interesting
   d. overpriced

Exercise 2

In reading comprehension, everything rests on your ability to understand the ideas in each sentence. If you don't know what a word means, you may completely misunderstand an important sentence—and that means you could misunderstand the whole passage.

So, here's another practice. This one may be more challenging, since these vocabulary words aren't exactly real words!

Take a careful look at one of the most famous poems in the English language, Lewis Carroll's "Jabberwocky." (Lewis Carroll is the author of the classic *Alice in Wonderland*.) Though you won't be able to determine exactly what the nonsense words in the poem mean, you should be able to make an educated guess based on their context.

Here are the first two stanzas of the poem. Read them carefully and then answer the questions that follow. Read the poem twice, at least one of those times out loud. (The lines of the poem are numbered to make the questions easier to follow.)

Jabberwocky

1 'Twas brillig, and the slithy toves
2 Did gyre and gimble in the wabe;
3 All mimsy were the borogoves,
4 And the mome raths outgrabe.
5 "Beware the Jabberwock, my son!
6 The jaws that bite, the claws that catch!
7 Beware the Jubjub bird, and shun
8 The frumious Bandersnatch!"

Circle the letter of the answer you think is correct.

1. What could *slithy toves* (line 1) be?
   a. some sort of food
   b. some sort of place
   c. some sort of animal
   d. some sort of vehicle

2. The *Jabberwock* (line 5) is probably
   a. a mean person.
   b. a dangerous creature.
   c. a harmless bird.
   d. a magical animal.

3. What does *shun* (line 7) mean?
   a. to avoid, keep away from
   b. to capture
   c. to make friends with
   d. to take care of

4. What does *frumious* (line 8) probably mean?
   a. friendly
   b. ugly
   c. dangerous
   d. poor

How to Determine Meaning from Word Parts

Occasionally the text or passage you are reading might not provide enough context to figure out the meaning of a word. Another strategy for tackling tough words is to break the word into smaller parts. The meaning of these parts can give important clues about the meaning of the word.

For example, the word *bicycle* is made of two parts, *bi* and *cycle*. The first part, *bi*, is a prefix. A **prefix** always appears at the beginning of the word. The prefix *bi-* means two, so *bicycle* means "two wheels." If you replaced *bi* with another prefix, it changes the word's meaning. A *unicycle* has one wheel, and a *tricycle* has three wheels.

A **suffix** appears at the end of a word. Compare the meanings of *theorize* and *theorist*. *Theorize* is a verb meaning to make theories, while a *theorist* is *the person* who makes theories. Although these words look very similar, recognizing the suffix helps you identify the meaning. Review the prefixes and suffixes shown in the table.

PREFIX	MEANING
anti-	against
co-	with, together
inter-	between
mis-	bad, false
pre-	before
post-	after
re-	again
sub-	below
trans-	across
un-	not

SUFFIX	MEANING
-able	able, can do
-dom	quality, realm
-er/or	one who
-ful	full
-ist	one who
-ize	to make
-less	without
-ment	an act, result
-ology	study of
-ous	full of

Word Roots

The English language borrows many word parts from other languages, especially ancient Greek and Latin. These are called **roots**, and they can appear at the beginning, middle, or end of a word. Consider the word *aquaphobia*. If you recognize its two root words, *aqua* (water) and *phobia* (fear), you'll have no trouble guessing that *aquaphobia* means a fear of water. But even if you only recognized part of the word, it would likely be enough of a clue to help you understand the word in context. Some common root words are shown in the table below.

ROOT	MEANING
bio	life
chron	time
cred	believe
dem	people
fin	end
geo	earth
ject	throw
pathy	feeling
therm	heat

Exercise 3

Use your knowledge of word parts to determine the meaning of the italicized words in the sentences below. Circle the letter of the answer you think is correct.

1. The newspaper will be a *credible* source for my essay.
   a. authentic
   b. believable
   c. convincing
   d. untrustworthy

2. The political movement lacked *cohesion*.
   a. leadership
   b. feeling
   c. validity
   d. unity

3. Simon was *vigorous* and brave.
   a. deceptive
   b. courageous
   c. strong
   d. feeble

4. The *postrevolutionary* period was difficult for many French peasants.
   a. after the revolution
   b. before the revolution
   c. adjustment
   d. conversion

Summary

Often, you can figure out what unfamiliar words mean from their **context**—the way they are used in a passage. Look carefully at the words and sentences surrounding the unfamiliar word. You'll often find clues that will tell you what the word means. Remembering a few common word parts can also be a big help when you run into unfamiliar words. Even if you can't figure out the exact meaning of a word, you can usually tell whether the word means something positive or negative and sort through your answer choices.

Answers

Exercise 1

1. b. If you are nervous, your voice is not likely to be booming and certainly not likely to be confident. You might speak quietly, but "so nervous" suggests that something unusual was happening to his voice.

2. c. The context here clearly suggests that *famished* has something to do with hunger, since the speaker hadn't eaten anything except a pear all day.

3. a. If the seller provided the signature, then the autograph must be a fake.

Exercise 2

1. c. Slithy toves could be some sort of animal. The toves "did gyre and gimble," which suggests that they are active and alive. They could also be some sort of bug or plant, but neither of these was listed as an option.

2. b. The Jabberwock is a dangerous creature. You can tell because the speaker says to "beware the Jabberwock" and describes "the jaws that bite, the claws that catch!" This is clearly a beast you want to stay away from!

3. a. Shun means to avoid, to keep away from. This word *is* in the dictionary.

4. c. The speaker says to shun the Bandersnatch in the same stanza as he warns against the dangerous Jabberwock and Jubjub bird. The Bandersnatch must also be dangerous, since the listener is told to keep away from it.

Exercise 3

1. b. Credible means believable, from the Latin root word *credere*, to believe. Think of words like credulous and credence.

2. d. Cohesion means unity or joining together as one. The prefix *co-* is the first clue, but you might also think of *cohesive* tape, which can stick things together. Think of words like coherent, cooperate, and cohort.

3. c. Vigorous means strong and *full of vigor*. The context tells you that this word is probably positive, so you can eliminate deceptive and feeble, and courageous is a synonym for brave. Think of words like invigorate and vigilant.

4. a. Postrevolutionary means *after* the revolution. The story's context gives you additional clues about whether this period was positive or negative, by describing it as difficult.

SKILL BUILDING UNTIL NEXT TIME

1. Before you look up any unfamiliar words this week, try to figure out what they mean from their context. For example, if you come across an unfamiliar word while you're surfing the Web, use the context around that word to determine its meaning. After you've made an educated guess based on the context, look each word up in a dictionary. Did you guess correctly?

2. Begin a vocabulary list of the words you look up as you work your way through this book. Many people feel insecure about their reading and writing skills because they have a limited vocabulary. The more words you know, the easier it will be to understand what others are saying and to express what you have to say.

4 ▶ DISTINGUISHING BETWEEN FACT AND OPINION

LESSON SUMMARY

One of the most important signs of a good reader is the ability to distinguish between *fact* and *opinion*. This lesson will show you how facts are different from opinions and why this difference matters.

As you know from your own experience, sometimes it's really important to know when someone is telling you what they *think*, not what they *know*. For example, let's say your friend wants you to come over, but you'd planned to work on your book report.

"Don't worry," your friend says. "Mr. Billings is really laid back. He won't care if you hand it in late."

You could be in big trouble if you assume that your friend is offering a fact and not just his opinion.

When you're working on that book report like the dedicated student you are, you might need to do some research, consult outside sources like newspapers or websites. You'll need to know fact from opinion so you can tell what to believe and what ideas you should mistrust.

Defining Fact and Opinion

Before we go any further, let's define these two important terms.

Facts are
- things *known* for certain to have happened.
- things *known* for certain to be true.
- things *known* for certain to exist.

Opinions are
- things *believed* to have happened.
- things *believed* to be true.
- things *believed* to exist.

The key difference between fact and opinion lies in the difference between *knowing* and *believing*. Opinions may be *based* on facts, but they are still what people think and believe, not what they know. Opinions are debatable; two different people could have two different opinions about the matter. Facts, however, are not debatable. Two different people would have a hard time debating a fact. They might not agree on how to *interpret* the facts, but they would have to agree on the facts themselves.

Consider this example: "Basketball is more exciting than football." This statement is debatable. You could argue that football is more exciting than basketball, or that they're both equally exciting, or even that they're both dreadfully boring. All these statements are opinions. Either opinion can be "true" or accurate depending on the speaker's taste in sports. "Jimmy hates football" could be a fact, but "football is boring" is Jimmy's opinion. But "Basketball is a team sport" is not debatable; it's impossible to disagree with this statement. It's something known to be true. Thus, it's a fact.

Asking Questions

A good test for whether something is fact or opinion, then, is to ask yourself two questions:

- Can this statement be debated?
- Is this something known to be true?

If you can answer "Yes" to the first question, it's probably an opinion. If you can answer "Yes" to the second question, it's probably a fact. For example, look at the following sentence:

> Our school's policy is that you must have a C average in order to participate in school sports.

Does this topic sentence express a fact or an opinion? Well, is it debatable? Can someone disagree? You could debate whether the policy is *fair*, but not what the policy *is*. It's a matter of *fact*, something that could be proven by a quick visit to the principal or the athletic department. On the other hand, look at the following claim. (Read it carefully; it's different from the previous example though it looks the same.)

> Our school should have a policy that you must have at least a C average to participate in school sports.

Now, is this something known to be true, or is this something debatable? Clearly, different people can have different opinions on this issue. It's an *opinion*, signaled by the phrase "should have"—the policy doesn't exist yet.

Looking for Clues

Writers often provide clues when they are expressing a fact or an opinion. Look at the following passage, for example. Use your active reading skills to annotate it.

> I think school days should be extended until 4:00. Many children go home after school to an empty house. These latchkey children are often alone for

hours until their parents come home from work. In fact, a recent survey in our school district found that more than 50% of fourth graders are home alone for two or more hours a day.

Of these four sentences, three express facts and one expresses an opinion. Can you tell which one is the opinion? It should be pretty easy to spot; after all, the sentence begins with "I think" and includes "should be." Of the other three sentences, one offers a clear clue that it is a fact. It begins with a signal phrase: "In fact."

There are other signal words, too. Opinions are often stated using words like "should," "ought," or "had better," as in the following examples.

- We *should* apologize for being rude.
- He *ought* to return those library books right away.
- I *had better* get to school before I'm late.

Words that show judgment or evaluation, like "good," "bad," "interesting," and "important," usually signal an opinion, too. Here are some examples.

- She is a *great* teacher.
- This was the *most significant* development in the history of science.
- It was a *fascinating* film.

WORDS AND PHRASES THAT OFTEN SIGNAL OPINIONS

bad	important
best	insignificant
boring	interesting
disappointing	I think
excellent	ought
fascinating	remarkable
good	should
great	terrible
had better	worst

Exercise 1

Determine whether the following sentences express a fact or an opinion. Write **F** for fact or **O** for opinion before each sentence.

_F_ **1.** People should spend less time on the Internet and more time with one another.

_F_ **2.** The Internet allows people to communicate with friends and strangers all around the world.

_O_ **3.** There ought to be better rules for protecting children on the Internet.

_O_ **4.** The Internet is an amazing research tool.

_F_ **5.** Angelina Jolie is a good role model.

_F_ **6.** Many children look up to top entertainers and athletes as role models.

_O_ **7.** Only a handful of entertainers and athletes are good role models.

_F_ **8.** Many professional athletes earn millions of dollars each year.

_O_ **9.** Many professional athletes are grossly overpaid.

When Facts and Opinions Are Mixed Together

It's usually easy to determine whether something is fact or opinion when it stands alone as in the preceding sentences. But what about when you're looking at a whole paragraph or a whole page? Unless you're reading a scientific or technical manual, you'll usually find a combination of facts and opinions. In fact, you'll often find fact and opinion together in the same sentence. One of the topic sentences from Lesson 2 is a good example:

> Wilma Rudolph, the child with disabilities who became an Olympic running champion, is an inspiration for us all.

The first part of the sentence, "Wilma Rudolph, the child with disabilities who became an Olympic running champion," is a fact. Rudolph developed polio as a child, and she did win medals in the 1956 and 1960 Olympics. But the second part of the sentence—that she "is an inspiration for us all"—is an opinion. It's probably not an opinion that many people would disagree with, but someone could argue that Rudolph is not an inspiration or only inspiring to other runners. Thus, it's an opinion. Here's another example.

> Winston was an absolute genius, but he died without any recognition or reward for his accomplishments.

Here, the first part of the sentence expresses an opinion, while the second part expresses a fact. Though "absolute genius" is emphatic, it's still subjective (and therefore an opinion). How would you measure or compare it to other expressions of genius?

Fact and Opinion Working Together

People have opinions about everything and anything. But some opinions are more *reasonable* than others. A *reasonable* opinion is one that is supported by relevant facts. That's what most writing is all about. Writers make claims about their subjects, which are often opinions. Then they offer facts to support those opinions to convince you. If you recognize that their supporting details are facts, you might agree with their interpretation. The Wilma Rudolph passage is a perfect example. The writer begins by offering her opinion—that Rudolph is an inspiration. Then she lists the facts of Rudolph's life as *evidence* that Rudolph is an amazing woman.

Good writers offer support for their opinions because they know that opinions are debatable. They know readers will want to see *why* writers think what they do. Most of their evidence will come in the form of facts. Of course, this doesn't mean that readers will agree with the writer's opinion. But an opinion supported by facts is much stronger than an opinion that stands alone or that is supported only by other opinions. For example, read the two paragraphs below. Use active reading techniques to mark phrases that signal facts and opinions (you might circle one and underline the other—be sure to make yourself a key to remember which is which). In one, the writer supports her opinion with facts. In the other, she does not. Which paragraph is stronger?

> Many people are afraid of snakes, but they shouldn't be. Snakes have an unfair reputation as dangerous animals. People think snakes are poisonous, have big fangs, and have slimy skin. They shouldn't feel that way about snakes. Snakes ought to have a better reputation because they make great pets and are some of the most interesting creatures around. The people who are afraid of snakes had better learn more about these reptiles. Snakes aren't dangerous at all.

> Many people are afraid of snakes, but most snakes aren't as dangerous as people think they are. There are more than 2,500 different species of snakes around the world, and only a small percentage of those species are poisonous. Only a few species have venom strong enough to actually

kill a human being. Statistically, snakes bite only 1,000 to 2,000 people in the United States each year, and only ten of those bites (that's less than 1%!) result in death. If you think about it, lots of other animals are far more dangerous than snakes. In fact, in this country, more people die from dog bites each year than from snake bites.

Why is the second paragraph so much stronger or more convincing than the first? Because the second paragraph offers you more than just opinions. It offers opinions *supported* by specific facts and examples. The first paragraph opens with a fact but then offers several unsupported opinions. The opinions are debatable because they state what the author *thinks* is true—that snakes make great pets and are very interesting—not what the author *knows* to be true.

Identifying Specific Facts and Details

In your classes and on your tests, you'll often be expected to identify and recall specific facts and details from what you read. For the passage about snakes, for example, you might be asked a question like the following:

> How many species of snakes are there worldwide?
> **a.** between 1,000 and 2,000
> **b.** less than 100
> **c.** less than 2,500
> **d.** more than 2,500

There are several numbers in this passage, and if you didn't read carefully, you could easily choose the wrong answer. The correct answer is choice **d**, more than 2,500 species. This fact is clearly stated in the second sentence.

How do you identify specific facts and details quickly and accurately, especially when you're reading a passage that's several paragraphs long? You can't be expected to remember every detail. But you can be expected to know *where and how to find* specific facts and details.

For example, in the question just mentioned, the key word that will help you find the exact information you need is "species." If you scan the second snakes paragraph for numbers, you can quickly identify the correct answer by finding the sentence with both a number and the word "species," without being distracted by the number of people or the percentage of fatal bites.

In addition, you can use the structure of the paragraph to help you find your answer. If you read carefully, you probably noticed that the paragraph talked first generally about snakes, then got more specific with why people fear them, persuasively arguing that snakes are less dangerous, bite less often, and kill fewer people than you might think. Thus you can use your understanding of the structure to guide you to the correct answer. You'll learn more about this pattern in the next section: moving from general to specific information.

To find specific facts and details, you can use two guidelines:

1. Look for key words and numbers in the question that you can locate in the passage.
2. Think about the structure of the passage and where that information is likely to be located.

Exercise 2

This exercise, which features a longer passage, will give you a chance to practice all the skills you learned in this lesson. Read the passage carefully (don't forget your active reading strategies) and then answer the questions that follow.

The Gateway Arch

(1) The skyline of St. Louis, Missouri, is fairly unremarkable, with one huge exception—the Gateway Arch, which stands on the bank of the Mississippi. Part of the Jefferson National Expansion Memorial, the Arch is an amazing structure built to honor St. Louis's role as the gateway to the West.

(2) In 1947 a group of interested citizens known as the Jefferson National Expansion Memorial Association held a nationwide competition to select a design for a new monument that would celebrate the growth of the United States. Other U.S. monuments are spires, statues, or imposing buildings, but the winner of this contest planned a completely different type of structure. The man who submitted the winning design, Eero Saarinen, later became a famous architect. In designing the Arch, Saarinen wanted to leave a monu-ment that would have enduring impact.

(3) The Gateway Arch is a masterpiece of engineering, a monument even taller than the Great Pyramid in Egypt. In its own way, the Arch is at least as majestic as the Great Pyramid. The Gateway is shaped as an inverted catenary curve, the same shape that a heavy chain will form if suspended between two points. Covered with a sleek skin of stainless steel, the Arch often reflects dazzling bursts of sunlight. In a beautiful display of symmetry, the height of the arch is the same as the distance between the legs at ground level.

1. "The skyline of St. Louis, Missouri, is fairly unremarkable" is
   a. a fact.
   b. an opinion.

2. Saarinen's winning design was
   a. modeled after other U.S. monuments.
   b. unlike any other monument.
   c. part of a series of monuments.
   d. less expensive to construct than other monuments.

3. The sentence "The Gateway Arch is a masterpiece of engineering, a monument even taller than the Great Pyramid in Egypt" follows which pattern?
   a. fact/fact
   b. fact/opinion
   c. opinion/fact
   d. opinion/opinion

4. The Gateway Arch is shaped like
   a. a rainbow.
   b. a rectangle.
   c. a pyramid.
   d. a square.

Summary

Facts are things that are known to be true and can be objectively verified. Opinions are things that are believed to be true. They are subjective and vary from person to person. To distinguish between fact and opinion, determine whether the claim is debatable or not. If it is debatable, it is probably an opinion. Good writers often support their opinions with facts; this makes their opinions more reasonable. To identify specific facts in a passage, use key words and structure as your guides and don't be afraid to question an author's premise—ask "how do you know that?" and "according to who?"

Answers

Exercise 1

1. **Opinion.** Even if you agree with an opinion, you should recognize it's still up for debate. The word "should" signals this is an opinion.
2. **Fact.** It is objectively true that people use the Internet to communicate.
3. **Opinion.** Reasonable opinions are still opinions, here signaled by the word "ought to." The speaker would need to respond to people who think there are already plenty of rules for protecting children on the Internet.
4. **Opinion.** While the Internet has a lot to offer, the adjective "amazing" is subjective and requires evidence to support it.
5. **Opinion.** Even fans of Angelina Jolie would have to acknowledge her status as a role model depends on your opinion of her accomplishments. "Good" is a subjective, unquantified measurement of value.
6. **Fact.** While the number of children covered by "many" is vague, this is a fact because it can be supported with evidence—fan clubs, ticket sales, etc.
7. **Opinion.** The speaker has likely made a judgment about which entertainers and athletes are good role models, and again, "good" is hard to measure.
8. **Fact.** Many professional athletes do earn millions of dollars, and their contract details are made public.
9. **Opinion.** "Grossly overpaid" according to who? Some people might think it's too much, others might think it's fair compensation for the physical risks that athletes take.

Exercise 2

1. **b.** Whether the skyline is "fairly unremarkable" is debatable. It is a matter of opinion.
2. **b.** The passage explicitly states the Arch is not modeled after other monuments (choice **a**); there's no indication the Arch was part of a series (choice **c**) nor does the passage go into the cost of the project (choice **d**).
3. **c.** The first part of the sentence, "The Gateway Arch is a masterpiece of engineering," is an opinion; it makes a judgment about the Arch and is debatable. If they wanted to, the author could have supported her or his opinion with facts to illustrate what about the engineering was advanced, or compared the Arch to other monuments in more ways than just height. The second part of the sentence, "a monument even taller than the Great Pyramid in Egypt," is not debatable; it is a matter of fact.
4. **a.** If the word "Arch" didn't give it away, the exact shape of the Arch is described in the third paragraph. It is an inverted curve and has no angles, so it cannot be a rectangle (choice **b**), a pyramid (choice **c**), or a square (choice **d**).

SKILL BUILDING UNTIL NEXT TIME

1. Listen to what people say around you. For example, make a list of statements that are made on a local or national news program. Do the reporters state facts or opinions? When they state opinions, do they support them?
2. Practice turning facts into opinions and opinions into facts. For example, turn the fact "Today is Wednesday" into an opinion, such as "Wednesday is the best day of the week." (Then you could support that opinion by offering a supporting fact: "Wednesday is the best day of the week because that's when I have music lessons.")

LESSON

5 ▶ PUTTING IT ALL TOGETHER

SECTION SUMMARY

This lesson reviews what you learned in Lessons 1 through 4: active reading strategies, finding the main idea, defining unfamiliar words, and distinguishing between fact and opinion. In the practice exercises, you'll get to use all these reading comprehension skills together.

I f you want to become good at basketball, you can practice your dribbling, work on your jump shots, and run through your layups over and over until your arms and legs ache. But you won't become really good unless you can successfully combine all these skills on the court and interact with your teammates. Similarly, when you read, you need to use a number of different reading strategies at the same time. Putting together the strategies that you've learned so far will take your reading skills to the next level and help you see how far you've come.

What You've Learned

These are the reading strategies you've learned so far.

Lesson 1: Becoming an Active Reader. You learned that active reading is the key to reading success. Active readers use five specific strategies to understand what they read:

- surveying ahead and jumping back
- highlighting key words and ideas
- looking up unfamiliar vocabulary words
- recording questions and reactions
- looking for clues

Lesson 2: Finding the Main Idea. You learned that the **main idea** is different from the **subject** of a text. The main idea makes an **assertion** about the subject. This idea is **general** enough to hold together all the ideas in a passage, but not so general it misrepresents the passage. It is the thought that controls the whole passage, and this thought is often expressed in a **topic sentence**. The other sentences in the passage provide support for the main idea.

Lesson 3: Defining Vocabulary. You learned how to figure out what unfamiliar words mean from their **context**—the surrounding words and ideas. You also looked for clues in the unfamiliar words by examining **word parts**, including the **prefix**, **suffix**, or **root**.

Lesson 4: Distinguishing between Fact and Opinion. You learned that a **fact** is something *known* to be true while an **opinion** is something *believed* to be true. Main ideas are often opinions. Good writers use facts to support their opinions.

If any of these terms or strategies are unfamiliar, take some time to review the term or strategy that is unclear.

Section 1 Practice

Read the passage below carefully. If you come across unfamiliar words circle them, but *don't* look them up until after you've answered all the questions. Take as much time as you need and remember to read actively. You'll develop your own system over time. Make a key if you need to—feel free to annotate the questions as well as the passage. (The sentences are numbered to make the questions easier to follow.)

Bicycles

(1) Today, bicycles are so common that it's hard to believe they haven't always been around. (2) But two hundred years ago, bicycles didn't even exist, and the first bicycle, invented in Germany in 1818, was nothing like our bicycles today. (3) It was made of wood and didn't even have pedals. (4) Since then, however, numerous innovations and improvements in design have made the bicycle one of the most popular means of recreation and transportation around the world.

(5) In 1839, Kirkpatrick Macmillan, a Scottish blacksmith, dramatically improved on the original bicycle design. (6) Macmillan's machine had tires with iron rims to keep them from getting worn down. (7) He also used foot-operated cranks similar to pedals so his bicycle could be ridden at a quick pace. (8) It didn't look much like a modern bicycle, though, because its back wheel was substantially larger than its front wheel. (9) In 1861, the French Michaux brothers took the evolution of the bicycle a step further by inventing an improved crank mechanism.

(10) Ten years later, James Starley, an English inventor, revolutionized bicycle design. (11) He made the front wheel many times larger than the back wheel, put a gear on the pedals to make the bicycle more efficient, and lightened the wheels by using wire spokes.

Sarveen Sangha

PUTTING IT ALL TOGETHER

(12) Although this bicycle was much lighter and less tiring to ride, it was still clumsy, extremely top-heavy, and ridden mostly for entertainment.

(13) It wasn't until 1874 that the first truly modern bicycle appeared on the scene. (14) Invented by another Englishman, H. J. Lawson, the "safety bicycle" would look familiar to today's cyclists. (15) This bicycle had equal-sized wheels, which made it less prone to toppling over. (16) Lawson also attached a chain to the pedals to drive the rear wheel. (17) With these improvements, bicycles became extremely popular and useful for transportation. (18) Today they are built, used, and enjoyed all over the world.

1. Highlight the passage. Which words and ideas should be underlined?

   _____

   _____

   _____

2. The main idea of this passage is best expressed in which sentence?
   a. **Sentence 1:** Today, bicycles are so common that it's hard to believe they haven't always been around.
   b. **Sentence 13:** It wasn't until 1874 that the first truly modern bicycle appeared on the scene.
   c. **Sentence 4:** Since then, however, numerous innovations and improvements in design have made the bicycle one of the most popular means of recreation and transportation around the world.
   d. **Sentence 18:** Today they are built, used, and enjoyed all over the world.

3. Which of the following would be the best title for this passage?
   a. Bicycles Are Better
   b. A Ride through the History of Bicycles
   c. Cycle Your Way to Fitness
   d. The Popularity of Bicycles

4. Which sentence best expresses the main idea of paragraph 2?
   a. Macmillan was a great inventor.
   b. Macmillan's bike didn't look much like our modern bikes.
   c. Macmillan's bike could be ridden quickly.
   d. Macmillan made important changes in bicycle design.

5. An *innovation*, as it is used in sentence 4, is
   a. a new way of doing something.
   b. a design.
   c. an improvement.
   d. a clever person.

6. *Revolutionized*, as it is used in sentence 10, most nearly means
   a. cancelled.
   b. changed drastically.
   c. became outdated.
   d. exercised control over.

7. The word *prone*, as it is used in sentence 15, means
   a. lying down.
   b. unbalanced.
   c. incapable of doing something.
   d. likely to do something.

8. Which of the following sentences from the passage represents the writer's opinion?
   a. Sentence 1
   b. Sentence 6
   c. Sentence 9
   d. Sentence 16

51

9. Sentence **8**, "It didn't look much like a modern bicycle, though, because its back wheel was substantially larger than its front wheel," follows which pattern?
   a. fact, fact
   b. fact, opinion
   c. opinion, fact
   d. opinion, opinion

10. Macmillan added iron rims to the tires of his bicycle to
   a. add weight to the bicycle.
   b. make the tires last longer.
   c. make the ride less bumpy.
   d. make the ride less tiring.

11. A gear system on bicycles was first used by
   a. H. J. Lawson.
   b. Kirkpatrick Macmillan.
   c. the Michaux brothers.
   d. James Starley.

12. Starley's addition of wire spokes made the bicycle
   a. lighter.
   b. less likely to tip over.
   c. more efficient.
   d. safer.

Answers

1. The passage should be highlighted or underlined as follows (answers may vary slightly, as you may have highlighted or underlined words or ideas that are particularly interesting to you). Here, we've underlined main ideas and key innovations in bicycle design. We did not underline the effects of these innovations or the problems with these new designs. By highlighting the innovations, though, we can quickly and easily find that related information. When you survey ahead and find out the passage is about bicycles and the development of the modern version, you know it makes sense to track the specific innovations throughout the essay.

Bicycles
(1) Today, bicycles are so common that it's hard to believe they haven't always been around. (2) But two hundred years ago, bicycles didn't even exist, and the first bicycle, invented in Germany in 1818, was nothing like our bicycles today. (3) It was made of wood and didn't even have pedals. (4) Since then, however, numerous innovations and improvements in design have made the bicycle one of the most popular means of recreation and transportation around the world.

(5) In 1839, Kirkpatrick Macmillan, a Scottish blacksmith, dramatically improved on the original bicycle design. (6) Macmillan's machine had tires with iron rims to keep them from getting worn down. (7) He also used foot-operated cranks similar to pedals so his bicycle could be ridden at a quick pace. (8) It didn't look much like a modern bicycle, though, because its back wheel was substantially larger than its front wheel. (9) In 1861 the French Michaux brothers took the evolution of the bicycle a step further by inventing an improved crank mechanism.

(10) Ten years later, James <u>Starley</u>, an English inventor, <u>revolutionized bicycle design</u>. (11) He made the <u>front wheel many times larger than the back wheel, put a gear on the pedals</u> to make the bicycle more efficient, and lightened the wheels by using <u>wire spokes</u>. (12) Although this bicycle was much lighter and less tiring to ride, it was still clumsy, extremely top-heavy, and ridden mostly for entertainment. (13) It wasn't until <u>1874 that the first truly modern bicycle</u> appeared on the scene. (14) Invented by another Englishman, H. J. Lawson, the "safety bicycle" would look familiar to today's cyclists. (15) This bicycle had <u>equal-sized wheels</u>, which made it less prone to toppling over. (16) Lawson also attached a <u>chain</u> to the pedals to drive the rear wheel. (17) <u>With these improvements, bicycles became extremely popular and useful for transportation.</u> (18) Today they are built, used, and enjoyed all over the world.

If you missed this question, revisit Lesson 1.

2. c. This is the only sentence general enough to encompass all the ideas in the passage. Each paragraph describes the innovations that led to the modern design of the bicycle, and this design has made it popular around the world. If you missed this question, revisit Lesson 2.

3. b. The essay describes the history of the bicycle, from its invention in 1818 to its modern design. It's not comparing bikes to other modes of transportation, focusing on bikes and fitness, or discussing how many bike owners there are. If you missed this question, revisit Lesson 2.

4. d. Macmillan may have been a great inventor, but this paragraph describes only his innovations in bicycle design. The first sentence in this paragraph expresses this main idea in a clear topic sentence. The rest of the paragraph provides specific examples of the improvements he made in bicycle design. If you missed this question, revisit Lesson 2.

5. a. An *innovation* is a new way of doing something. The first clue is in sentence **3**, which describes the first bicycle—"it was made of wood and didn't even have pedals." Clearly, bicycles have changed dramatically. Other clues can be found in the following paragraphs, which describe the various changes made to bicycle design. Each bicycle designer came up with a new way of building a bicycle. If you missed this question, revisit Lesson 3.

6. b. *Revolutionized* means changed drastically. If you examine the two word parts, *revolution•ize*, you'll know that it means "to make a revolution." Starley's changes to the bicycle were major changes that enabled the development of the modern bicycle. If you missed this question, revisit Lesson 3.

7. d. Although *prone* does also mean "lying down," that is not how it is used in this sentence. Here, the context clues tell us that the best answer is "likely to do something." Since Lawson's design was called the "safety bicycle," we can assume it was less likely to tip over because of his innovations. If you missed this question, revisit Lesson 3.

8. a. Of the four sentences, this is the only one that is debatable. If you missed this question, revisit Lesson 4.

9. c. The first part of the sentence, "It didn't look much like a modern bicycle," is an opinion; it is debatable. The second part of the sentence, "its back wheel was substantially larger than its front wheel," is a fact. If you missed this question, revisit Lesson 4.

10. b. Since the question is asking for a specific fact about Macmillan's design, you should know to look in the second paragraph. Then you can find the sentence with the key words "iron rims"—the second sentence—to find the correct answer. This phrase is easy to find if you underlined or highlighted specific innovations. If you missed this question, revisit Lesson 4.

11. d. If you highlighted the various innovations, then all you have to do is scan the highlighted parts of the passage. Otherwise, you can reread paragraphs 2, 3, and 4 to find the correct answer. If you missed this question, revisit Lesson 4.

12. a. Again, the question is asking for a specific fact about a specific inventor's design, so you know to go directly to the paragraph about Starley. Then, look for the key words "wire spokes." They should be easy to find because you've highlighted the various innovations. If you missed this question, revisit Lesson 4.

SKILL BUILDING UNTIL NEXT TIME

1. Review the Skill Building sections from each lesson in this section. Try any Skill Builders you didn't already do.

2. Write a paragraph or two about what you've learned in this section. Begin your paragraph with a clear topic sentence and then write several supporting sentences. Try to use at least one new word you learned this week as you write. Ask a friend or family member to look over it for you.

S E C T I O N

2 ▶ STRUCTURE

Now that you've covered the basics of active reading and understanding, you can begin to focus on an important reading strategy: recognizing and understanding structure. How do writers organize their ideas?

Think of a writer as a chef. A meal must have a certain number of ingredients. But how much of each there is and how they are combined is up to the chef. The same goes for a piece of writing. How the sentences and ideas are arranged is entirely up to the writer. Writers must decide which ideas go where and move from one idea to another in an organized way.

Writers generally use one of several basic organizational patterns when they design a text. These basic patterns help writers organize their ideas effectively. Fiction stories follow a certain pattern to build a plot. Both fiction and nonfiction writing, such as essays and articles, can contain content arranged in a variety of ways.

In a fictional story or a novel, you might look for exposition or background, rising action, conflict, and resolution. (Lesson 6)

In essays and articles, as well as other nonfiction forms like reviews, you can find the following patterns:

- chronological order: beginning to end (Lesson 7)
- order of importance: building to the most important or starting big and getting smaller (Lesson 7)

- comparing and contrasting: examining elements of a topic one at a time (Lesson 8)
- cause and effect: this, therefore, that (Lesson 9)

In Section 2, you'll learn how to recognize these patterns, and you'll understand why writers use them. Then you'll practice two ways to take useful, organized notes about what you read. When you begin to notice the underlying structure, the skeleton, of a piece of writing, you will become a stronger reader *and* writer.

6 ▶ THE PARTS OF A PLOT

LESSON SUMMARY

In works of fiction, the plot is the story's plan, or its sequence of events. Plots are usually built around a conflict, or problem, and the conflict is usually resolved by the end of the story. This lesson will show you how to recognize the four parts of a plot: exposition, rising action, conflict, and resolution.

What are the ingredients of a good story? You might like to read about a strange, clever, or funny character. But what if that character simply sat in his house all day and nothing happened to him? In most stories, the main character is very active. What the main character does or says begins a sequence of events that moves the story from beginning to end. The *sequence of events* in a story is called the **plot**. The plot events follow a chain of cause and effect to reach the climax of the story. The plot reveals the *meaning* behind the characters' actions and the conflicts they face.

Exposition

When we start to read a book or story that engages us, we become instant detectives. We search relentlessly for clues about the story—*who* the characters are, *where* they live, *when* the story take place, *what* will happen to them, and *why* these elements are important. The reader can usually get a pretty good idea of *who* and *what* the story is about in the first few paragraphs. The author's setup for the story is called the **exposition**. This setup, which might also be called the premise or background, appears before the main action of the story, and it introduces the reader to the characters, their situations, and their motives. As you read the opening lines of *Goldilocks and the Three Bears*, notice the information that the author reveals.

Goldilocks and the Three Bears
Once upon a time, a family of bears lived in a house in the forest. The Papa bear was large and fierce, but he loved his family and protected them loyally. The Mama bear took pride in her house and cared diligently for her little son, called Baby Bear. One day, the bears decided to go for a walk while waiting for their hot porridge to cool.

In the first paragraph of this familiar tale, we are introduced to the major characters (a family of three bears) and the setting (the bears' forest home), and we can begin to make predictions about the story. Something is going to happen to the bears on their walk or to the porridge they leave behind.

Setting

The two basic elements of a setting are *time* and *place*. *Time* could mean the historical era, such as "during the Civil War" or "1352 BCE." It might also mean the season or even the time of day when the story occurs.

Place means the physical location of the story, such as "Norway" or "inside Ben's grandmother's house." Writers do not always want to be obvious about establishing place and time. Sometimes they want the reader to pick up on more subtle clues, or reveal something surprising later in the story.

Why is it important to understand a story's setting? Let's imagine a story about a girl named Maya. Does Maya live in a high-rise apartment in Paris, or on a slave plantation in South Carolina? Is she the daughter of an Egyptian king or a Russian astronaut? The setting that the writer chooses will determine much about who Maya is and what she will experience. Read this scene carefully, and pay close attention to the underlined setting clues.

"There are more coming on the road," the <u>head nurse</u> called wearily. Maya reluctantly poked her head through the dingy window. Waves of <u>soldiers</u> had been dragging their wounded friends to the <u>makeshift hospital</u> <u>all afternoon</u>. The <u>beds</u> were nearly all full, and their supplies of <u>bandages and splints</u> were running low. <u>Cannon fire</u> still thundered ferociously in the distance, but the battle was interrupted by stretches of silence. Maya hoped the silence would last forever. But until then, these men were counting on her. She wiped her hands on her blood-stained dress, and ran to the door to meet them.

Each underlined detail tells us something about the setting. We've learned that Maya and another nurse work in a hospital in a war zone. *Afternoon* tells us the time of day, but it also suggests that the battle has been going on for a long while, because the beds are full of wounded people. The *bandages and splints* and *cannon fire* suggest that the setting is before the invention of modern medical and military technology. There are still many details we *don't* know, but we can start to build a mental picture of the setting.

Recognizing the setting also helps you define your expectations. For the story above, we expect Maya to meet some soldiers, but she probably will not meet a wicked witch on a flying broomstick. As we read more of a story, our mental picture of the setting becomes more complete. For example, a tale that takes place in the Middle Ages won't have cars or telephones, just as a story set in Manhattan probably won't have knights or joust tournaments.

Exercise 1

Here is the first paragraph of a short story. Read it twice; the second time, underline clues that tell the reader about the setting and the main character. Then answer the questions that follow.

Aboard the *Portello*

The candle sputtered, dripping hot wax on the half-filled journal page. "Oh, no!" Mario moaned. "That's the third time tonight!" He pushed back his chair and stood up, tucking his journal carefully into the tiny drawer. He had only written a few sentences, and it was making him depressed. In the first days of their journey, it had been fun to write about the ship and its crew. Each day had brought new discoveries— the portholes and rope reels, the anchor as big as a horse, the cook's pantry full of potatoes and flour, where Mario had been warned not to touch anything. But it had been more than a week and he had yet to find anyone his age. Well, there were a few girls, but they were stiff and boring in their long dresses. They had even told him that they were not curious to explore the ship, but that was probably a lie. Still, the crew was too busy to humor him for long, and he began to wish he had stayed at home in Naples with his mother and sisters.

1. Who is Mario?
   a. a father
   b. a fisherman
   c. a cook
   d. a young boy

2. Where does this scene take place?
   a. in a library
   b. on a rowboat
   c. in Mario's room
   d. in Naples

3. What is the likely setting for the story's main action?
   a. a ship
   b. Naples
   c. a library
   d. Mario's room

4. In what historical era is the story probably set?
   a. ancient Rome
   b. the Age of Exploration
   c. the twenty-first century
   d. the future

Rising Action

Plot is more than just a bunch of events; it is a *sequence* of events. That means there is a relationship, usually cause and effect, between the events. A series of random events would be hard to make sense of, but a good plot will seem *logical* and even *inevitable*. Each event leads to the next, and the **rising action** builds to a **climax**, the turning point in the action.

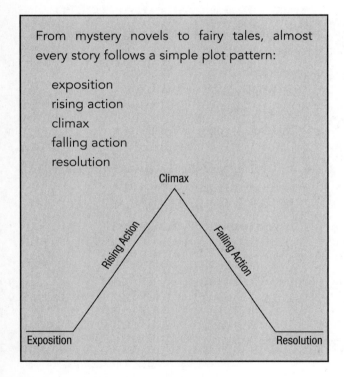

From mystery novels to fairy tales, almost every story follows a simple plot pattern:

exposition
rising action
climax
falling action
resolution

Exercise 2

Read the remainder of the story about Mario, and pay close attention to the events of rising action. Then respond to the questions that follow.

(1) Mario's weary feet carried him up the narrow metal staircase to the upper deck. With his lantern in hand, he checked the lounge and the dining room, but his father was nowhere to be seen. Most of the men had retired to their cabins for the night. If his father wasn't dining or playing cards with the other officers in the lounge, the surest place to find him was the captain's library. His father kept scores of books at home, but they had packed only a few favorite volumes in their luggage. Some evenings, his father liked to sit in the cramped ship's library, poring over heavy, salt-stained books about the places they would soon visit.

(2) Mario wound his way through the dark corridors, guided only by the splash of light from his lantern. Suddenly, he heard a funny sound, like a stifled sneeze, he thought. He spun around, looking for the source of the sound, but he couldn't see anyone else in the passage. Shrugging, he continued down the hall until—"Achoo!" A real sneeze erupted in the narrow hall.

(3) "Who's there?" Mario called. There was no answer. Maybe those girls were playing a trick on him, trying to scare him. Holding his light high, he began to search the walls, looking for a door or window where someone might be hiding. There was only a narrow grate, about three feet high. He lifted his lantern and peered into the darkness beyond. When his light reflected in two dark eyes, he sprang back with a yelp.

(4) "Who are you? What are you doing in there?" he cried.

(5) After a long silence, a whisper came through the grate. "Don't tell anyone, please, sir. I boarded the ship to escape my cruel father, but if they find me, they will send me back to him, or make a slave of me, or worse!"

(6) Mario's fear dissolved as the boy spoke. "I'm called Mario," he offered. "What is your name?"

(7) "Benito," the boy replied.

(8) "Come out of there, Benito," Mario insisted. "My father would never let anyone harm you. You must be starving. Come out, and we'll have apples and bread, and you can sleep on a cot in our cabin." More long moments followed as the stowaway considered his options. Finally there was a creak as he unscrewed the grate and pushed it open. A hungry-looking boy unfolded his long limbs from the small refuge and stood on unsteady legs.

(9) "Let's go find my father," Mario said. "This voyage is turning out to be a good adventure, after all!"

1. Why does Mario go to the upper deck?
   a. to find something to eat
   b. because he heard a sneeze
   c. to find his father
   d. because a storm is coming

2. Why are the corridors empty and quiet?
   a. There are no other passengers on board.
   b. The passengers and crew have gone to bed.
   c. There is a rule against walking around at night.
   d. The corridors are haunted.

3. What happens immediately after Mario hears a sneeze?
   a. Mario searches the corridors for a hidden door or window.
   b. Mario takes Benito to his father.
   c. Mario's lantern reflects in Benito's eyes.
   d. Benito emerges from a grate.

4. Why is Mario pleased to discover Benito?
   a. He can turn him in for reward money.
   b. He has found someone to make the voyage interesting.
   c. He can impress his father.
   d. He can surprise the crew.

Conflict

Conflict is the single most important ingredient for any story. A **conflict** is a struggle between two forces. It is usually introduced early in the story, and during the course of the action, the problem is resolved. The conflict shows us *why* the characters act the way they do.

The most common conflicts include:

- character versus character
- character versus self
- character versus nature
- character versus society

In the story you just read about Mario and Benito, the central conflict is that Mario is lonely for a friend. This type of conflict is "character versus self," because Mario's loneliness is internal. When he finds a new friend, Benito, the conflict is resolved.

In *Goldilocks and the Three Bears*, the conflict is between Goldilocks and the bears, a "character versus character" conflict (and maybe a little bit of Goldilocks versus herself).

Climax

The rising action eventually builds to a climax. The **climax** is the highest point in the action, when the conflict is faced head-on. In a love story, it might be the scene where the protagonists finally declare their feelings for one another. In an action story, it might be a battle or dramatic rescue. In a mystery story, it is the moment when the criminal is discovered. In short, it's the *big moment* that the reader has been waiting for. The climax usually appears near the end of the story, and it has an important effect on the characters.

(1) When we last left Goldilocks and the Three Bears, Papa, Mama, and Baby Bear had gone off for a walk while their porridge cooled.

(2) After the three bears disappeared down the road into the forest, a little girl named Goldilocks, who had long curly blonde hair and a very curious disposition, came walking from the opposite direction. She spied the Bears' cozy house and smoking chimney and decided to knock on the door. It swung open at her touch and she saw the three bowls of porridge on the table. She was very hungry, so she rushed in and sat down before the biggest bowl, which belonged to Papa; she helped herself to a spoonful.

(3) "Ouch!" she cried, "This porridge is too hot!"

(4) She scooted down the bench to the second bowl, which was medium-sized and belonged to Mama Bear.

(5) "Brrr!" she exclaimed, "This porridge is too cold!"

(6) She slid down the bench a little further, to Baby Bear's small bowl.

(7) "This porridge is just right!" she exclaimed, and then she ate every bit of it.

(8) After her snack, Goldilocks found she was tired, so she wandered through the empty house until she found the Bears' bedroom. First she stretched out on the biggest bed, near the door, and found it was stiff as a board.

(9) "My!" she said, "This bed is too hard!"

(10) She got up and moved to the next bed, which was just Mama's size. She sank down into it until she almost couldn't see over the edge.

(11) "Goodness!" she said, "This bed is too soft!"

(12) She clambered out of the bed and moved to the littlest one, which of course belonged to Baby Bear, and fit her like a glove.

(13) "Ah," she sighed, "this bed is just right," and before she knew it, she'd fallen fast asleep.

Just in case you've forgotten the rest, the three bears come home, Baby Bear is distraught to find someone has eaten his porridge, then the family discovers Goldilocks asleep in their bedroom.

Which statement shows the climax of the Goldilocks tale?
   a. The baby bear's bed looked so comfortable that Goldilocks decided to take a nap.
   b. Baby Bear said, "Who's been eating my porridge?"
   c. Baby Bear said, "Someone's been sleeping in my bed . . . and she's *still here*!"

The climax is choice **c**, when the bears finally confront the girl. When Goldilocks lies down in Baby Bear's bed and falls asleep, the reader starts to anticipate the moment when the bears come home and find her. And as the bears explore their house, finding evidence of a stranger's presence, the *suspense* builds until—aha! They find her, and the conflict is resolved.

Resolution

After the climax, there usually follows some **falling action** as the author ties up loose ends in the plot. The **resolution** is how the author resolves the conflict and concludes the story. Authors usually (but not always!) tell us what happens to the main characters after the conflict.

Compare these three conclusions to the Goldilocks story. Which resolution do you like best?

1. Goldilocks apologized for her behavior. Mama Bear accepted the apology and invited Goldilocks to share their porridge. The bear family invited her to come back and visit any time.

2. Goldilocks ran, screaming, down the stairs, through the bears' house, out the door, and all the way back to her mother's cottage. She swore she would never roam alone in the forest again.

3. Baby Bear began to cry, and Goldilocks felt guilty for eating his porridge, sitting in his chair, and sleeping in his bed. Goldilocks gave him a hug and asked him to come visit her house the next day for tea and cookies.

Exercise 3

The following events from a myth about Pandora are scrambled. Read the story, then label each part as exposition, rising action, climax, or resolution.

1. Finally, one day as Epimetheus lay fast asleep, Pandora couldn't control her curiosity any longer. She stole the key and crept into the next room with the box in her hands. With great anticipation, she opened the box. Out flew every kind of trouble that people had never known. There was Sickness, Worry, Crime, Hate, Envy, Poverty, and all sorts of other bad things. They looked like ugly little bugs. Pandora tried to shut the box before they escaped, but she couldn't, and they began to fly away, out the windows and into the world. She tried to catch them and put them back inside the box, but it was too late. They were gone.

2. To punish mankind for the theft of fire, Zeus, king of the Ancient Greek Gods, created a beautiful clay figure of a woman, and then brought it to life. She was the most exquisite and charming woman ever, and he named her Pandora, meaning "all gifts." He then sent her to Earth, where she married a man named Epimetheus. Before she left, Zeus gave Pandora a little locked box and told her to take good care of it. He also stipulated that she must never, ever open it. He gave the key to Epimetheus for safekeeping.

3. Pandora was very sorry that she had opened the box, and she sat down on the floor and began to cry. Then, a strange thing happened. Out of the box flew one more thing, but it was not ugly like the others had been. No, it was beautiful. It was Hope, which Zeus had sympathetically sent to keep humans going when ugly things occur. So it is that even today, when things get really bad, you can always hang on to Hope.

4. The young couple settled down to begin a happy life. But Pandora always wondered what was in the little box that Zeus had given her. As she became more and more curious, she begged her husband to let her open the box, just for a little peek inside. He, feeling it was his obligation to follow Zeus' order, always refused. Time after time, Pandora tried to sweet-talk and convince her husband to open the box just a bit, but to no avail.

Summary

Some stories have an obvious problem to resolve and big action. In other stories, you may have to read closely to recognize the conflict. But almost every fiction story uses the same recipe: the *exposition* introduces the setting and characters, then the *action rises* to a *climax*, when the *conflict* is *resolved* and the characters are somehow changed.

Answers

Exercise 1

1. d. Mario mentions his mother and sisters, so he is probably still a child. He says that the crew are too busy for him, so he must not be a crew member.

2. c. You might assume that the scene takes place on a ship, especially if you know that ship names are usually italicized and capitalized as proper nouns, but that is not one of the answer options. We know that Mario stores his private journal in his desk, though, so this scene likely takes place in his room. There's no evidence to suggest he is in a library, even if the ship had one (choice **a**); there would not be enough room for him to look around for his father if they were only in a row boat (choice **b**); since Mario has left his mother and sisters behind in Naples, he can't still be there (choice **d**).

3. a. Although the first scene takes place in his cabin room, the conflict—Mario's loneliness and boredom—will probably take him out of his room to explore the ship.

4. b. Ancient Rome (choice **a**) is probably too early for a boy to be exploring the seas on a big ship and because Mario uses candles and a lantern, the story likely takes place before the twenty-first century (choice **c**), which means it's definitely not the future (choice **d**). The Age of Exploration (choice **b**), also called the Age of Discovery, took place in the 1600s and early 1700s, which matches the feel of this story's setting.

Exercise 2

1. c. The story explicitly says Mario is checking the lounge and the dining room in search of his father. The passage tells us it's too late at night, after dinner, so he's probably not looking for food (choice **a**). He doesn't hear the sneeze (choice **b**) until he is already exploring, and there's no evidence a storm is coming (choice **d**).

2. b. The first paragraph mentions most of the other men on board had retired to their cabins for the night. We know there are other passengers because Mario has met them, so choice **a** cannot be correct; there's no indication that Mario is forbidden from wandering around at night (choice **c**), and no suggestion that the ship might be haunted (choice **d**).

3. a. Paragraph 3 tells us Mario first looks for doors or windows where someone might be hiding. Choices **b**, **c**, and **d** all happen eventually after Mario hears the sneeze, but only choice **a** happens immediately.

4. b. Mario's reaction to Benito is not that he can turn him in for a reward (choice **a**), but that the voyage is looking more like an adventure, so choice **b** is correct. There's no reason to think his father will be impressed by the discovery of a stowaway (choice **c**), nor that he will tell the whole crew (choice **d**).

Exercise 3

1. **Climax.** When you read the scrambled story, you learn that first Pandora was given a box, then she wanted to open it, then she opened it, then she closed it just in time. This is the passage where she opens the box, and since the story leads up to this dramatic moment, this is the climax.

2. **Exposition.** This passage describes the set-up for the story, where we meet the main characters for the first time and the pivotal plot device, the box, is given to Pandora.

3. **Resolution.** Now that the worst has happened and Pandora has opened the box, the story concludes with the suggestion that hope remains.

4. **Rising Action.** This passage is building suspense for the climactic moment when Pandora opens the box; Pandora becomes "more and more" curious and pleads with her husband "time after time" so you know the story is leading to the moment she finally opens the box.

SKILL BUILDING UNTIL NEXT TIME

1. Flip through your favorite book. Where does the rising action start? Which chapter includes the climax? Is the conflict resolved after the climax? (If the book is part of a series, the author might leave part of the conflict unresolved!)

2. Choose a familiar fairy tale, such as *Cinderella* or *Jack and the Beanstalk*. What is the *climax* of the story? Do you like the tale's resolution? Brainstorm another possible ending for the story, and write your own version.

3. Next time you watch a movie or a TV show, consider how they clue the viewer in on necessary backstory. Notice how and when they depict conflict.

7 ORGANIZING PRINCIPLES

LESSON SUMMARY

Authors can organize their ideas, arguments, or plots in a variety of ways. One of the basic organizing principles is time, and you'll learn how writers organize ideas chronologically. The content could also be presented in order of importance, starting with either the most important or the least important point. In this lesson you'll learn to recognize these organizational patterns.

There are many ways to tell a story. Some stories start in the middle and flash back to the beginning. A few stories actually start at the end and tell the story in reverse. But most of the time, stories start at the beginning, describe what happened first and then what happened next, and next, and so on until the end. When writers tell a story in the order in which things happened, they are using **chronological order**.

Another common organizational pattern is **order of importance**. With this pattern, writers use *value* instead of time as their organizing principle. That is, the first idea a writer describes isn't what *happened* first; it's the idea that's most or least *important*. Writers can start with the most important idea and then work down the line to the least important idea. Or, they can do the opposite—start with the least important idea and build up to the most important.

Keeping Track of Time: Transitions

Much of what you read is arranged in chronological order. Newspaper and magazine articles, instructions and procedures, and essays about personal experiences usually use this pattern. In fact, several of the passages you've read so far—about Wilma Rudolph, Goran Kropp, and the history of bicycles—use time to organize ideas. First, we learned about Wilma's childhood illnesses, then her struggle to learn to walk again as a teenager, and then her Olympic success as a young woman. Similarly, we read (first) about Goran Kropp's journey to Mount Everest, then his ascent up the mountain, and finally his return to Sweden. The bicycle passage relates the history of bicycles from their invention in 1818 to 1874 through several stages of redesign.

Each of these passages provides several clues to show the chronological order. **Transitional words and phrases** connect the ideas and events within the text. For example, the bicycle passage uses dates to tell us the order in which the bicycle evolved. Without these dates and transitional phrases, we would have no sense of the time frame in which these changes in design took place. Transitions are often so important that we'd often be lost without them.

COMMON TRANSITIONAL WORDS AND PHRASES

There are many ways writers signal time order in a chronological passage. Below is a list of some of the most common transitional words and phrases.

afterward	eventually	later	suddenly
as soon as	finally	meanwhile	then
at last	first, second, third	next	when
before, after	immediately	now	while
during	in the meantime	soon	

Exercise 1

Here is a paragraph with all the transitional words and phrases removed. Read it carefully. Then, choose from the list of transitions that follows to fill in the blanks and create a smooth, readable paragraph.

It was just one of those days. _____, I woke up half an hour late. _____, _____ rushing to get ready, I realized that the shirt I was wearing had a big stain on it. _____ I quickly changed, grabbed a granola bar and banana for breakfast, and raced out the door. _____, I was standing at the bus stop wondering where my bus could be. _____ I remembered that I was supposed to set my clock back an hour for the end of daylight savings time. _____ I realized I wasn't late—I was a whole hour early!

a few minutes later	suddenly
after	that's when
first	then
so	

The Right Sequence of Events

Transitions are very important, but even transitions can't do much for a passage if the ideas are all out of order. Imagine, for example, that you were trying to follow a recipe that didn't list the steps in the proper sequence. You'd probably end up ordering a pizza instead! If ideas aren't in the proper sequence—if you aren't given instructions in a coherent order—you're going to have lots of trouble.

One of the most obvious sequencing clues is a numbered list, as in a recipe. Instead of using numbers, writers may sometimes use the transitions *first*, *second*, *third*, and so on to indicate proper order. In addition, writers can show the sequence of events with carryover clues that show a relationship between two events. For example, the instruction "Drizzle the melted chocolate over the cake" must come after "Melt the chocolate in a double boiler." If you got to "melted chocolate" and still had a bag of chocolate chips in front of you, you would know you'd missed something.

Exercise 2

A jam recipe includes instructions for sterilizing the jam jars. These steps are listed below in random order. Place them in the proper order by numbering them from 1 through 7. Use the carryover clues that link the events together to find the correct sequence. (The first step has been identified to get you started.)

____ Boil gently and uncovered for 15 minutes.

____ Place washed jars in a pan with a rack and cover with hot water.

____ Wash inspected jars in hot, soapy water.

____ Let jars stand in the hot water until 5 minutes before you are ready to fill with jam.

__1__ Examine the tops and edges of jars and discard any with chips or cracks, because they will prevent an airtight seal.

____ Remove pan from heat but keep jars in the hot water. Cover.

____ Heat water in pan to boiling.

When the Sequence Is Scrambled

Sometimes authors intentionally scramble the order of events. A writer might include flashbacks, memories, or dreams of the future to tell parts of the story. Or a story might be told from the perspective of more than one character. When the plot is not arranged in chronological order, pay careful attention to the transitions and carryover clues to follow the development of the story.

Order of Importance

It's a scientifically proven fact: People remember beginnings and endings better than middles. In the classroom, for example, you're most likely to remember the topics covered at the beginning and end of class. Writers have instinctively known this for a long time. That's why many pieces of nonfiction writing are organized by *order of importance*. Writers will decide to start with either the most important or the least important idea, and they will choose carefully because each choice has a different effect.

Most Important to Least Important

Organizing ideas from most important to least important puts the most essential information *first*. This is often the best approach when writers are offering advice or when they want to be sure readers get the essential information right away. A newspaper article is a good example. News reports generally don't read chronologically; instead, they begin with the most important information. Writers give us the *who*, *what*, *when*, *where*, and *why* information about the event. Here's an example from a school newspaper article:

Chess Team Wins First Championship!
(1) Yesterday the Oakville High Chess Team won its first state championship in an exciting victory over Winslow High. The team, led by captain Vassil Matic, was losing four matches to three when Magdalena Lukas, a sophomore,

won a decisive game against Winslow High captain Julian Mille. Matic then won the tie-breaker to defeat Winslow and bring home the trophy.

(2) This was only the second time the team qualified for the state championship. Two years ago, the team made it to the state championship for the first time but was eliminated during the first round of competitions. The chess team was formed in 1994 by former students Ainsley Pace, Mark Waters, and Shane Trombull. Mr. Trombull is now an advisor for the team.

Notice how this article begins with the most important information: the chess team's victory. Chronologically, this was the *last* event in the series of events described in the article, but here it comes first because it is most important. Next, the article describes the decisive moments in the match—the second most important information. Finally, the article offers some history of the chess club. This information may be interesting, but in terms of the event, it isn't all that important.

Newspaper articles are organized this way for a reason. A newspaper contains so much information that readers rarely read an entire article. In fact, newspaper readers will often read only the first few paragraphs of an article and skim—or skip—the rest. Other texts use this strategy for similar reasons. They want readers to know right from the start what's most important. The best way to do that is to put it first.

Exercise 3

Here is a passage about safety on the Internet. Read it carefully and actively. Then answer the questions that follow. Use active reading techniques to flag transitions.

Net Safety

Though it may seem like cyberspace is a pretty safe place, in reality, the Internet poses some very real dangers for teens. To be safe when you're online, follow these guidelines. First and foremost, protect your privacy. Never give your real last name, address, or telephone number to anyone. Second, never agree to meet with someone you've talked with on the Internet without asking permission from your parents first. Third, remember that people are not always what they seem. Someone who is very nice to you online could turn out to be someone eager to hurt you in person. Finally, trust your instincts. If someone uses bad language or mentions things that make you uncomfortable, don't respond; log off instead. If you come across a site where the content makes you uncomfortable, exit it as quickly as possible.

1. According to this passage, what's the most important thing you can do to be safe on the Internet?

   _____

   _____

2. What is the second most important thing?

   _____

   _____

3. What is the third most important thing?

_____

_____

4. What is the fourth most important thing?

_____

_____

ORDER OF IMPORTANCE TRANSITIONS

Here's a list of the most common transitions writers apply when using the order of importance organizational pattern.

above all
first and foremost
first, second, third
last but not least
more importantly
moreover
most importantly

Least Important to Most Important

Sometimes instead of *starting* with the most important idea, writers prefer to *end* with the most important idea. This takes advantage of the momentum, the buildup or force that a writer gets from starting with what's least important and moving toward what's most important. With this order, writers can also create suspense, since the reader has to wait for the final and most important idea.

Writers often use the least-to-most-important structure when they are presenting an **argument**, because they need to build their case piece by piece and win readers over point by point this kind of structure is more convincing. It's like the way you learned to

support your opinion with facts in the last section. If your less important points make sense to the reader, then your more important points will come off stronger. Writers often save the best for last because that's where the best has the most impact.

Take a look at the following student essay, for example. Notice how the writer builds her case, piece by piece, saving her strongest and most important point for last. As you read, mark up the text by underlining her main idea and her key supporting points.

Make Us Volunteers!

(1) There's been a proposal to add a new requirement to the eighth grade curriculum: 10 hours of volunteer work each quarter. Some will argue that this is forced volunteerism, and therefore not volunteerism at all. But I think that's beside the point. What matters is that students will benefit enormously from such a program.

(2) For one thing, volunteer work is a confidence booster. When you help someone else, when you make someone else feel good, it makes you feel better about yourself. Students will go through the year knowing that they are helping others and making a difference in their community. They will know that they have the power to make people's lives better.

(3) More importantly, volunteering will help students become more compassionate and tolerant. They will see that there are all kinds of people in the world with all kinds of problems. But underneath those problems, they're still people just like you and me.

(4) But the most important benefit of this program is that it will teach students that they have a responsibility to other people. We have a duty to help others whenever we can. Students will learn that other people are counting on

them to meet very real and important needs. They will learn that when they fail to fulfill their responsibilities, they may hurt other human beings. They will learn that when they make a commitment, it is important to honor it.

What is the writer's main idea? Did you identify it as the idea stated in the last sentence of the first paragraph—that "students will benefit enormously from such a program"? Good. Next, did you correctly identify her three supporting ideas? They are:

- Volunteering will boost students' confidence.
- Volunteering will help students become more compassionate and tolerant.
- Volunteering will teach students that they have a responsibility to others.

These points are listed from least important to most important. The transitions are our biggest clues to this structure. Here are the transitions in the order in which they're used:

- for one thing
- more importantly
- but the most important benefit

This structure works well for this argument. The first point is difficult to disagree with; we all know how good it feels to help someone else. The second point is a little more controversial. Some readers might be hesitant about working with people they feel are different. The third point is the one the author thinks is most important, and it's also perhaps the most controversial. Some people would argue that we are not duty bound to help others. But this point is easier to accept if we've already accepted the writer's previous two points. If the author began by insisting that we

have an obligation to others, and you disagreed, you might not be persuaded by her assertion that volunteering also builds confidence.

Summary

Two of the most common organizational patterns that writers use are chronological order and order of importance. The organization that writers choose depends upon their purposes. Stories of events are often told in the order in which they happen. Persuasive essays and newspaper articles typically order their topics by rank instead of time. You can identify the organizational strategy by looking closely at the transitional words and phrases used.

Answers

Exercise 1

Here's the paragraph with the transitions in place. Your answers may vary slightly:

> It was just one of those days. <u>First</u>, I woke up half an hour late. <u>Then</u>, <u>after</u> rushing to get ready, I realized that the shirt I was wearing had a big stain on it. <u>So</u> I quickly changed, grabbed a granola bar and banana for breakfast, and raced out the door. <u>A few minutes later</u>, I was standing at the bus stop wondering where my bus could be. <u>Suddenly</u> I remembered that I was supposed to set my clock back an hour for the end of daylight savings time. <u>That's when</u> I realized I wasn't late—I was a whole hour early!

Exercise 2

The correct order is as follows. The sequencing clues are underlined.

1. Examine the tops and edges of jars and discard any with chips or cracks, because they will prevent an airtight seal.
2. Wash <u>inspected jars</u> in hot, soapy water.
3. Place <u>washed jars</u> in a pan with a rack and cover with <u>hot water</u>.
4. Heat <u>water in pan</u> to boiling.
5. <u>Boil</u> gently and uncovered for 15 minutes.
6. <u>Remove pan from heat</u> but keep <u>jars in the hot water</u>. Cover.
7. Let jars stand <u>in the hot water</u> until 5 minutes before you are ready to fill with jam.

Exercise 3

1. Protect your privacy: Don't give out your name, address, or phone number.
2. Never agree to meet someone you met online without your parents' permission.
3. Remember that people are not always what they seem.
4. Trust your instincts.

Notice that this passage uses the *first, second, third* transitions we saw in the last lesson on chronological order. Here, however, these transitions don't indicate a *sequence* of doing things; rather, they indicate the *rank* of these safety suggestions.

SKILL BUILDING UNTIL NEXT TIME

1. As you read today, put the events you read about in chronological order. A newspaper article, for example, will often start with the most important information first and then provide some historical background. Revise the order so that everything proceeds chronologically.
2. Listen carefully to a commercial on television. Notice how the ideas are presented. If advertisers are trying to convince you of something, how do they organize their ideas? If they are giving advice, are their ideas organized in a different way?

SIMILARITIES AND DIFFERENCES: COMPARISON AND CONTRAST

LESSON SUMMARY

This lesson explores another organizational pattern writers often use: comparing and contrasting similarities and differences.

Imagine for a moment that an alien landed in your backyard. How would you describe this alien to your friends? Chances are you'd rely heavily on **comparison** and **contrast**. You might say, for example, that the alien looked a lot like an octopus (comparison), except that it had twelve tentacles instead of just eight (contrast). Or you might say the alien looked exactly like the alien in the movie *E.T.* (comparison), only about ten times as large (contrast).

When you show how two or more things are similar, you are **comparing** them. When you show how two or more things are different, you are **contrasting** them. This technique gives you a way to classify or judge the items you're analyzing. By placing two (or more) items side by side, for example, you can see how they measure up against each other. How are they similar or different? And why does it matter? For example, you might say that *The Hunger Games* series was even better than the *Harry Potter* books. Both featured young people with special skills, coming-of-age narratives, and the fight against an evil, oppressive force (**comparison**). But in *The Hunger Games*, the fighters relied on their physical strength and agility rather than magical skills and wizardry, which are the main tools used by the *Harry Potter* characters (**contrast**). *The Hunger Games* featured a female protagonist whose skills are as strong as (or even stronger than) her male best friends', where *Harry Potter* featured a male hero whose talents are exceptional (though his friend Hermione Granger had more book-smarts than anyone else) (**contrast**).

Main Idea in Comparison and Contrast

In writing, whenever an author is comparing and contrasting two or more items, he or she is doing it for a reason. There's something the author wants to point out by putting these two items side by side for analysis. This reason or point is the main idea, which is often stated in a topic sentence. For example, let's take another look at a more developed *Hunger Games* and *Harry Potter* comparison and contrast.

(1) Two of the best films ever made from books are *The Hunger Games* and *Harry Potter and the Sorcerer's Stone.* I've seen both movies at least a dozen times. While I always will be a loyal *Harry Potter* fan, I do have to say that *The Hunger Games* is an even better story.

(2) Both films feature warriors with special powers. In *Harry Potter and the Sorcerer's Stone*, Harry Potter, a young wizard, has innate magical abilities that make him very good at spells and charms. Similarly, in *The Hunger Games*, Katniss Everdeen has wilderness training and physical strength that she's developed in order to survive. The characters in *Harry Potter* rely heavily on their wands to battle each other. The tributes in *The Hunger Games*, in contrast, do all their fighting with whatever tools they can get their hands on, from a bow and arrow to artfully laid traps and, when desperate, their own hands. What they're forced to do to survive is much more impressive and dramatic than anything Harry Potter manages to accomplish in his first year at Hogwarts.

Right from the beginning of the passage the author's main idea is clear. The writer wants to compare and contrast these two films to show they're both great, but that *The Hunger Games* is even better. This idea is stated clearly in the last sentence of the first paragraph (a good example of a topic sentence). Then, the second paragraph looks at one aspect of both films—that they both feature warriors with special powers. After this comparison, the writer shows how different they are within this similarity. It's a nice, strong paragraph because it provides specific evidence for the overall main idea. It also states its own main idea clearly in the last sentence: "What they're forced to do to survive is much more impressive and dramatic than anything Harry Potter manages to accomplish in his first year at Hogwarts."

Exercise 1
The following passage is a more complete comparison and contrast of *Harry Potter* and *The Hunger Games*. Read the passage carefully and actively, noting how each paragraph provides support for the overall main idea. Then answer the questions that follow the passage.

The Best of the Best
(1) Two of the best films ever made from books are *The Hunger Games* and *Harry Potter and the Sorcerer's Stone.* I've seen both movies at least a dozen times. While I always will be a loyal *Harry Potter* fan, I do have to say that *The Hunger Games* is an even better story.

(2) Both films feature warriors with special powers. In *Harry Potter and the Sorcerer's Stone*, Harry Potter, a young wizard, has innate magical abilities that make him very good at spells and charms. Similarly, in *The Hunger Games*, Katniss Everdeen has wilderness training and physical strength that she's developed in order to survive. The characters in *Harry Potter* rely heavily on their wands to battle each other. The tributes in *The Hunger Games*, in contrast, do all their fighting with whatever tools they can get their hands on, from a bow and arrow to artfully laid traps and, when desperate, their own hands. What they're forced to do to survive is much more impres-

sive and dramatic than anything Harry Potter manages to accomplish in his first year at Hogwarts.

(3) More importantly, *The Hunger Games* empowers its female character more thoroughly than *Harry Potter* does. In *Harry Potter*, Hermione Granger is a supporting character; the story is told through Harry's point of view despite the fact that Hermione works harder, studies more, and takes magic more seriously than Harry does. In *The Hunger Games*, however, Katniss is a much better fighter than Peeta, the other tribute from her district; the story is told from her point of view and Peeta cedes to her authority when it's time to make decisions. There is a broad range of female characters in both films. In addition to Katniss, we meet her mother who is gifted at practicing medicine, Effie Trinket, who manages their schedule, the women of District 12, who work hard to care for their families, Rue, who is sweet and loyal, and the Katniss' prep team at the Capitol, who are colorful, unusual characters. In *Harry Potter*, there's the stern but good Professor McGonagall, the warm and nurturing Mrs. Weasley, Harry's female classmates, other professors, and some evil allies of Lord Voldemort's.

(4) The best thing about *The Hunger Games*, though, is Katniss' story. While *Harry Potter* is a great story about good wizards against evil wizards, *The Hunger Games* is a great story about a personal rebellion that all young people can relate to. Katniss becomes the figurehead of a rebellion against the society that wants to control the lives of young people and their families. Who wants to be condemned to a life of poverty in an impoverished district, at the whim of a tyrannical Capital? Katniss has grown up evading the law and breaking the

rules. When she refuses to harm Peeta, who has become her friend and ally during the Games, she challenges the authority of the game makers and sparks rebellion across the country of Panem. Katniss doesn't know how to handle her role as the symbolic face of the revolution, though, and struggles to find her place as both a Hunger Games champion and a rebel fighter. If she had been able to channel her problem with the establishment into political activism, she might have become a real leader instead of a figurehead. Katniss' story shows us that the ability to fight for survival is crucial, but a willingness to lead people who want to follow you is just as important.

1. What is the similarity discussed in paragraph 3?

_____

_____

2. What is the difference discussed in paragraph 3?

_____

_____

3. What is the similarity discussed in paragraph 4?

_____

_____

4. What is the difference discussed in paragraph 4?

_____

_____

5. What is the main idea of paragraph 4?

_____

_____

Multiple Strategies

Organizational patterns are a bit like main ideas. While there is usually one **overall organizing principle** (as there is one overall main idea), there can be other organizing principles in each paragraph (like the main ideas that hold each paragraph together). There can even be two different organizational patterns working together in the same paragraph. For example, the *Harry Potter/Hunger Games* passage uses comparison and contrast as its main organizing principle. But it also uses another strategy to organize the characteristics it compares. Notice how the transitions give this secondary structure away:

> Paragraph 2: Both films feature . . .
> Paragraph 3: More importantly . . .
> Paragraph 4: The best thing about *The Hunger Games*, though . . .

If you didn't notice it before, it should be clear now that this comparison and contrast also uses order of importance (least to most) to organize its ideas.

Transitions

One of the keys to a good comparison and contrast is strong transitions. It's important to let readers know when you're comparing and when you're contrasting. As a reader, it's important to watch for these transitions.

WORDS AND PHRASES THAT SHOW SIMILARITY	
and	just as
also	like
both	likewise
in a like manner	similarly
in the same way	

WORDS AND PHRASES THAT SHOW DIFFERENCE	
but	on the other hand
conversely	unlike
however	while
in contrast	yet
on the contrary	

Notice, for example, how the writer uses transitions in one of the paragraphs comparing *The Hunger Games* and *Harry Potter*:

> **Both** films feature warriors with special powers. In *Harry Potter and the Sorcerer's Stone*, Harry Potter, a young wizard, has innate magical abilities that make him very good at spells and charms. **Similarly,** in *The Hunger Games*, Katniss Everdeen has wilderness training and physical strength that she's developed in order to survive, **while** the characters in *Harry Potter* rely heavily on their wands to battle each other. The tributes in *The Hunger Games*, **in contrast,** do all their fighting with whatever tools they can get their hands on, from a bow and arrow to artfully laid traps and, when desperate, their own hands. What they're forced to do to survive is much more impressive and dramatic than anything Harry Potter manages to accomplish in his first year at Hogwarts.

Structure in Comparison and Contrast

We've seen how comparing and contrasting works to support a main idea, and we've looked at how a comparison and contrast uses transitions. Now it's time to look at the comparison and contrast structure.

The Point-by-Point Technique

Comparison and contrast passages are usually organized one of two ways: the point-by-point or block technique. Take a look at the following paragraph, for example:

> I'm the oldest of five kids. Yesterday, my youngest sister said she wished she was the oldest. Ha! Let me tell you, being the youngest is better any day. For one thing, the oldest has tons of responsibility. What about the youngest? None. My sis simply has to be there. She doesn't have to do chores, watch the other kids, or help make dinner. For another, the oldest has to "break in" the parents. Since I was the first, my parents had to learn how to be parents—and if they made mistakes, well, I was the one who suffered. Lucky Emily has parents who've already been through this four times. Unlike me, she has parents who are already "well trained."

Notice how this paragraph first states the main idea—"being the youngest is better any day"—and then supports this idea point by point. That is, each time the writer makes a point about what it's like to be oldest, he counters with a point about what it's like to be youngest. Thus, the structure is as follows:

> *Topic sentence:* youngest is better than oldest
> *Characteristic one:* responsibility (oldest, youngest)
> *Characteristic two:* parents' experience raising children (oldest, youngest)

For each characteristic, the writer directly compares or contrasts A (oldest) and B (youngest). Then, the writer moves on to the next characteristic and compares or contrasts A and B again. A point-by-point passage, then, uses an AB, AB, AB structure.

The Block Technique

The block technique, on the other hand, discusses all the characteristics of A and *then* discusses all the characteristics of B. That's why it's called the block technique; we get a block of text about one item that's being compared and then get a block of text about the other item. Here's our previous example rewritten with the block comparison and contrast structure:

> I'm the oldest of five kids. Yesterday, my youngest sister said she wished she was the oldest. Ha! Let me tell you, being the youngest is better any day. For one thing, the oldest has tons of responsibility. I always have to do chores, watch the other kids, and help make dinner. For another, the oldest has to "break in" the parents. Since I was the first, my parents had to learn how to be parents—and if they made mistakes, well, I was the one who suffered. What about the youngest? What kind of responsibility does my sister have? None. My sis simply has to be there. Lucky Emily also has parents who've already been through this four times. Unlike me, she has parents who are already "well trained."

Here, we have an AA, BB structure—first both of the characteristics of being the oldest, then both of the characteristics of being the youngest.

Comparing and Contrasting Matching Items

Although these two youngest/oldest child comparison and contrast passages use two different organizational techniques, they do have one very important thing in common. In both cases, the *characteristics are comparable.* When the writer makes a point about A, she also makes a point about the *same characteristic* in B. She's talking about the same issues for both—responsibility and parent experience using parallel structure. Look at what happens when the characteristics aren't comparable.

> I'm the oldest of five kids. Yesterday, my youngest sister said she wished she was the oldest. Ha! Let me tell you, being the youngest is better any day. For one thing, the oldest has tons of responsibility. I have to do chores, watch the other kids, and help make dinner. My sister, on the other hand, is always getting her way. Whatever she wants, she gets, from the latest Barbie accessory to tacos for dinner.

This version has a major problem: The two characteristics the writer wishes to compare *aren't the same*. Responsibility and the ability to get one's way are two entirely different issues. As a result, the writer is not really proving the point she makes in the topic sentence. We can't see, from this comparison, that the youngest sister doesn't have the same amount of responsibility or that the writer never gets her way. This sort of structure would be like AA55—you're comparing two categories too different to have a relationship to one another.

Exercise 2

Suppose you wanted to compare or contrast readers (Item A) to detectives (Item B). Following are five characteristics of being a reader and five characteristics of being a detective. Only three characteristics in each list match.

Find the matching characteristics and draw a line between the columns to connect them. Label whether the characteristics are similarities or differences.

READERS (ITEM A)	DETECTIVES (ITEM B)
1. look for clues to understand meaning	1. have a dangerous job
2. have many different types of books to read	2. get better at solving crimes with each case
3. can choose what book to read	3. require lots of training
4. build their vocabulary by reading	4. don't get to choose which cases to work on
5. become better readers with each book	5. look for clues to solve the crime

Exercise 3

Now that you've matched comparable characteristics, write a short comparison and contrast paragraph. Make sure you have a clear main idea and use strong transitions.

_____

_____

_____

_____

_____

Summary

Writers use the comparison and contrast structure to show how two things are alike and how they are different. Look for topic sentences that show the writer's focus (main idea). Watch for transitions, too, that signal comparison or contrast. A comparison and contrast passage may be organized point by point or in blocks. In either case, the characteristics should be comparable.

Answers

Exercise 1

1. In both movies, a broad range of female characters are presented.
2. In *The Hunger Games*, the story is from the female protagonist's perspective. In *Harry Potter*, the protagonist is male and the female lead is just a supporting character.
3. They're both great stories.
4. They're different kinds of stories. *Harry Potter* has broad, universal themes of good versus evil. *Hunger Games* features a personal story of rebellion that young people can relate to.
5. The main idea of paragraph 4 is stated in the first sentence, "The best thing about *The Hunger Games*, though, is Katniss' story."

Exercise 2

Reader 1 corresponds with Detective 5 (similarity).
Reader 3 corresponds with Detective 4 (difference).
Reader 5 corresponds with Detective 2 (similarity)

Exercise 3

Answers will vary. Here's one possibility (the transitions are in boldface type):

You may not realize it, but readers are a lot like detectives. An important part of both jobs is looking for clues. **Just as** a detective looks for clues to solve a crime, a reader looks for clues to solve the mystery of a text (its meaning). **Another similarity** is that **both** readers and detectives get better at their jobs with practice. A reader gets better at reading comprehension and builds vocabulary with each book. **Likewise,** a detective becomes better at solving crimes with each case. **One difference, however,** is that while readers get to choose which books they want to read, a detective doesn't have much choice about which case he or she has to work on. Make sure you used either AABB or ABAB structure, included transitions, and have a clear main idea.

SKILL BUILDING UNTIL NEXT TIME

1. Today, compare and contrast things around you. For example, you might compare and contrast this year's English class with last year's, or compare and contrast two sports, like football and soccer (you'll have a better comparison if you compare two team sports or two individual sports rather than comparing a team sport with an individual sport). How are these two things alike? How are they different? Make sure all the characteristics you choose are comparable. For example, if you compare and contrast football and soccer, you might consider the way the ball is handled, the way goals/points are earned, and the danger level of each sport.
2. As you make these comparisons, try arranging them in both the point-by-point and block structures.

9 ▶ CAUSE AND EFFECT

LESSON SUMMARY

"One thing leads to another"—that's the principle behind cause and effect. This lesson explains these two important concepts. You'll learn how to tell the difference between cause and effect, how they're related, and how to judge opinions about cause and effect.

Much of what you read is an attempt to explain either the cause of some action or its effect. For example, an author might try to explain the causes of global warming or the effects of a diet with too much sugar. Or an author might explore the reasons behind a change in school policy or the effects that an injury had on an athlete. As you might expect, authors describing cause and effect often use one of a few general patterns to organize their ideas.

Distinguishing between Cause and Effect

"For every action," said the famous scientist Sir Isaac Newton, "there is an equal and opposite reaction." Every action results in another action (a *reaction*). Or, in other words, for every action, there is an *effect* caused by that action. Likewise, each action is *caused* by a previous action. In other words, each action has a **cause**—something that made it happen—and an **effect**—something that *it* makes happen. Cause and effect, then, work together; you can't have one without the other. That's why it's very important to be able to distinguish between the two.

> **Cause:** a person or thing that makes something happen or creates an effect
> **Effect:** a change created by an action or cause

A passage about **cause** explains *why* something took place. You might ask, for example: Why did Elaine decide to quit the basketball team?

A passage about **effect**, on the other hand, explains *what happened after* something took place. What happened as a result of Elaine's decision? How did it affect the team? How did it affect Elaine?

Thus, we might identify a cause and effect from the previous example as follows:

> Because Elaine quit the team, she had enough free time to join the drama club.

What happened? Elaine quit the team (the cause). What was the result? She was able to join the drama club (the effect).

Exercise 1

To help you distinguish between cause and effect, try this exercise. Read the following sentences carefully and identify which is the cause and which is the effect in each sentence.

Example: Robin got 10 points taken off his grade because he handed in his paper late.
Cause: Robin handed in his paper late.
Effect: Robin got 10 points taken off his grade.

1. This new detergent has caused a rash on my arms.

   Cause: _____

   Effect: _____

2. Since I joined the track team, I've made a lot of new friends.

   Cause: _____

   Effect: _____

3. I realized that the rash on my arms wasn't created by the new detergent, but by my allergy to wool.

   Cause: _____

   Effect: _____

4. As a result of the new volunteer program, I spend every Thursday night helping in the local soup kitchen.

   Cause: _____

   Effect: _____

5. Because I help feed the homeless, I feel really good about myself.

   Cause: _____

   Effect: _____

Transitions and Other Clues

You probably had a lot of success with Exercise 1 because of the clues the writers left for you. Just as certain key words indicate whether you're comparing or contrasting, other key words indicate whether things are causes or effects. Here is a partial list of these important clues.

WORDS INDICATING CAUSE	WORDS INDICATING EFFECT
because (of)	as a result
caused (by)	consequently
created (by)	hence
since	so
	therefore

Exercise 2

Reread the sentences in Exercise 1. Are there any signal phrases that indicate cause or effect? If so, underline them.

Chain Reactions

The difference between cause and effect may seem clear, but it's not always easy to separate the two. For one thing, the two work very closely together. For another, effects often *become causes* for other events. Here's an example. Imagine that you lost your house keys (cause). As a result, you might have to stay in the school library until one of your parents can pick you up (effect). But that *effect* could then *cause* another event. That is, getting stuck in the library might give you two hours of uninterrupted time to get started on your research paper assignment. And *that* might mean that you can go to the baseball game this weekend instead of doing research.

Thus, A caused B, B caused C, and C caused D.

A causes → **B** effect (becomes) cause → **C** effect (becomes) cause → **D** effect

Effects, then, often become causes for other effects. So one event could be described as either a cause *or* an effect. It's often important to be able to tell which stage the writer is talking about.

Here's an example of a short chain of cause and effect. Read the passage below carefully and actively. Notice the clues that indicate cause and effect. Underline these transitions as you read.

> Yesterday my mother told me I was grounded for life. I was supposed to pick up my sister from her playdate at Ellie's house at 4:00. But I was playing JudoMaster-Extreme at Charlie's house, and I'd actually made it to the fourth level for the first time. So I decided to keep playing. I figured Rosie would enjoy the extra playtime. But Ellie's mom had an appointment and couldn't leave until someone picked up Rosie. She had to call my mom, who had to leave an important meeting to get Rosie.

Notice that this paragraph's purpose is to explain *why* the narrator was grounded for life. This idea is expressed in the topic sentence that begins the paragraph. This sentence reveals that this passage will explain *cause*. But the paragraph talks about *several* different causes. And it also talks about *several* different effects.

Like most events, the narrator's trouble wasn't caused by just *one* thing. Instead, it was caused by a *series* of actions and reactions—a chain of cause and effect. This particular chain began when the narrator reached the fourth level in JudoMaster. Because of that, he decided to keep playing instead of picking up his sister as he was supposed to do.

COMMONLY CONFUSED WORDS

Never mistake "affect" for its homonym, "effect."

Most commonly, effect is the noun and affect is the verb:

Example: The heat affects my ability to think clearly, and the effect of that is I lose my train of thought.

But! Someone's manner of speaking is also called their affect, and effect is used as a verb in the expression "to effect change." Read attentively and always consult a dictionary if you're unsure.

Exercise 3

There are three other sets of cause and effect in the preceding passage. What are they? List them below. The first link in the chain is provided to get you started.

Cause 1: He reached the fourth level.

Effect 1: He decided not to get Rosie on time.

Cause 2: He decided not to get Rosie on time.

Effect 2: _____

Cause 3: _____

Effect 3: _____

Cause 4: _____

Effect 4: _____

When One Cause Has Several Effects

Sometimes one cause may have several effects. That is, several things may happen as a result of one action.

For example, imagine you lie to a close friend and tell her you can't come over on Friday night because you are grounded—but the truth is that you have another friend coming over. This action could actually create several distinct effects:

1. You might feel pretty guilty for lying.
2. You'd have to make sure you stay home on Friday in case your friend calls.
3. You'd have to make sure your other friend is quiet if your friend calls.
4. You'd have to make sure no one in your family mentions your other friend's visit.

When One Effect Has Several Causes

While one cause can have several effects, one effect can also have several causes. For example, read the following paragraph carefully.

Yesterday my mother told me I was grounded for at least a month. I need to be more responsible and get myself together, she said, and I guess she's right. For one thing, I haven't cleaned my room since last summer—and trust me when I tell you, it's a disaster. And I admit I haven't been doing my other chores around the house. She's also mad because my grades slipped last semester—my As slid into Bs and my Bs into Cs. We both know I can do better. And she's right—I've been pretty disrespectful to everyone in my family for the past couple of weeks.

Here, the narrator probably wouldn't have been grounded for a month if he'd only done *one* thing wrong. But we can see from this paragraph that there were actually four different causes leading to his being grounded. These aren't causes in a chain of cause and effect; each cause individually *contributed* to this result.

Exercise 4

Questions

List the four separate reasons (causes) that the narrator was grounded.

1. _____

2. _____

3. _____

4. _____

Opinions about Cause and Effect

Sometimes, when the facts of the causes aren't clear, a writer will offer his or her *opinion* about why something happened. Or a writer may predict what he or she thinks the effects of a certain event will be. If this is the case, you need to consider how reasonable those opinions are. Are the writer's ideas logical? Does the writer offer support for the conclusions he or she offers?

A good example is the extinction of the dinosaurs. There have been many proposed causes, such as an asteroid, a devastating disease, even an attack by aliens. For each argument, you'd have to consider the evidence that the writer offers. Does the writer's evidence support the claim that *that* particular cause led to their extinction?

Similarly, imagine your school board was considering a proposal to require students to wear uniforms. In this case, writers might offer their opinions about possible effects of such a policy. Again, you'd have to consider what kind of evidence the writers offered to support their opinions. Take a look at the two following paragraphs, for example:

Paragraph A

The proposal to require public school students to wear uniforms is a bad idea. Can you imagine what it would be like? Everyone will look the same. We'll walk around school like a bunch of zombies in a bad horror movie. Teachers won't even be able to tell us apart. Our personalities will be hidden by the clothes. We will never be able to express ourselves through what we wear. The school will have to have uniform police to make sure everyone is alike.

Paragraph B

I disagree with the proposal to require public school students to wear uniforms. The intentions may be good, but the results will be bad. We should be encouraging individuality. But a uniform policy will tell students that individuality doesn't matter. After all, the way we dress is an important way we express who we are. Worse, the uniform policy will tell kids that conformity is the rule, and if they don't conform, they'll be punished. Kids who don't abide by the uniform dress code will be suspended. Are clothes more important than education?

Both authors predict certain effects of a school uniform policy. You may not agree with either author, but you should be able to see that the second paragraph is much more reasonable than the first. Most of the predicted results in the first paragraph are not very likely to happen. They're exaggerated and not supported by facts. The second paragraph, however, offers some support for its predictions. In addition, the predicted results are much more reasonable and therefore Author B's opinion is much more acceptable.

Exercise 5

Imagine that a friend has suggested you both fake being sick to miss school on the day of a test instead of studying for it. In a short paragraph, explain to your friend some of the negative effects that would result from skipping instead of just studying as best you can.

_____

_____

_____

_____

_____

_____

_____

_____

_____

Summary

Understanding cause and effect is important for reading success. All events have at least one cause (what made it happen) and at least one effect (the result of what happened). Some events have more than one cause, and some causes have more than one effect. An event is also often part of a chain of causes and effects. Causes and effects are usually signaled by important transitional words and phrases.

Answers

Exercise 1

1. Cause: the new detergent
   Effect: a rash on my arms
2. Cause: I joined the track team.
   Effect: I made a lot of new friends.
3. Cause: my allergy to wool
   Effect: sneezing
4. Cause: the new volunteer program
   Effect: I spend every Thursday night helping in the local soup kitchen.
5. Cause: I help feed the homeless.
   Effect: I feel really good about myself.

Exercise 2

The signal phrases are underlined below.

1. This new detergent has <u>caused</u> a rash on my arms.
2. <u>Since</u> I joined the track team, I've made a lot of new friends.
3. I realized that the rash on my arms wasn't <u>created</u> by the new detergent, but by my allergy to wool.
4. <u>As a result</u> of the new volunteer program, I spend every Thursday night helping in the local soup kitchen.
5. <u>Because</u> I help feed the homeless, I feel really good about myself.

Exercise 3

Cause 2: He decided not to get Rosie on time.
Effect 2: Ellie's mom couldn't leave for her appointment.

Cause 3: Ellie's mom couldn't leave for her appointment.
Effect 3: She called Rosie's mom.

Cause 4: She called Rosie's mom.
Effect 4: Rosie's mom had to leave a big meeting.

Exercise 4

1. He hasn't cleaned his room in more than a month.
2. He hasn't done his other household chores.
3. His grades have slipped.
4. He has been disrespectful to his family.

Exercise 5

Answers will vary. Here's one possibility.

Blowing off school sounds like fun but it probably wouldn't be worth it. First of all, we'd only get further behind. If we don't show up, we might get a zero on the exam, and depending on how many absences you have already, it could affect your grade for the class. If not, we'd have to make up the test anyway. Besides, my parents would ground me—we might as well study together instead!

SKILL BUILDING UNTIL NEXT TIME

1. Consider the effects of a recent change in your home, school, or neighborhood. For example, imagine that a new movie theater is being built a few blocks away from your home. How will that affect traffic on your street? How will it affect your own and your family's leisure time? How will it affect the level of noise in your area at night?
2. Consider recent events at home or school. What might have caused them? For example, imagine that your hockey team has been losing a lot of games lately. What might be causing this slump?

10 ▶ SUMMARIES AND OUTLINES

LESSON SUMMARY

Taking good notes is a valuable skill for both readers and writers. This lesson will introduce two useful ways to organize your reading notes. It will also help you decide when to use each method to create the most effective notes.

Can you remember every sentence you have read in this book so far? Of course not! When we read longer works such as books and articles, we usually remember only a few important points, or an idea that seemed really interesting. Two of the best ways to record these important ideas are summaries and outlines. A summary consists of a few sentences that briefly explain the main ideas. But if the reading has several interesting details, an outline may be the best way of organizing your notes. Summaries and outlines are useful tools for keeping track of the really significant information in a source.

When you're an active reader, outlines and summaries nearly write themselves—you can start by transcribing (writing down in a notebook or typing up on your computer) your annotations and notes, since you've been underlining or circling main ideas and supporting details.

Summaries

When you recommend a great book or movie to a friend, you probably give your friend a short summary of the story. A **summary** is a retelling of the content in your own words. The summary should briefly paraphrase the main idea and supporting ideas or arguments. The main idea can usually be stated in one sentence, but a summary is often two or more sentences.

Read the following story carefully, and think about how you would summarize it.

(1) Shiloh swung her leg back and clobbered a clump of dirt. It sailed over the sidewalk and shattered on the grass beyond. "Goal!" she sang. "One point for Shiloh Fanin!" As she continued the long walk home, she kicked at other dirt clumps and even a pile of dry leaves, though they didn't fly far. Fat tears welled in her brown eyes, but she wouldn't let them fall. For weeks she had been practicing her dribbling, long-range kicks, and passing. Every evening after dinner her father had brought out the scuffed soccer ball for an hour of running around the yard, and she had even outrun him a few times. But the hours of practice hadn't done her any good. Today's soccer team tryouts had been dismal. Nearly thirty girls had assembled on the field after school, and many of them were taller, stronger, and more experienced than Shiloh. After they had finished the tryouts, the coach explained that only fifteen girls could be chosen, and Shiloh wasn't surprised to be among those sent home. Now she would have to explain to her father that she wasn't good enough to play.

(2) As she wandered down the last block to her house, something hit her in the back of the leg. A soccer ball! She spun around and saw Ashley, another girl who hadn't made the team. "Hey, Shiloh," Ashley called. "Would you like to sign up for the community soccer league with me? You were really good today, and I need a few more girls for our team."

(3) Shiloh smiled. Maybe she could make her father proud after all.

Now look at two possible summaries. Which one seems more effective?

Shiloh didn't make the school soccer team. Then a friend asked her to join a different soccer team.

Shiloh was hoping to join the school soccer team. Despite hours of practice, she was not chosen for the team. She was upset and disappointed until a friend asked her to join a community soccer team.

The first summary is brief and concise. It tells *who* and *what*. If you were taking notes for yourself, this version might be sufficient to help you remember what the story was about. But the second version gives a bit more information—*how* Shiloh felt about these events and *why* the events were connected. If you wanted to summarize this story for a friend, these details would help explain the mood of the story and the relationship between the events. Thus, the second example is a more complete and effective summary of the story.

Exercise 1

As you read the following article, underline the main ideas. Then write your own summary on the lines that follow the article.

Northern Spotted Owl under Threat
Thirty years ago, the Northern spotted owl was one of the most common owls in the Pacific Northwest. But these owls live in old-growth forest, and logging caused much of their habitat to be lost. In 1991 the federal government

passed laws to protect the land where the owls live. Now, though, the owls face a new threat—competition with the barred owl. Barred owls are larger and more aggressive, and they scare the spotted owls away from nesting and hunting grounds. Scientists have tried several ways to protect this endangered bird. Some track the owl nests to monitor when their eggs hatch. Some scientists have even tried to reduce the population of barred owls. Environment specialists are working hard to protect this species, but more research is needed. The Northern spotted owl is also threatened by climate change and competition with other birds of prey.

_____

_____

_____

_____

Be Selective

Because a short summary cannot include every detail, you will have to decide which information is most important. Sometimes the supporting ideas can be grouped together. For example, an article may include several dates or names of people and places. Not all these names and dates have to appear in your summary. As you read this newspaper excerpt, underline the most important information.

On January 3, Swiss native Jens Kipper became the first person to swim across Lake Delgado. Kipper practiced for more than eight months before attempting the 3,250-meter swim across the chilly mountain lake. A special wetsuit allowed him to retain body temperature, and a medical crew closely followed him in a boat in case of any mishap. He completed the crossing in just over five hours. Kipper trained in Lake Superior, one of the Great Lakes bordering

northern Wisconsin and Michigan, and claimed that the weather conditions there helped him to prepare for Lake Delgado. Several people have attempted the Lake Delgado crossing before; Seamus Rich, of Ireland, made it two-thirds of the way across the lake in 2006 before high waves forced him to quit, and Frenchman Jacques Isther made several unsuccessful attempts in the late 1900s.

Unlike the article about the history of bicycles you read in Section 1, most of the names and dates in this article are not essential details. You can summarize these details in one general statement. Your summary might look like this:

Jens Kipper recently became the first person to swim across Lake Delgado. He trained for months and wore a special wetsuit. Several other people had previously attempted this crossing but failed.

The main idea of the article is Kipper's record. The article supports this main idea with details about his training, his equipment, and other swimmers who have tried the task before. If you tried to record all of these details in your summary, it might end up as long as the original article! **Keep in mind that a summary provides a very brief version of the content, and some details will have to be left out.**

Exercise 2

Here are three summaries of a story about Xerxes' attack on the Greeks. The summaries are lettered for easy reference. Read each version, then answer the questions that follow.

    a. In 484 BCE, the Persian king Xerxes attacked the Greeks.

    b. In 484 BCE, the Phoenicians joined Persia in a war against the Greeks. Their warships and sailing expertise helped King Xerxes fight the Greek navy.

c. In 484 BCE, the Persian king Xerxes asked the Phoenicians to help him make war on the Greeks. The Phoenicians contributed 300 warships and helped build a bridge of ships across the Hellespont. Xerxes' army crossed on the bridge to reach the mainland. There they began to attack the Greek cities.

1. Which summary provides only the main idea?

_____

2. Which summary provides the most supporting details? Do these details seem important?

_____

_____

3. Which summary do you think is the most effective? Why?

_____

_____

_____

When to Use Summaries

You probably summarize all the time—when you tell a friend about an argument with your mother, for example, or when you recommend a favorite comic book or television show. When you need to take notes on a reading, ask yourself, "What is this reading *about*?" This will help you focus on the main idea rather than the events or supporting details.

A summary is usually the best way to record the main idea of a fiction story. The four stages of a plot, which you discovered in Lesson 6, might be tough to arrange in outline form.

The type of notes you take will depend on what type of notes will be the most *useful* to you. Let's look once more at the story of St. Louis's Gateway Arch:

The Gateway Arch

(1) The skyline of St. Louis, Missouri, is fairly unremarkable, with one huge exception—the Gateway Arch, which stands on the bank of the Mississippi. Part of the Jefferson National Expansion Memorial, the Arch is an amazing structure built to honor St. Louis's role as the gateway to the West.

(2) In 1947 a group of interested citizens known as the Jefferson National Expansion Memorial Association held a nationwide competition to select a design for a new monument that would celebrate the growth of the United States. Other U.S. monuments are spires, statues, or imposing buildings, but the winner of this contest was a plan for a completely different type of structure. The man who submitted the winning design, Eero Saarinen, later became a famous architect. In designing the Arch, Saarinen wanted to leave a monument that would have enduring impact.

(3) The Gateway Arch is a masterpiece of engineering, a monument even taller than the Great Pyramid in Egypt. In its own way, the Arch is at least as majestic as the Great Pyramid. The Gateway is shaped as an inverted catenary curve, the same shape that a heavy chain will form if suspended between two points. Covered with a sleek skin of stainless steel, the Arch often reflects dazzling bursts of sunlight. In a beautiful display of symmetry, the height of the arch is the same as the distance between the legs at ground level.

If you are reading this passage just to get the main idea, you'll want to know *what* the Arch is, *where* it is located, and *why* it is important. You would include only the most important details that you want to remember or refer to later. Your summary might look like this:

The Gateway Arch is a remarkable monument on the bank of the Mississippi River in St.

Louis. The stainless steel Arch was designed by Eero Saarinen in the 1940s to honor St. Louis as the gateway to the West.

But suppose you were writing an essay comparing the Arch to another monument. The names, dates, and other details about the Arch would be important to remember, so you could use an outline instead.

Outlines

Outlines may include single words, short phrases, or complete sentences. Include as much information as you need. Taking detailed, organized notes can save you a lot of time in the long run!

A summary uses complete sentences to explain what a reading is about. But if the reading contains many important or interesting details, you might use an outline. An **outline** shows the main idea and supporting details in a *list*. Outlines can be used to take notes on fiction stories, but they are best for readings that contain lots of facts and information. Outlines usually are formatted like this one:

Surfing
I. History
    A. Polynesian culture
    B. Captain Cook's travel notes
    C. Modern surfing
II. Equipment
    A. Surfboards
        1. Longboards
        2. Funboards
        3. Shortboards
    B. Wetsuits
    C. Board wax

Note that the topic appears at the top; if you are taking notes from a book or article, include the au-

thor's name or the book title as well. This sample outline uses three *levels* to list the two main topics and several smaller details. The main ideas should be the first level in your outline. Usually the first level of the outline uses Roman numerals (I, II, III, IV, V, and so on). The second level uses capital letters, and the third level uses regular Arabic numbers. These levels help you show how the details are related.

Exercise 3

Read the paragraph about the Northern spotted owl once more, and this time organize your notes as an outline on the lines that follow. You might use headings such as *current threat*, *other threats*, and *possible solutions*.

Northern Spotted Owl under Threat
Thirty years ago, the Northern spotted owl was one of the most common owls in the Pacific Northwest. But these owls live in old-growth forest, and logging caused much of their habitat to be lost. In 1991 the federal government passed laws to protect the land where the owls live. Now, though, the owls face a new threat—competition with the barred owl. Barred owls are larger and more aggressive, and they scare the spotted owls away from nesting and hunting grounds. Scientists have tried several ways to protect this endangered bird. Some track the owl nests to monitor when their eggs hatch. Some scientists have even tried to reduce the population of barred owls. Environment specialists are working hard to protect this species, but more research is needed. The Northern spotted owl is also threatened by climate change and competition with other birds of prey.

_____

_____

_____

_____

_____

_____

When to Use Outlines

Outlines are best when you want to remember *specific details* from a reading. Remember that outlines show not only the ideas, but also the *relationship* between the ideas. Thus, when you take notes as an outline, you have to decide how to organize the details. This is much easier when you see how the *author* organized the ideas in the text as we learned in the previous lesson on organization. Suppose you are reading an article comparing wind power to solar power. Here are two possible ways to organize your outline:

I.	History	I.	Wind power
	A. Wind power		A. History
	B. Solar power		B. Advantages
II.	Current use		C. Disadvantages
	A. Wind power	II.	Solar power
	B. Solar power		A. History
III.	Future potential		B. Advantages
	A. Wind power		C. Disadvantages
	B. Solar power		

The outline on the left is arranged point by point. The outline on the right is arranged in blocks. Remember AABB and ABAB? Even if the author uses one arrangement, you could still reorganize the ideas to fit a different pattern. But when you understand the *structure* of the article, you'll have a good idea of how to organize your notes.

Other Ways to Organize

An outline is one type of graphic organizer; it is a way to organize information using both illustration and words. The outline still uses a lot of words, but the way they are arranged adds to your understanding. A web-shaped **cluster diagram** is another type of graphic organizer. It shows a topic or character name in a central circle. Lines are drawn to smaller circles containing details related to the main topic or character. A cluster diagram helps you make connections between concepts and characters. A **time line**, showing a list of dates of events, is also a graphic organizer. A time line helps you organize information chronologically, or by time. You will probably use time lines in your history classes. When taking notes, use the organizer that will work best for the topic or content. You might need to experiment with more than one method to decide which will be most helpful.

Summary

Good readers take notes on what they read; notes help us to organize ideas, make connections, and remember the most important points. The content will probably determine what type of note-taking strategy you choose. Summaries briefly restate the story or main ideas in your own words, while outlines arrange the main ideas in a list.

Answers

Exercise 1

There are several ways to summarize this article, but your summary should include most of these ideas:

> The Northern spotted owl is endangered because of competition with barred owls. The owl is also threatened by climate change and logging in its habitat. Scientists are trying several methods to protect the owl.

Exercise 2

1. a. This summary presents the topic and the main idea, but no supporting details.

2. c. The third summary presents numerous details, but the number of ships, the location of the ships, and the sequence of events are probably more information than we need.

3. b. The second summary is most effective because it includes the main idea and some supporting details without being too specific.

Exercise 3

This outline includes the suggested topic headings, but other headings are certainly possible. You may have included short key words or longer phrases to help you remember the major points of this article. Your outline should include most of these details:

Northern Spotted Owls Endangered

I. Current threat ← Main idea
  A. Competition with barred owls for food and nesting sites ← Supporting detail/ fact
II. Other threats
  A. Logging and loss of habitat
  B. Climate change
  C. Competition with other birds of prey
III. Possible solutions
  A. Monitoring spotted owl chicks
  B. Reducing barred owl population
  C. More research needed

SKILL BUILDING UNTIL NEXT TIME

1. Write a brief summary (up to four sentences) of your favorite book. Try to summarize the *main idea* of the story. If it seems tough to leave out all the character names and plot twists, look at some short book or movie reviews in the newspaper to see how they summarize long stories.
2. Read a news or magazine article that interests you. Build an outline by writing down the main ideas of the article, and then add the supporting details. Don't be afraid to erase, cross out, or reorganize!

11 ▶ PUTTING IT ALL TOGETHER

SECTION SUMMARY

This lesson pulls together what you've learned about structure in Lessons 6 through 10. It also gives you more practice in the basics from Lessons 1 through 4.

Like chefs preparing a meal, writers need a plan for how they will organize their ideas. In the last section, you learned to recognize the parts of a fictional plot. You learned some organizational strategies that writers use: arranging ideas according to time, order of importance, similarities and differences, and cause and effect. You also learned how to take effective notes about fiction and nonfiction readings. Now it's time to review these strategies and combine them with the basics of active reading, word recognition, finding the main idea, and distinguishing fact from opinion you learned in Section 1.

What You've Learned

Here's a quick review of each lesson about structure.

Lesson 6: The Parts of a Plot. You examined the four stages of plot development in fiction stories: exposition, rising action, climax, and resolution. Each stage reveals important details about the characters and the meaning behind their actions while advancing the story.

Lesson 7: Organizing Principles. You learned that ideas are often presented in chronological order—the order in which they occurred or should occur. Writers often provide sequence clues through transitions. Ideas can also be organized by value. They can begin with the most important idea and work to the least important idea, or vice versa to build momentum, from the least important to the most important.

Lesson 8: Similarities and Differences: Comparison and Contrast. You saw how ideas are arranged to illustrate similarities and differences. Writers match corresponding features of two or more topics and show how they are alike or different. Ideas can be presented either point by point (ABAB) or in blocks (AABB).

Lesson 9: Cause and Effect. Here, ideas are organized so that readers can see what caused an event to take place or what effect(s) an event had. Sometimes writers describe a chain of cause and effect as well as multiple causes and multiple effects.

Lesson 10: Summaries and Outlines. You learned how to build your own notes in summary form, as complete sentences, or in outline form, as an organized list of ideas. By identifying the structure of the piece of writing, you can decide which type of notes will be most helpful.

If any of these terms or strategies are unfamiliar, STOP. Take some time to review the term or strategy that is unclear.

Section 2 Practice

Although writers often have one overall organizing principle, they often combine two or more organizational strategies as they write. Keep this in mind as you read through the practice passages below. As you read, look for clues to determine the overall structure and watch for smaller sections that organize ideas in a different way *within* the main structure. Read each passage actively and carefully. Then answer the questions that follow.

Exercise 1

(1) Too much sun exposure can be deadly. (2) First of all, too much sun can dry your skin, which in turn reduces its elasticity and speeds up the aging process. (3) Second, too much sun can burn unprotected skin and lead to permanent discoloration and damage to the dermis (the second layer of skin). (4) Most important, long-term exposure of unprotected skin can cause skin cancer.

1. Which two organizational patterns does this paragraph use?
   a. chronology; cause and effect
   b. order of importance; cause and effect
   c. order of importance; comparison and contrast
   d. cause and effect; comparison and contrast

2. Which sentence expresses the main idea of this passage?
   a. Sentence 1
   b. Sentence 2
   c. Sentence 3
   d. Sentence 4

3. According to the passage, what is the most important reason to avoid too much sun?
  a. It can dry skin.
  b. It can speed up the aging process.
  c. It can burn skin.
  d. It can cause skin cancer.

4. Which of the following can result from dry skin?
  a. burns
  b. a rash
  c. reduced elasticity
  d. permanent discoloration

Exercise 2

Note: Exercise 2 is considerably longer than any other passage you've seen so far—but it's about the length you'll expect to see on standardized tests. If the length seems a bit scary, don't worry. Just read the story carefully and actively as you would any other passage.

This passage has been numbered for your reference. If you're ever faced with an unnumbered test, just write them in yourself!

The Tryout

(1) A lark—that's what Alexander's family called him because he sang all the time. Personally, Alexander believed he sounded more like a crow, but it didn't concern him. He simply liked singing. He sang in the shower, he sang while he did his homework, and he sang while he walked to school. He couldn't have cared less what he sounded like, until Kevin started talking about the tryouts for the City Boys' Choir.

(2) "Yeah, I'm attending the tryouts this weekend," he heard Kevin bragging one day in class. "With my voice, I'm pretty much guaranteed a spot. I imagine they'll want me to perform lots of solos, too." Everyone around school knew that Kevin had a fantastic singing voice. Normally, Alexander just ignored him, but while he was walking home from school (singing as usual), he kept imagining himself as a member of the boys' choir. Wouldn't it be fun, he thought, to sing competitively with other kids and have someone actually teach him about singing?

(3) Bright and early Saturday morning, Alexander's mom dropped him off at the auditorium where the tryouts were being held. Alexander took a deep breath, walked into the building, registered at a large table, and then joined the other boys who were all chattering nervously in the hallway. The only one who didn't look nervous was Kevin. And why should he be? Kevin had been taking lessons for years and had won numerous competitions. Alexander, on the other hand, had never taken a music lesson in his life, much less performed for an audience.

(4) Fortunately, before Alexander had a chance to get too nervous, the choir director, Mr. Robeson, walked in and immediately got things started. He had each boy stand up on the auditorium stage, announce himself, and sing a song. When Alexander's turn came, he pretended he was singing in the shower and did his best to ignore the scribbling of the people sitting in the front row, who were diligently taking notes on his performance. He felt satisfied when he was done, at least until Kevin's turn came. As Kevin's confident voice filled the room, Alexander realized that he would never sound that good.

(5) After the boys had finished their individual performances, Mr. Robeson put them into groups of four or five and asked them to sing again, this time as a group. Alexander thoroughly enjoyed singing with the other boys. He did his best to blend his voice with theirs. Kevin's group sang right after Alexander's, and even with four other boys singing, Kevin's voice was clear, distinct, and completely unmistakable; it seemed to reach the farthest corners of the auditorium.

(6) When the groups finished singing, Mr. Robeson began the interview process. He asked Alexander about his performance experience, any music lessons he'd had, any training he'd received. All Alexander could say was, "I just really enjoy singing. I sing all the time, and I want to learn more." He kept imagining the lengthy and detailed answers Kevin would give to each of Mr. Robeson's questions.

(7) Afterward, Alexander slunk miserably out of the building and climbed into his mother's car.

(8) The next afternoon, Alexander anxiously pedaled his bicycle over to the auditorium where a list of new members was supposed to be posted. He didn't think his name would be on the list, but he was curious to see who'd made it. Quickly, he scanned the list, and then he read it again more carefully. There must have been some mistake. His name was on the list, and Kevin's name was not.

(9) Just then the door opened and Mr. Robeson strolled out. "Um, excuse me, Mr. Robeson," stammered Alexander. "What happened? How did I make the choir?"

(10) "You love singing, and what better quality could a choir member have? Your voice isn't the best I've ever heard, but with training I think it will improve quite a bit. That improvement will take a lot of practice, however. You are willing to practice, aren't you?"

(11) "Of course I am. But, what about Kevin? Why didn't he make it? He has such a good voice."

(12) "Talent alone is not enough," said Mr. Robeson. "We need boys who are willing to work hard. Even the best singers in the world must continue to practice. Just think about it, Alexander. This is a choir where all the members are equal. We weren't looking for soloists. We were looking for boys who seemed to have the right voice and attitude to be part of a choir. Enough about tryouts, though. Will we see you at choir practice this week?"

(13) "Absolutely, Mr. Robeson!" Alexander said. He climbed back onto his bicycle and rode home, singing all the way.

5. What is the overall organizing principle of this passage?
   a. chronology
   b. order of importance
   c. comparison and contrast
   d. cause and effect

6. Which organizational pattern is used *within* the third paragraph?
   a. chronological
   b. order of importance
   c. comparison and contrast
   d. cause and effect

7. Why did Alexander try out for the choir?
   a. because he has a terrific voice
   b. because he loves to sing
   c. because he practiced hard
   d. because he was good friends with Kevin

8. According to this story, in what way are Kevin and Alexander *alike*?
   a. They both love to sing.
   b. They both have great voices.
   c. They both made the choir.
   d. They both tried out for the choir.

9. Which is the correct order of events that took place during the tryout?
   a. singing in a group, singing alone, interviewing with Mr. Robeson
   b. singing in a group, interviewing with Mr. Robeson, singing alone
   c. singing alone, singing in a group, interviewing with Mr. Robeson
   d. interviewing with Mr. Robeson, singing alone, singing in a group

10. Reread the following sentence from the story.

    When Alexander's turn came, he pretended he was singing in the shower and did his best to ignore the scribbling of the people sitting in the front row, who were diligently taking notes on his performance.

    The word *diligently* in this sentence probably means
    a. carefully and attentively.
    b. slowly.
    c. loudly and rudely.
    d. sloppily.

11. What type of conflict develops in this story?
    a. Alexander versus another character
    b. Alexander versus himself
    c. Alexander versus society
    d. Alexander versus nature

12. Which event is the climax of the plot?
    a. Mr. Robeson interviews Alexander.
    b. Mr. Robeson explains why Alexander has been chosen.
    c. Alexander sees his name on the list of new members.
    d. Alexander decides to try out for the boys' choir.

13. According to Mr. Robeson, what characteristic does Alexander have that Kevin does not?
    a. Alexander has the right attitude.
    b. Alexander has a better schedule for coming to practice.
    c. Alexander was brave enough to try out.
    d. Alexander didn't want to be a soloist.

14. In which of the following sentences is Mr. Robeson expressing an *opinion*?
    a. "Will we see you at choir practice next week?"
    b. "We weren't looking for soloists."
    c. "Your voice isn't the best I've ever heard, but with training I think it will improve quite a bit."
    d. "You love singing."

15. Which of the following statements best summarizes the story?
    a. Alexander loves to sing, so he wants to join a boys' choir. He auditions and is accepted.
    b. Alexander wants to join a boys' choir. He is nervous at the auditions because Kevin is a better singer. But Alexander is chosen because he loves to sing and has the right attitude.
    c. Alexander and Kevin are rivals. Alexander is shocked when he is chosen for the boys' choir instead of Kevin.
    d. Alexander likes to sing in the shower and while he walks to school. When Alexander joins the boys' choir, Mr. Robeson encourages him to keep practicing to improve his singing skill.

Answers

Exercise 1

1. b. This paragraph lists three effects of too much sun and lists them from least to most important. If you missed this question, revisit Lesson 7 and Lesson 9.

2. a. The first sentence is a topic sentence that clearly expresses the main idea of the paragraph. If you missed this question, revisit Lesson 2 and Lesson 7.

3. d. The beginning of the fourth sentence tells us that this is the most important effect. If you missed this question, revisit Lesson 4 and Lesson 7.

4. c. The second sentence explains that dry skin can have two results (effects): It can reduce its elasticity and speed up the aging process. If you missed this question, revisit Lesson 4.

Exercise 2

5. a. This is a story organized chronologically, from Alexander's interest in trying out for the choir to the results of his tryout. The story also uses comparison and contrast and cause and effect, but chronology is the only organizing principle that works throughout the entire story. If you missed this question, revisit Lesson 7.

6. c. At the end of the third paragraph, the author directly contrasts Alexander's singing experience to Kevin's. If you missed this question, revisit Lesson 8.

7. b. The first paragraph stresses just how much Alexander likes to sing, and the second paragraph tells us he thought it would "be fun" to sing competitively and learn more about singing. This is also the best answer because none of the other possible answers are true: He did not have a terrific voice, he did not practice hard (he only sang for fun), and he was not good friends with Kevin. If you missed this question, revisit Lesson 4 and Lesson 9.

8. d. The only similarity clear in the story is that they both tried out for the choir. We can guess that Kevin loves to sing, but that is never mentioned in the story, and the fact that he does not have the right attitude suggests that maybe he doesn't like to sing all that much. We know that Alexander does not have a great voice, so choice **b** is incorrect, and we also know that Kevin did not make the choir, so choice **c** can't be the correct answer. If you missed this question, revisit Lesson 8.

9. c. When Mr. Robeson gets things started, he **first** "had each boy stand up . . . and sing a song." **Then,** "After the boys had finished their individual performances, Mr. Robeson put them into groups." **Finally,** "When the groups finished singing, Mr. Robeson began the interview process." Notice the carryover clues in both the second and third steps. If you missed this question, revisit Lesson 7.

10. a. Diligently means carefully, attentively. Given the context of the sentence, this is the meaning that makes the most sense. There seem to be a lot of boys competing for the choir, and there are three separate steps in the tryout, so the process seems to be taken very seriously. If you missed this question, revisit Lesson 3.

11. a. The conflict is between Alexander and Kevin, as both characters are competing for a place in a choir. Nature and society are not really part of the story, and it is not an internal conflict for Alexander because he does not control the outcome though he does have to defeat his nerves. If you missed this question, revisit Lesson 6.

12. c. Alexander's decision to try out is the exposition, the setup for the story, while the audition marks the rising action, and Mr. Robeson's explanation is part of the story's resolution. Thus choice **c**, the moment he learns of his acceptance, is the climax. If you missed this question, revisit Lesson 6.

13. a. Mr. Robeson's answer is all about attitude. He likes the fact that Alexander loves to sing and seems willing to work hard and practice. He tells Alexander, "We were looking for boys who seemed to have the right voice and attitude to be part of a choir," and Kevin was more focused on standing out than cooperating. If you missed this question, revisit Lesson 8.

14. c. The first choice is a question, so it is neither a fact nor an opinion. Both choices **b** and **d** state facts: Robeson and the others "weren't looking for soloists"—they wanted boys who wanted "to be part of a choir"—and of course the fact that Alexander loves to sing is repeated throughout the story. In addition, the phrase "I think" is a good clue that choice **c** offers an opinion. If you missed this question, revisit Lesson 4.

15. b. This summary introduces the main characters and explains the story's conflict and its resolution. If you were trying to jog a friend's memory about this story, this choice would do it. By contrast, choice **a** ignores the story's conflict, while choice **c** focuses only on the conflict without explaining the characters or the resolution. Choice **d** includes irrelevant details and leaves out the main ideas. If you missed this question, revisit Lesson 10.

SKILL BUILDING UNTIL NEXT TIME

1. Look again at the passages you read in Lessons 1 through 5. What organizational structures do you notice at work in those paragraphs?
2. As you read (and write) in the next few days, be aware of the structure of each paragraph and of passages as a whole. Choose one of the passages you like a lot, and try to identify the author's overall organizational strategy as well as other strategies he or she may use throughout the text.

3 ▶ LANGUAGE AND STYLE

In most of the passages you've read so far, the author's ideas and purpose have been very clear. But what happens when they're not? What if the writer doesn't provide a topic sentence that clearly expresses the main idea? Maybe they're trying to be subtle or maybe they were having an off day. What about stories and poems? How do you figure out what the author is trying to say?

The good news is that if you read carefully, you'll find plenty of clues about the meaning of any kind of text. Some of the most helpful clues are found in the writer's *language* and *style*. How does the author write? What types of words does the author use? What types of sentences? What point of view does he or she represent? What was her or his motivation for writing?

The lessons in this section are all about language and style. You'll learn about:

- point of view (Lesson 12)
- word choice (Lesson 13)
- style and tone (Lesson 14)
- literary devices (Lesson 15)

You'll see how authors use these elements to create meaning. Then you'll put it all together in Lesson 16.

LESSON

12 ▶ POINT OF VIEW

LESSON SUMMARY

This lesson is about point of view: the perspective that writers use to tell a story. You'll learn the three main points of view and the effects each point of view has on the reader.

Imagine that you're at a magic show. On stage, the magician is sawing his assistant in half. From the tenth row, it looks like he really has cut her in two! But she's alive and smiling. Magic!

Now imagine that you're still at the magic show, but this time you're not in the audience—you're backstage. From where you are, what do you see now? The trick looks quite different. From this point of view, you can see the assistant open a trap door for her legs. You can see the magician place a curtain over part of her body. You can see, in fact, how the "magic" works—and it's just an illusion after all.

In both cases, the magician and his assistant did the same thing. But what you saw was very different, because what you saw depended upon your point of view.

Point of view (also often called *perspective*) is the person or position through which you see things. You can look at an object from many different points of view. You can look at it from above, below, behind, beside, and so on. What you see when you view the object and its surroundings often depends on your position. Remember facts and opinions?

You can look at ideas and events from many different points of view, too. This is true of most things in life, and that's why it's so important to be aware of point of view.

In writing, the point of view is like a filter. It's the voice through which the writer shares his or her ideas. It may come across as a bias. What readers hear depends upon who is telling it to them. Thus, point of view is an important decision for writers to make and for readers to consider critically. Who will talk to the reader? Who will **narrate** the story? (In stories, the person who tells the story is called the narrator.)

The Three Points of View

There are three points of view writers can use: the **first-person**, **second-person**, and **third-person** point of view. Each point of view is available to writers, and each has a specific effect. That's because each point of view works differently and creates a different relationship between reader and writer.

The First-Person Point of View

In the first-person point of view, the writer uses the pronouns *I*, *me*, *my*, *we*, and *us*. The writer or narrator shares his or her own feelings, experiences, and ideas with the readers, which is why nonfiction writers often choose this option when writing in their own voices. Fiction writers frequently set novels in the voice of the main character. Writing in first-person is like seeing through your own eyes. Here are two examples.

> I couldn't wait for the weekend. I would finally get to meet my relatives from Romania, the people I'd been writing to for years but had never seen.

> We wandered around for hours and finally admitted that we were hopelessly lost. What were we going to do now?

The Second-Person Point of View

The second-person point of view uses the pronoun *you*. By doing so, the writer or narrator puts the reader in his or her shoes or in the situation he or she is describing. Here are the examples rewritten in the second-person point of view:

> You couldn't wait for the weekend. You would finally get to meet your relatives from Romania, the people you'd been writing to for years but had never seen.

> You wandered around for hours and finally admitted that you were hopelessly lost. What were you going to do now?

To write in second-person, imagine seeing through someone else's eyes and describing what you see for them, speaking directly to them.

The Third-Person Point of View

The third-person point of view offers readers the voice of an outsider. There is usually no direct reference to the writer or narrator (the first person *I* or *we*). Instead, the writer uses the pronouns *he, she, it,* or *they*. When writing in the third-person, imagine two people having a conversation, with a third person standing nearby to describe their actions. Reporters and critics often choose this perspective in order to be more objective. Writers of fiction use this technique if they want to tell a story from multiple perspectives. Here are our examples again, rewritten in the third-person point of view:

> She couldn't wait for the weekend. She would finally get to meet her relatives from Romania, the people she'd been writing to for years but had never seen.

> They wandered around for hours and finally admitted that they were hopelessly lost. What were they going to do now?

Determining Point of View

Of course, writers can't be restricted to one pronoun, so sometimes you need to read carefully to determine which point of view the writer is using. For example, read the following sentence:

> I was watching her carefully, wondering what she would say to you.

Here, we seem to have all three points of view, don't we? There's the first-person *I*, the second-person *you*, and the third-person *her* and *she*. But really this sentence uses only *one* point of view. The question to ask is, *who* is talking? Who is telling the story or sharing the information? The answer should tell you the correct point of view. In this case, it is clearly a first-person perspective.

Exercise 1

Determine the point of view in the following sentences by circling the letter of the correct answer.

1. As Xavier held tightly to the rope, Paul used all his strength to pull his friend up out of the gorge.
   a. first person
   b. second person
   c. third person

2. By now you're settled into your routine. You wake up at 5:00 A.M., walk the dogs, shower, gulp down a quick breakfast, and meet Mr. Walton in the cafeteria for a challenging game of chess before school.
   a. first person
   b. second person
   c. third person

3. I thought and thought but could not come up with any reason why she would be angry with me.
   a. first person
   b. second person
   c. third person

4. We'd never talked much before, and he always thought I was a shy person, so he couldn't believe how much I talked when we went out to dinner.
   a. first person
   b. second person
   c. third person

5. They knew that he wanted to join their club, but they were afraid to make an exception for him.
   a. first person
   b. second person
   c. third person

The Effect of Point of View

As we've already stated, point of view is important because each point of view creates a different effect.

The Relationship to the Reader

Perhaps the most important difference among the points of view is the kind of relationship they create between reader and writer. Read the two paragraphs below to see for yourself. The first paragraph is from *The Tryout*, which you read in Lesson 11 and which is told in the third person.

> The next afternoon, Alexander anxiously pedaled his bicycle over to the auditorium where a list of new members was supposed to be posted. He didn't think his name would be on the list, but he was curious to see who'd made it. Quickly, he scanned the list, and then he read it again more carefully. There must have been some mistake. His name was on the list, and Kevin's name was not.

This paragraph is the same passage rewritten in the first-person point of view.

> The next afternoon, I anxiously pedaled my bicycle over to the auditorium where a list of

new members was supposed to be posted. I didn't think my name would be on the list, but I was curious to see who'd made it. Quickly, I scanned the list, and then I read it again more carefully. There must have been some mistake. My name was on the list, and Kevin's name was not.

Although these paragraphs tell the same story, the effects are quite different. When the story is told from the first-person point of view, there's suddenly a *direct contact* between the reader and the storyteller. Here, we are identifying with Alexander, sharing his experience. When the story is told in the third person, *someone else*, an outside narrator, is telling Alexander's story to us. There's no direct contact.

The first-person point of view, then, tends to create a sense of *closeness* or identification between reader and writer (or narrator). The writer shares his or her feelings and ideas with us. The relationship between reader and writer is personal, internal, often informal, friendly, and open.

The third-person point of view, on the other hand, creates more *distance* between reader and writer. With the third-person point of view there's no direct person-to-person contact. Instead, someone else (often an unnamed narrator) is speaking to the reader, telling them about an external series of events. The relationship between the reader and the writer is therefore more formal, less friendly, and less open.

Exercise 2

Make the following sentences less formal and more personal by switching the point of view.

1. The ad makes readers feel good about themselves.

_____

_____

_____

2. The students are upset about the change in the lunch menu.

_____

_____

_____

3. People often feel betrayed when someone breaks a promise.

_____

_____

_____

Subjectivity versus Objectivity

Another important difference between the points of view is the level of subjectivity or objectivity they create. Sometimes, it's important *not* to be too friendly and informal. The first-person point of view may make the reader feel close to the writer, but the first-person point of view is a *personal* point of view. It is therefore **subjective**. Ideas often carry more weight if they are presented in an **objective** way. An objective person is outside the action; he or she is not personally involved. Therefore, his or her ideas are more likely to be fair to everyone. But someone involved in the action is subjective and therefore affected by the situation. His or her ideas may be based on personal feelings and desires and may be limited by what he or she was able to see.

Subjective: based on the thoughts, feelings, and experiences of the speaker or writer (first-person point of view)
Objective: unaffected by the thoughts, feelings, and experiences of the speaker or writer (third-person point of view)

To see the difference, read the following sentences carefully.

A: I think a school uniform policy would hurt us more than it would help us.

B: A school uniform policy would hurt students more than it would help them.

Which sentence offers a subjective point of view? Which is more objective? Clearly, Sentence A is written from the first-person point of view—and not just any first person, but the point of view of a student who will be personally affected. Sentence B, on the other hand, may still have been written by a student, but it is written in an objective, third-person point of view.

If you were making an argument against a school uniform policy, the objective, third-person point of view would probably be more convincing. Why? Because it suggests that you are not directly involved in the action or situation and therefore don't have a personal stake in the issue. It suggests that you have a more objective (and therefore more reasonable) opinion on the issue because you are an outsider. A first-person point of view, on the other hand, suggests that you are directly involved and have something personal at stake, which might skew your ability to see it from all sides.

Of course, writers often use the third-person point of view to state very subjective opinions. But with the third-person point of view, opinions appear more objective—and that makes a bigger difference than you might think.

Exercise 3

The following sentences use the first-person point of view. Change the point of view to the third person to make the statements seem more objective.

1. Teacher: "I think we deserve an additional period each day for class preparation because we have many papers to grade."

_____

_____

_____

2. Student: "We should get less homework. I often feel overwhelmed by how much schoolwork I have to do at home."

_____

_____

_____

3. Parent: "I often wonder if I'm doing the right thing for my children."

_____

_____

_____

What about the Second-Person Point of View?

When do writers use the second-person pronoun, and what are its effects?

Referring to the Reader

When writers write, they must decide how to refer to themselves or to the narrator. They must also decide how to refer to the reader. They can address the reader in two ways: with the second-person *you* or with the third-person *he*, *she*, or *it*.

Writers use the second-person *you* to address the reader directly. Here's an example. Imagine that on your first day of school, you get the following letter.

Welcome to South Mountain High! In addition to a nationally recognized teaching staff, South Mountain also offers you many extracurricular activities to enhance your learning experience. You might want to join the Drama Club, the Math Team, or the South Mountain Student Volunteer Association. Please read the attached description of student clubs and activities and let us, in Student Services, know if you have any questions. Club Day will be held on Thursday, September 19.

Now imagine that you got this letter instead.

Welcome to South Mountain High! In addition to a nationally recognized teaching staff, South Mountain also offers students many extracurricular activities to enhance the students' learning experiences. Students can join the Drama Club, the Math Team, or the South Mountain Student Volunteer Association. Please read the attached description of student clubs and activities. Any questions should be addressed to Student Services. Club Day will be held on Thursday, September 19.

Which letter would you rather receive? The first letter speaks directly to you. With the second-person pronoun. In this letter, you are an individual, not a category (students). The first letter also comes *from* a person—the folks in Student Services, who use the first person *us* to refer to themselves. The result is a friendly person-to-person communication.

In the second letter, on the other hand, the reader isn't addressed at all. The letter never names *you* as the new student. This isn't necessarily because the writers mean to be impersonal, though. It could be that the writers intended this letter for a much wider audience, including parents and teachers, not just students.

Getting the Reader Involved

Writers also use the second-person point of view for another reason: to make readers feel directly involved in the action. Imagine, for example, that the writer of *The Tryout* put *you* in Alexander's shoes.

The next afternoon, you pedal anxiously over to the auditorium where a list of new members is supposed to be posted. You don't think your name will be on the list, but you're curious to see who's made it. Quickly, you scan the list . . . and then you read it again more carefully. There must have been some mistake! Your name is on the list, and Kevin's name is not.

Some readers enjoy the second-person voice. There's a whole series of books called *Choose Your Own Adventure*, that specifically inserts you into the story. Others might have a more negative reaction, and think "I don't know how to sing! Why am I auditioning?"

How do you feel after reading this passage? Could you imagine yourself in Alexander's shoes?

Writers also use the second-person point of view in arguments when they want readers to imagine themselves in certain situations. Take the school uniform policy situation once more as an example, and read the following passage.

Imagine what it would be like if every morning, when you woke up, you knew exactly what you were going to wear. In fact, you'd know exactly what *everyone* in school was going to wear, because you are all required to wear uniforms. As you walk down the hall, you wouldn't be able to recognize your friend by her favorite sweater. You wouldn't be able to wear the stylish and comfortable pants you got for your birthday. You'd look just like everyone else in your navy blue sweater, white oxford shirt, and navy blue skirt.

As an introduction to an argument against a school uniform policy, this would probably be pretty effective—and certainly more effective than the same paragraph in the third-person point of view.

Exercise 4
Read the following sentences and decide which point of view is best for each writing situation. Explain why you believe this point of view would be effective.

1. You are the president of the new South Mountain High School Student Volunteer Association and you are writing a description of the association for a school brochure.

   _____
   _____
   _____

2. You are writing an editorial for the school newspaper. Your purpose is to convince students to keep the school property clean.

   _____
   _____
   _____

3. You are writing a letter to your school's PTA. Your purpose is to thank the PTA for an award you received.

   _____
   _____
   _____

Summary

In writing, the point of view is the person through whom the writer tells the story or shares information. The first-person point of view uses the pronouns *I*, *me*, and *we*. It is a personal point of view because the writer or narrator is speaking directly to the reader; therefore, it is also the most subjective point of view. The second-person point of view uses the pronoun *you*, putting the reader in the writer's or narrator's shoes. The third-person point of view presents information from an outsider's perspective and uses the pronouns *he*, *she*, *it*, or *they*.

You can see by now how important point of view is in writing, for each point of view creates a different effect. Sometimes it brings the reader and writer closer together (the first-person point of view); sometimes it pushes them apart (the third-person point of view). Sometimes it makes an argument more convincing through third-person objectivity, because the speaker is not directly involved in the action. Sometimes an argument is more convincing through second-person involvement. Still other times the argument is more convincing in the first-person point of view because of the intimacy that perspective creates.

Answers

Exercise 1

1. **c.** third person—we're on the outside looking at Xavier and Paul; we're not inside their heads.
2. **b.** second person—"you" are the one with the routine.
3. **a.** first person—we're invited to imagine ourselves as the one with the problem, as you can see by the personal "I."
4. **a.** first person—the first person pronoun is included in that initial "we."
5. **c.** third person—we as readers are outside the group, identified as "they" instead of "we."

Exercise 2

1. The ad makes me feel really good about myself.
2. We're very upset about the change in the lunch menu.
3. I often feel betrayed when someone breaks a promise.

Exercise 3

Answers may vary slightly, but some may look like this.

1. Teachers deserve an additional period each day for class preparation because they have many papers to grade.
2. Students should be assigned less homework. They often feel overwhelmed by how much schoolwork they have to do at home.
3. Parents often wonder if they're doing the right thing for their children.

Exercise 4

Answers may vary slightly, but here are some possibilities:

1. For this letter, the third-person point of view is probably best. Any description will probably be read by a large audience, including students, parents, teachers, and administrators, so it would be best if you aimed for an official and objective point of view.
2. For this letter, you might use the second-person point of view to help readers imagine themselves looking at the trash around campus and feeling good about cleaning it up.
3. For this letter, the first-person point of view is definitely best. You would want your letter to be warm and personal.

SKILL BUILDING UNTIL NEXT TIME

1. Think about the last conflict you had with someone. Describe the conflict first from your point of view using the first-person pronoun *I*. Then, tell the story again from another person's point of view, but keep using the first-person pronoun *I*. Finally, tell the story from an outsider's perspective using the third-person point of view. How does the story change when the point of view changes? Which accounts are subjective? Which account is most objective?
2. Take something that you read today and change its point of view. For example, say you read a short story told in the first person. Change it to third person. How does the new point of view change the story and how you feel about the characters?
3. Using the second-person, write directions for how to get to school or make your favorite meal. Include enough details and organize the steps carefully.

LESSON

13 ▶ WORD CHOICE

LESSON SUMMARY

This lesson focuses on diction, the words writers choose to express meaning. A small change in word choice can have a big impact. You'll learn how to watch for word choice clues that reveal meaning.

What made Sherlock Holmes such a good detective? Was he just that much smarter than everyone else? Did he have some sort of magical powers? Could he somehow see into the future or into the past? No. Sherlock Holmes was no fortune-teller or magician. So what was his secret? His powers of **observation** and the strong control of detail that Sir Arthur Conan Doyle, his author, had.

In Lesson 1, you learned how to become an active reader. One of the things active readers do is *look for clues*. So far you've learned, among other things, to look for clues for determining the main idea, the structure, and the point of view. Now we're going to focus on the clues writers offer through **diction**: the specific words writers choose to describe people, places, and things. A writer's word choice can give away an awful lot about how the writer feels about his or her subject.

Making Observations and Drawing Conclusions

As a writer, you make a lot of decisions. You decide what to say and how to say it. You choose whether to clearly state your ideas or *suggest* them. If you only suggest them, then you need to decide what clues to leave for your readers, who must find and interpret those clues.

By looking closely at the work of writers you like, you can see the clues that will help you understand the text and learn to include clues in your own writing. Search for hints in:

- particular words and phrases that the author uses
- the way those words and phrases are arranged in sentences
- word or sentence patterns that are repeated
- important and subjective details about people, places, and things

Reading like a detective is a two-part process. First, you must find the clues. But the clues alone don't solve the case. You must also **draw conclusions** or **inferences** based on those clues. Inferences are conclusions based on reasons, facts, or evidence.

What is the writer trying to say? Good conclusions come from good observations. To be a better reader, be more like Sherlock Holmes: be more observant. To become a better writer, think like Sir Arthur Conan Doyle—be thoughtful and deliberate about your decisions and choices. In *The Adventures of the Blanched Soldier*, Sherlock Holmes tells a client: "I see no more than you, but I have trained myself to notice what I see." To be a good reader, you just have to train yourself to notice what you see! Then, as a writer, you have to imagine how your readers will see it.

Observing Word Choice

Here's a quick test of your observation skills. Read the next two sentences.

A: A school uniform policy would reduce disciplinary problems.

B: A school uniform policy would minimize disciplinary problems.

In sentence A, the writer says the policy will *reduce* disciplinary problems; sentence B, on the other hand, uses the word *minimize*. No big deal, right? After all, both sentences say that the uniform policy will lead to fewer disciplinary problems. But there is a difference. One sentence is much stronger than the other because one *word* is actually much stronger than the other. To reduce is just to make fewer. To *minimize* is to reduce to the smallest possible amount. Thus, while both writers agree that a uniform dress code would lessen disciplinary problems, the writer of sentence B feels that it would nearly eliminate them, or at least eliminate as far as is humanly possible. The writer doesn't need to spell this out for you because his *word choice* should make his position clear.

Here's another example.

A: The school board instituted a strict new dress code.

B: The school board instituted a tyrannical new dress code.

Both *strict* and *tyrannical* show that the dress code is tough, but they suggest very different levels of toughness. A *strict* dress code is not as tough as one that is *tyrannical*. Nor is it as troubling. *Tyrannical* means controlling others through force or threats. While *strict* suggests that the policy is tough, but may be acceptable, *tyrannical* suggests that the policy is tough and unacceptable.

Denotation and Connotation

Mark Twain once said, *"The difference between the right word and the almost right word is like the difference between lightning and the lightning bug."*

Even words that seem to mean the same thing have subtly different meanings and sometimes not-so-subtle effects. For example, look at the words *meticulous* and *finicky*. If you say your aunt is *finicky*, that means one thing. If you say she is *meticulous*, that means something a little bit different. That's because *meticulous* has a different **connotation** from *finicky*. Connotation is a word's *suggested* or implied meaning; it's what the word makes you think or feel. *Meticulous* and *finicky* have almost the same **denotation**—their dictionary definition—but *finicky* suggests a pickiness that might be irritating, where *meticulous* is a more positive word. It suggests that your aunt is cautious and detail-oriented. *Finicky*, on the other hand, suggests that your aunt is hard to go to lunch with. *Finicky* and *meticulous*, then, have different connotations. So the word you choose to describe your aunt can tell others a lot. It also says something about you.

Be very aware of the connotations and denotations of the language you use—some language has hurtful or offensive connotations, and it's your responsibility to be clear.

Exercise 1

Below are several sentences with a blank. Following each sentence are three words or phrases that all have similar denotations, but different connotations. See how the sentence sounds with each word in the blank. Then rank those words by connotation, marking the word with the most extreme connotation 3 (whether it's positive or negative) and the word with the weakest, or most neutral, connotation 1.

Example: I'm feeling kind of _____ today.
_____ down
_____ depressed
_____ discouraged

Ranked by connotation:
__1__ down
__3__ depressed
__2__ discouraged

1. Joe has been looking a little _____ lately.
_____ unwell
_____ sick
_____ under the weather

2. Our new neighbors are _____.
_____ well off
_____ rich
_____ loaded

3. It takes a lot of _____ to do what he did.
_____ courage
_____ guts
_____ confidence

4. I'm totally _____.
_____ worn out
_____ beat
_____ exhausted

5. She told him a _____.
_____ lie
_____ fib
_____ half-truth

6. This is clearly a _____ situation.
_____ risky
_____ dangerous
_____ life-threatening

Reading between the Lines

Paying attention to word choice is particularly important when the main idea of a passage isn't clear. A writer's word choice doesn't just *affect* meaning; it *creates* it. For example, look at the following description from a teacher's evaluation for a student applying to a special foreign language summer camp. There's no topic sentence, but if you use your powers of observation, you should be able to tell how the writer feels about her subject.

> As a student, Jane usually completes her work on time and checks it carefully. She speaks French well and is learning to speak with less of an American accent. She has often been a big help to other students who are just beginning to learn the language.

What message does this passage send about Jane? Is she the best French student the writer has ever had? Is she one of the worst? Is she average? Would she do well at a foreign language summer camp? To answer this question, and decide whether to admit Jane or not, you have to make an inference, and you must support your inference with specific observations. What makes you come to the conclusion that you do?

The diction of the paragraph reveals that this is a positive evaluation, but not a glowing recommendation. Here are some of the specific observations that support this conclusion:

- The writer uses the word *usually* in the first sentence. This means that Jane is good about meeting deadlines for work, but not great; she might hand in her work on time.
- The first sentence also says that Jane checks her work *carefully*. Although Jane may sometimes hand in work late, at least she usually makes sure it's quality work. She's not often sloppy.

- The second sentence says Jane speaks French *well*. This is a positive word, but not a very strong one. Again, she's good, but not great. A stronger word like *fluently* or *masterfully* would make a big difference. But like in "The Tryout," the camp might want people who are still developing.
- The second sentence also tells us she's "learning to speak with less of an American accent." This suggests that she has an accent and needs to improve in this area. It also suggests that she is already making progress.
- The third sentence tells us that she often helps "students who are just beginning to learn the language." From this we can conclude that Jane has indeed mastered the basics. Otherwise, how could she be a big help to students who are just starting to learn? We also learn that she works generously with others.

By looking at the passage carefully, then, you can see that the teacher thinks Jane would be a good addition to the summer camp.

Exercise 2
Read the paired sentences below, making careful observations as you read. Then answer the inference questions that follow. Be sure to support your answers with specific observations from the sentences.

Pair 1
  A. Let's get together as soon as possible.
  B. Let's meet as soon as we can.

1. Which sentence suggests that the writer has a more formal relationship with the reader?

_____

_____

2. Which sentence suggests that the writer is more anxious to meet with the reader?

_____

_____

Pair 2

  A. Thomas has a very colorful way of speaking.

  B. Thomas has a very showy way of speaking.

3. Which sentence is more critical of Thomas? How can you tell?

_____

_____

Pair 3

  A. They have been meeting in the hope of clearing up their differences.

  B. They have begun negotiations in an attempt to resolve their conflict.

4. Which sentence seems more hopeful about the outcome?

_____

_____

5. Which sentence describes a more serious situation?

_____

_____

6. Which sentence suggests a more informal relationship between the parties that are meeting?

_____

_____

Summary

Sherlock Holmes' secret was his power of observation. Arthur Conan Doyle's was his imagination for detail. You, too, can learn to notice what you see by looking carefully at what you read. Notice the specific words the writer has used, and what that says about the subject and the writer themselves. Remember that writers choose their words carefully. They know that each word has a specific effect, and they want just the right word to convey their ideas.

Answers

Exercise 1

1. 2 (unwell), 3 (sick), 1 (under the weather)
2. 1 (well off), 2 (rich), 3 (loaded)
3. 2 (courage), 3 (guts), 1 (confidence)
4. 2 (worn out), 1 (beat), 3 (exhausted)
5. 3 (lie), 2 (fib), 1 (half-truth)
6. 1 (risky), 2 (dangerous), 3 (life-threatening)

Exercise 2

1. Sentence **B** suggests a more formal relationship between reader and writer. In sentence **B**, the writer uses the word *meet* while the writer of sentence **A** uses the less formal *get together*.
2. Sentence **A** suggests that the writer is more anxious to meet with the reader. In sentence **A**, the writer uses the phrase *as soon as possible*, while the writer of sentence **B** uses the less urgent phrase *as soon as we are able*.
3. Sentence **B** is more critical. The word *showy* suggests that he's a bit *too* colorful.
4. Sentence **A** seems more hopeful, since it uses less serious words throughout: *meeting* instead of *negotiations*; *in the hope* instead of *in an attempt*; *clearing up* instead of the more serious *resolve*; and *differences*, which is much milder than *conflict*.
5. Sentence **B** clearly describes a more serious situation. See the answer for 4.
6. The word choice in sentence **A** suggests a more informal relationship between the parties. They are *meeting*, not *negotiating*; they hope to *clear up* rather than *resolve*; they have *differences*, not a *conflict*. These words are not only less serious; they're also less formal.

SKILL BUILDING UNTIL NEXT TIME

1. Think about how you choose your words. Do you use different words for different people? Imagine you are describing an event to a family member and then to a classmate. Would you describe it the same way? Or would your word choice be different? Do you think carefully about what you say and which words you will use? How aware are you of your word choice? Write down both descriptions and compare them.
2. Take another look at something you read recently. This could be an ad or a full-length article. What words does it use to appeal to its audience? Why are they effective?
3. Consider what a piece of writing tells you about its author. What other words could they have used to give different connotations?

STYLE

LESSON SUMMARY

Writers think carefully not only about the words they use but also about the kind of sentences they write. Will they be long or short? Full of description or right to the point? What kind of tone does this produce? Some writers make choices instinctively, others edit and revise to shape their voice and pace. This lesson shows you how to analyze a writer's style and how style helps create meaning.

What distinguishes an adventurous quest novel from a travel memoir? Both take you to exciting new places, but their tone and purpose will be very different. Their style also distinguishes one from the other.

Actually, understanding style is very important to reading success. Writers use different structures to organize their ideas, and they also use different styles to express those ideas. Being aware of style helps you see what writers are up to.

Style is also important because it's often what makes us like or dislike certain writers or types of writing. For example, some people like stories with a lot of description and detail, while others like stories with lots of right-to-the-point action. You may not change your taste after this lesson, but you should be able to appreciate, identify, and understand all kinds of writers and styles.

Before we go any further, let's define **style**.

> **Style:** a way of doing something—writing, speaking, dressing, and so on; the manner in which something is done.
>
> In writing, style generally consists of four elements:
> - sentence structure
> - level of description and detail
> - level of formality
> - tone

Sentence Structure

Think about a table for a moment. How many different ways could you put a table together? It could have four legs, or just one in the middle. It could be round, rectangular, or square—or any other shape, for that matter. It could be thick or thin. It could be made of wood, plastic, or metal. It could seat two people or twenty. The possibilities and combinations are virtually endless.

The same goes for sentences. They can come in all kinds of shapes and sizes. They can be short and simple or complex, with lots of ideas packed together. Good writers use a range of sentence sizes and styles. Sometimes sentences will all sound the same; other times sentences will vary in word order, length, and structure.

Here are examples of two very different styles.

Paragraph A
A team works best when it is organized. The leader should have clear goals. All team members should understand those goals. The team members should have well-defined roles. Everyone should have specific deadlines.

Paragraph B
The key to an effective team is organization. The team leader must have clear goals, and it's the team leader's job to make sure the team members understand those goals. But how

should you meet those goals? Deciding who does what is just as important. Team success depends on everyone knowing exactly what is expected of him or her. Finally, all team members should have very specific deadlines for each job they are assigned.

Notice the following differences between these two paragraphs.

Paragraph A
- uses simple sentences.
- uses the same sentence structure (type of sentence) throughout.
- does not provide transitions between sentences.
- has limited word choice, simple vocabulary.

Paragraph B
- uses complex sentences.
- has a lot of variety in sentence structure.
- uses strong transitions between sentences.
- has variety in word choice and a more sophisticated vocabulary.

Which style do you prefer? Paragraph A is simple and clear, but it may sound dull because all the sentences follow the same simple pattern. They are all short, and there aren't any transitions. As a result, the paragraph sounds choppy.

Paragraph B flows well. The sentences are longer and more varied. They sound more natural, because it reflects how the narrator might speak.

Here are two more passages with different sentence structures.

Paragraph A
Emma stared sadly out the window of the bus. Only 50 miles outside town was the farm. She thought about it all the time. She remembered the view from her bedroom window. She remembered the creaky wooden floors of the old farmhouse. She especially remembered the animals.

Paragraph B
Emma stared sadly out the window of the bus. The farm was only 50 miles outside town. She thought about the farm all the time, the breathtaking view from her bedroom window, the creaky wooden floors of the old farmhouse, and especially the animals.

Again, we have two paragraphs that say the same thing but say it in very different styles. The second paragraph has only three sentences instead of six; it combines sentences three through six into one long sentence, with more details like "creaky" and "breathtaking." But unlike the previous example, here the shorter sentences in paragraph A *don't* sound awkward or choppy. Instead, the repetition of "she remembered" creates a certain rhythm that makes us spend more time on each image instead of flowing from one to the next. This kind of *purposeful* repetition of a sentence pattern is called **parallelism**.

Exercise 1

Combine sentences in the following paragraph and rewrite them to create a new style.

Bicycles have always been popular forms of transportation. They are used for work and play. They are found on city streets and in small towns. They are even found in the mountains. The first mountain bikes were built in 1975. They were made to ride over rocky terrain. In order to handle the rocks and bumps on these trails, bicycles were built with heavy, balloonlike tires. They only had one speed. They also had coaster brakes.

_____

Level of Description and Detail

When we talk about the level of description and detail, we're looking at two things:

1. How **specific** is the author? Does he write "dog" (general) or "golden retriever" (specific)? Does she write "some" (general) or "three and a half pounds" (specific)?
2. How much **description** does the author provide? Does he write, "Mr. Gupta is my teacher" (nondescriptive) or "Mr. Gupta, my teacher, is a tall man with warm brown eyes and a curly mustache" (descriptive)?

Look carefully at these two sentences as an example:

A. Jing-Mae just got a new bike.
B. Yesterday morning Jing-Mae went to Cycle World and bought an emerald green, 18-speed Diamondback mountain bike.

Both sentences tell you the same thing (that Jing-Mae bought a new bike), but the second version gives you a lot more information. The first writer keeps things general; he does not provide any description or detail. The second writer gets specific and offers description and details.

The level of detail can reveal important information about the relationship between the reader and the writer. Sometimes, if a writer doesn't include a lot of detail, it's because the writer assumes the reader already knows certain information. For example, in the sentence "Let's meet after school on the corner," we can assume that the reader knows exactly which corner and what time to meet. It might also imply the writer isn't very observant or doesn't care to be descriptive.

Description and detail are also important because they can help to draw out our emotions by helping us imagine a situation. For example, look at the following sentences.

A. When Paul heard the news, he jumped for joy.
B. When Paul heard the news, he jumped up and down on the couch, waving his arms wildly and screaming, "I did it! I did it!"

In sentence B, we can see just how happy Paul was when he heard the news, and we also learn the news was related to an achievement or accomplishment of Paul's.

Exercise 2

Change the styles of the sentences below by adding specific description and detail.

1. He ate breakfast this morning.

Descriptive/detailed version:

_____

_____

_____

2. The car drove down the street.

Descriptive/detailed version:

_____

_____

_____

3. The new computer lab has lots of equipment.

Descriptive/detailed version:

_____

_____

_____

Level of Formality

The third element of style is level of formality. Would you say to the President of the United States, "Hey, dude, what's up?" Probably not. But you certainly might talk that way to your friends. You think about how formal or informal you should be before you talk to someone. The same goes for writing. Writers must decide how formal or informal they need to be when they write. They make this decision based on their audience (who they're writing for) and their purpose (why they're writing).

Writers can use slang, which is very informal; formal or ceremonious language; provocative or placating; or something in between. They can address readers by their first names (casual) or by their titles (formal). For example, look at the different levels of formality in the following sentences.

A: "Amelia, can I see you up here?"
B: "Ms. Bravehart, please proceed to the front of the room immediately."

The first sentence is informal while the word choice in the second creates a much higher degree of formality. Here's another example.

A: "I couldn't believe it. I mean, who would have guessed? I sure didn't! I had no clue, no clue at all. And I was the last person to find out, too. It figures."
B: "I was deeply shocked; I had never suspected such a thing. Not surprisingly, I was the last person to become aware of the situation."

Notice the drastic difference in style. Though they both tell the same story and both use the personal, first-person *I*, there's clearly a different relationship to the reader. From the word choice and style—the short sentences, the very casual language—we can tell that the writer of passage A has a more informal, more friendly relationship with the reader than the writer of passage B. You feel the emotion of the writer in passage A much more strongly, too, because the language is more informal, more natural. You get the idea that passage A is addressed to a friend while passage B might be addressed to a journalist.

Exercise 3

Rank the sentences below according to formality. Put a 3 next to the sentence that is most formal, a 1 next to the sentence that is most casual, and a 2 for a midrange sentence.

1. _____ Your grades have improved.
   _____ These calculations show that your class average has increased.
   _____ Your grades are up!

2. _____ You're doing great work, Sierra.
   _____ Nice job, Sierra.
   _____ Your performance is above our expectations, Sierra.

Tone

When you speak, your **tone** of voice actually conveys more meaning than your words. The same is true in writing. To understand what you read, you need to *hear* the writer's tone.

> **Tone:** the mood or attitude conveyed by words or speech.

But how do you hear tone in writing? How can you tell how the words should sound? Think about how tone is created in speech. We create tone by how quickly or slowly we say a word, how loudly or softly we say it, and by our facial expressions and body language.

When you read, you can't hear *how* the writer says something, but you can use your powers of observation to determine the tone. Authors often leave clues to the tone in the type of words used, the point of view, and the length of the sentences. Sometimes, the writer's clues make it easy. For example, look at the following sentence:

> "Ellen always gets her way! It's not fair!" Ginger shouted angrily.

The key words *shouted* and *angrily* tell us what tone to hear in our heads when we read this passage.

Looking for Clues

Sometimes writers provide this kind of clue when they're writing dialogue, but sometimes they don't. Some of the texts you'll read won't include any dialogue at all. So what clues do you look for when an author doesn't tell you how a character said something?

To answer that question, let's look at an example.

> "I just quit, that's all," Toby said, still looking down at the ground. "I just . . . quit."

How do we know *how* Toby says this? To determine tone, we need to look carefully at exactly what he says and what he is doing while he says it (the context).

First, notice that Toby repeats himself: He says, "I just quit" two times. The first time, he also says, "that's all"—a phrase that suggests he doesn't know what else to say or how to explain what happened. We can infer that he's upset about the situation and doesn't want to talk about it. You can also conclude that it was a difficult decision for Toby to make.

The second time Toby says, "I just quit," he includes a pause, which we can "read" from the . . . , called an ellipsis. Again, this pause suggests that he's uncertain of what to say or how to say it—that he doesn't want to talk about it. **Punctuation** can be an important clue in determining tone. An exclamation point, for example, tells you that someone is expressing a strong emotion. You'd then have to determine from the context (what words are being exclaimed or what adjectives describe the speech) whether that feeling is anger, joy, or some other emotion.

Another clue is that Toby is "still looking down at the ground." What Toby is doing suggests a few things: (1) that he's unhappy with his decision, (2) that he's embarrassed by it, and/or (3) that he knows he has disappointed the person he is speaking to (and therefore can't look that person in the eye).

With these three important observations and the inferences you can draw from them, you can take a pretty good guess at the tone. Does Toby say this loudly or softly? Probably quite softly. Most likely, Toby's words were said with a mixture of anger and sadness—more anger in the first part, more sadness in the second.

The more you practice "listening" for tone while you read, the better your "hearing" will become. If you find yourself struggling, practice reading along with an audiobook or reading aloud to yourself.

Exercise 4

To strengthen your understanding of tone, try this exercise. Change the tone of the following passages so that they convey a new mood. You can change words, add words, or delete words if necessary. Change the sentence structure if you like, too.

> **Example:** The tickets are sold out.
> Change from: *matter-of-fact tone* to *disappointed tone*
>> Man, I can't believe the tickets are already sold out. What a bummer!

1. I'm really, really sorry I got you in trouble.
Change from: *apologetic tone* to *indifferent tone*

_____

_____

2. Now what do you want?
Change from: *annoyed tone* to *respectful tone*

_____

_____

3. Oh no—he's here!
Change from: *fearful tone* to *joyful tone*

_____

_____

Summary

Style is an important aspect of reading comprehension. Sentence structure, the level of description and detail, the level of formality, and the tone of the writing can reveal a lot about the writer's relationship to the reader. These also tell us about the writer's purpose and help us see and feel what the writer is describing.

Answers

Exercise 1

Answers will vary slightly. Here's one way to combine the sentences:

> Bicycles have always been popular forms of transportation. Used for both work and play, they can be found on city streets, in small towns, and even in the mountains. Built in 1975, the first mountain bikes were made to ride over rocky terrain. In order to handle the rocks and bumps on these trails, bicycles were built with heavy, balloonlike tires. They had only one speed and coaster brakes.

Exercise 2

Answers will vary. Here are some possible responses.

1. As usual, he ate a huge breakfast this morning: three eggs over easy, a dozen banana pancakes, ten strips of bacon, a pear, two pieces of buttered rye toast, a glass of 2% milk, and a glass of orange juice.

2. The red convertible sped down Riverside Drive doing about 80 miles per hour.

3. The new computer lab on the fourth floor has ten PCs, ten Mac laptops, a color inkjet printer, and a scanner.

Exercise 3

1. 2 (Your grades have improved), 3 (These calculations show that your class average has increased), 1 (Your grades are up!)

2. 2 (You're doing great work, Sierra), 1 (Nice job, Sierra.), 3 (Your performance is above our expectations, Sierra)

Exercise 4

Answers will vary. Here are some possibilities:

1. Too bad you got in trouble.

2. How can I help you?

3. At last! He's here!

SKILL BUILDING UNTIL NEXT TIME

1. As you read, think about how things would sound if you changed the style. Make the sentences more formal or more casual. Add or cross out details and description. Change the sentence structure by combining sentences or breaking long sentences into shorter ones. How does the new style sound? Does it create a different tone? Does it change meaning?

2. Look through things you've read recently to find examples of different writing styles. Consider why these authors have chosen different styles. Imagine what you'd do differently if you were adapting a comedy into a drama or an action movie into a romance.

LESSON 15 ▶ LITERARY DEVICES

LESSON SUMMARY
Writers can use a variety of tools called literary devices to tell a story. This lesson will show you how to recognize these devices and understand how they affect meaning.

What do a plumber, an architect, and a writer have in common? Each uses a special set of tools to do a job. A plumber's toolbox might contain wrenches and pipes, an architect has rulers and graph paper, but what does a writer's toolbox contain?

Writers have many storytelling tools to help communicate their ideas. These tools, called **literary devices**, enhance the writing to make it more powerful, creative, or interesting. This lesson explains four literary devices that authors commonly use; learning to recognize them makes you a more advanced reader, and learning to use them will make you a more developed writer.

- figurative language
- personification
- alliteration
- irony

Figurative Language

Our first important literary device is **figurative language**. Figurative language includes similes and metaphors, language that represents and enhances the object or person being described. A **simile** compares two things using the words *like* or *as*. A **metaphor** is stronger than a simile because it makes the comparison *without* the words *like* or *as*. Here's an example.

> **No figurative language**   He was tall.
> **Simile**   He was as tall as a skyscraper.
> **Metaphor**   He was a skyscraper.

Figurative language is so effective because it helps readers picture what the writer is describing in an imaginative way. The writer could have said, "He is seven feet, two inches tall," and that would have been very specific—one way to give us a clear picture of how tall he is. By using a simile or metaphor, though, the writer creates a different picture, borrowing the qualities of whatever the metaphor's subject is. It may be less exact, but it certainly is more powerful.

Exercise 1

Create similes and metaphors for the following sentences.

1. He has a violent temper.

Simile: _____

Metaphor: _____

2. She was running around crazily.

Simile: _____

Metaphor: _____

NOTE

You might have been tempted to say "She was running around like a chicken with its head cut off." True, this is a simile, but it's also a **cliché**—an overused phrase. Try to avoid clichés in your writing. Instead, come up with a fresh image.

NOTE

For similes and metaphors to work, the two things being compared must be sufficiently different. For example, it doesn't enhance the idea of a butterfly to compare it to a moth. However, comparing the way a butterfly's wings move and the way curtains flutter in the wind creates a more vivid, imaginative picture for the reader.

Finding an Implied Metaphor

Writers often *suggest* a metaphor rather than making an outright comparison. The implied metaphor might be a key to the whole meaning of the story, poem, or article, so you don't want to miss it. For example, notice the implied dog metaphor in this short paragraph.

> Ezra tried to leave the classroom as quickly as possible, but there was no escaping Trey. The sixth grader was right on Ezra's heels as they waded into the crowded hall, practically wagging his tail in excitement.

The second sentence uses key phrases, "right on Ezra's heels" and "wagging his tail," to make the reader picture the puppylike actions of the character. If you didn't notice these phrases, you might underestimate the relationship between Ezra and Trey.

To demonstrate how this works in literature, let's look at a poem: "A Poison Tree," from William Blake's *Songs of Innocence and Experience*. It has four stanzas. A stanza is a group of lines in a poem, much as a paragraph is a group of lines in an essay or story.

Read the poem carefully and read it out loud, too, because poetry is meant to be heard as well as read. Then read it actively—underline, circle, and write in the margins. Several words have been defined for you to the right of the poem.

A Poison Tree

1   I was angry with my friend:
2   I told my wrath, my wrath did end.   *wrath = anger*
3   I was angry with my foe: *foe = enemy*
4   I told it not, my wrath did grow.

5   And I water'd it in fears,
6   Night and morning with my tears;
7   And I sunned it with smiles,
8   And with soft deceitful wiles.   *deceitful = making others believe what isn't true*
                                                wiles = trickery, deceit

9   And it grew both by day and night,
10 Till it bore an apple bright;
11 And my foe beheld it shine,   *beheld = saw*
12 And he knew that it was mine,

13 And into my garden stole
14 When the night had veil'd the pole;   *veil'd = hidden*
15 In the morning glad I see
16 My foe outstretch'd beneath the tree.

The entire poem builds on an implied metaphor, so we need to recognize it to understand the author's ideas. First, you need to look carefully at *what* happened and then look at *why* it happened. The poem is organized both chronologically and by cause and effect, so let's break down the action in the first stanza, using the word *speaker* to refer to the narrator of the poem.

In the first four lines, Blake sets up two situations. First, the speaker is angry with his friend (line 1) and he tells his friend about it (line 2). As a result, the anger goes away (line 2—"my wrath did end"). But he acts differently with his enemy. He doesn't tell his foe about his anger (line 4), and as a result, the anger grows (line 4).

Now look at the second stanza. It's important to know what "it" refers to in line 5. What is "it"? Tears? Smiles? Wrath? Reread the first stanza carefully and then read the second stanza.

One of the things that can make poetry seem tough is the way it is broken up into lines. Sometimes ideas are carried from one line to another, so that the end of a line doesn't mean the end of a thought. An experienced reader of poetry knows to pause for breath where the punctuation is, not at every line break. A line is not always a sentence. Likewise, ideas can be carried from one stanza to the next. Here in line 5 "it" refers back to the first stanza. "It" is the speaker's wrath. You can tell because "wrath" is the last thing mentioned in the first stanza.

In the second stanza, the speaker "water'd" his wrath in fears and "sunned" his wrath with smiles and wiles. How can this be? Can you water and sun your anger?

No, not *literally*. The difficulty and beauty of poetry lies in this kind of language. Blake isn't being literal here; rather he's drawing a comparison between the speaker's anger to something that grows with water and sun. How do you know exactly what it is? Blake tells you in three key places: It's some kind of plant that grows fruit (the "apple bright" in line 10). The poem is called "A Poison Tree," and "Tree" is mentioned again in the last line of the poem.

Pay close attention to similes and metaphors, because they enrich meaning. Blake, for example, could have compared the speaker's anger to anything, but he chose to compare it to a tree. Why? Trees have deep, strong roots and often flower or bear fruit. They need sun and water to grow. As a result, the narrator's anger isn't generic, it has the characteristics and specific qualities taken from the image of a poisoned apple tree. Keep these traits in mind as you work through the rest of the poem.

Exercise 2

Now that we've walked through the first half of the poem, it's your turn to try. Reread the entire poem from beginning to end. Circle the letter of the correct answer.

1. In the third stanza, the foe
   a. grows his own apple tree.
   b. shines the speaker's apple.
   c. sees the speaker's apple.

2. In the fourth stanza, the foe
   a. sneaks into the speaker's garden at night.
   b. invites the speaker into his garden.
   c. attacks the speaker at night.

3. At the end of the poem, the foe
   a. is waiting to kill the speaker with an apple.
   b. has been killed by the poisonous apple.
   c. has been killed by the speaker.

Remember that this poem is not a *literal* description of events, but a drawn-out metaphor that creates the poem's meaning. Is it a *good thing* that the speaker helped his anger grow into a tree? Depends on how vengeful a person you are. Look again at the action. What does the speaker do? He tells his friend about his anger, and it goes away. What *doesn't* the speaker do? He *doesn't* tell his enemy about his anger. What happens to his anger, then? It grows and grows and it offers fruit that tempts his enemy. And what happens to his enemy? He steals the apple, but it is the fruit of anger. It is poisonous and it kills him. Thus, the author uses the tree metaphor to show that anger kept a secret grows out of control and eventually becomes poisonous. This is the poem's *theme*, which you'll read more about in Lesson 17.

Personification

Writers are often motivated by the desire to communicate an image or a strong emotion. A useful literary device to recognize and use is **Personification**, which means giving human characteristics to something that is not human. Readers are more strongly affected by comparisons to human behaviors because we instinctively recognize them; they correspond to our existing experiences. Which of these sentences creates a more powerful image?

1. The dawn turned the sky pink and purple.
2. The dawn put on her robes of pink and purple and shook out her golden hair against the sky.

The first example might make you think of the sky. The second example **personifies** the dawn by suggesting that it is a woman, with a body to clothe with robes and hair to shake out. It produces a stronger visual image for the reader—it has motion, color, texture, and requires your imagination. It also creates a **character** of the dawn by giving her an active part in the story.

Next is a poem called "The Eagle," written by Alfred Lord Tennyson. Read the poem actively and try to locate the personification. Read it both silently and out loud.

The Eagle

clasp = grab; crag = steep, rugged rock

1 He clasps the crag with crooked hands;
2 Close to the sun in lonely lands,
3 Ringed with the azure world, he stands.
4 The wrinkled sea beneath him crawls;
5 He watches from his mountain walls,
6 And like a thunderbolt he falls.

The poet says that the eagle ("he") "clasps" the rock "with crooked hands" and watches from mountain walls. Do eagles have hands or walls? No, they don't. The poet has given the eagle human features. This device helps the reader to picture the scene and understand the *character* of the eagle.

Alliteration

There's another literary device in this poem, too. Read the first line out loud again. Do you hear the repetition of the /k/ sound? "He clasps the crag with crooked hands." This repetition of a specific sound, especially at the beginning of words that appear near each other, is called **alliteration**. Alliteration helps create mood in a poem and enables the poem to *make music*. It's one of the favorite tools of poets.

Exercise 3
Now, reread "The Eagle" carefully and actively. For each question, circle the answer(s) you think are correct. There may be more than one.

1. Line 1 of the poem uses alliteration. Which other line(s) uses alliteration?
   a. line 2
   b. line 3
   c. line 4
   d. line 5
   e. line 6

2. Line 1 also uses personification. Which other line uses personification?
   a. line 2
   b. line 4
   c. line 6

3. The last line of the poem reads, "And like a thunderbolt he falls." Which tool does this line use?
   a. personification
   b. metaphor
   c. simile

4. The poem compares the eagle to a thunderbolt. How do you think the speaker feels about eagles?
   a. he has great respect for eagles.
   b. he is glad there aren't any eagles around.
   c. he feels sorry for eagles.

Irony

Irony is a powerful literary device, but it can also be tricky to recognize. The types of irony include:

Verbal irony: The words mean something different than they first appear to.
Situational irony: An event or result is the opposite of what was expected.

The first type of irony, verbal irony, is similar to sarcasm. The author expects the reader to *know* the hidden meaning of the words. A classic example of this type of irony is Jonathan Swift's essay "A Modest Proposal." Swift argues that the solution to Ireland's famine is to start eating human babies. Did the author really think that was a good solution? Of course not! He was parodying (mocking by imitation and exaggeration) the attitude of Irish public policy towards poor families. The reader gets clues to the author's use of *irony* by paying attention to the tone and the words he uses. Is the author saying something ridiculous or implausible? Can you trust that the author is exaggerating?

The second type, situational irony, is part of the plot. It occurs when what happens is the *opposite* of what you (or the character) expected or thought possible. It is *not* necessarily ironic every time something bad or unexpected happens.

Shi had stayed up all night working on his research paper. Finally, by 6:00 A.M., he had everything ready: cover page, essay, Works Cited page, and illustrations. This was the best essay he'd ever written, and he couldn't wait to present it to the class. He smiled as he showered and got ready for school. He smiled to everyone he passed on his way to the bus stop and smiled at the bus driver. He sat down in his usual seat and hummed to himself for a little while. Then he opened his bag. He wanted to admire his paper once more before his presentation. Of course, he'd left his paper on the kitchen table.

Here, Shi had stayed up all night preparing his paper and presentation. He had everything ready, and he was excited about presenting his work. But his satisfaction and excitement turned into disappointment because he'd left his work at home. The irony is heightened by the way he smiles happily and confidently until he discovers his error.

Exercise 4

Read the scenarios below and circle the ones that are *ironic.*

1. Kevin really hated writing. He hated it so much that he finally decided to write a book about it.

2. Liam woke up late, missed the bus, and failed his spelling test.

3. Meg wanted to go to a concert, but her parents said she was grounded for the weekend. She secretly bought the ticket anyway, and as she was preparing to sneak out of the house, her parents knocked on her door. "Surprise!" they said. "You've been so good all week that we decided to buy you a ticket to that concert."

Summary

Literary devices are tools used to express meaning in a creative, poetic way. Watch for similes and metaphors, and think about the comparisons the writer is making. Listen for the sounds of alliteration and picture the image created by personification. Pay attention to tone and style clues to recognize irony. Remember, writers choose their words carefully because they want to create a certain effect.

Answers

Exercise 1

Answers will vary. Here are some possibilities:

1. **Simile:** He has a temper like a tornado.
   Metaphor: His temper is a tornado.
2. **Simile:** She was running around like the Mad Hatter.
   Metaphor: She was the Mad Hatter.

Exercise 2

1. **c.** See lines 10 and 11: "it bore an apple bright" / "my foe beheld it shine."
2. **a.** See line 13: "And into my garden stole."
3. **b.** You know the speaker's garden had a tree, and you know that this tree is a metaphor for the speaker's anger. You know that this tree had an apple, and you know that the poem is called "A Poison Tree." Finally, at the end of the poem, the foe is "outstretch'd beneath the tree." What do all of these clues add up to? The foe sneaked into the garden and ate the apple, but the apple was poisonous.

Exercise 3

1. **d.** Line 2 repeats the /l/ sound in "lonely lands." Line 5 repeats the /w/ sound in "watches" and "walls."
2. **b.** The sea "crawls" like a baby or a turtle.
3. **c.** Remember, a simile is a comparison using *like* or *as*. Here, the eagle is compared to a thunderbolt. This helps readers picture the eagle's flight. It also tells you something about the eagle—it's like an incredible force of nature.
4. **a.** Tennyson compares the eagle to a thunderbolt to show how powerful and fast eagles are. He obviously has a great deal of respect for them.

Exercise 4

1. *Ironic.* The character did the very opposite of what we (and he) expected him to do.
2. *Not ironic.* The character had bad luck, but nothing happened that was the opposite of the reader's or the character's expectation.
3. *Ironic.* The outcome of the situation was the opposite of what the character expected to happen.

SKILL BUILDING UNTIL NEXT TIME

1. Read a poem on your own. Do you see any similes? Metaphors? Alliteration? Personification? Irony? Can you determine the tone? What happens? What does it add up to? What's the message?
2. Read a short story and apply the technique you used to understand poems to look for some literary devices.

16 ▶ PUTTING IT ALL TOGETHER

SECTION SUMMARY
This lesson reviews Lessons 12 through 15 and pulls together what you've learned in this section. You'll use point of view, word choice, style, and literary devices to interpret what you read.

You've learned a lot about how writers use language to create meaning and how you as a writer can make deliberate choices. Now you can add this to what you already know about being a good reader. But first, let's review the last four lessons.

What You've Learned

Here's a quick review of each lesson about language and style:

Lesson 12: Point of View. You learned that writers choose a specific **point of view** to express their ideas. They can use the first-person (*I, we*), second-person (*you*), or third-person (*he, she, it*) point of view. The first-person point of view creates closeness between the reader and writer and is a very subjective point of view. It directly expresses the feelings and ideas of the writer or narrator. The second-person point of view puts readers into the action and makes them feel involved. The third-person point of view is the most objective because the writer or narrator is not involved in the action; it creates distance between the reader and writer.

Lesson 13: Word Choice. You learned to look carefully at the words writers use. Each word has a specific **connotation**, so different words will have a different impact even if their **denotation** is nearly the same. It's your responsibility to choose words with the right connotation for your message. You learned to look closely at **diction** and draw conclusions based on your observations.

Lesson 14: Style. You learned that **style** consists of four main elements: sentence structure, level of description and detail, level of formality, and tone. Looking carefully at style can help you draw conclusions about the relationship between the writer and reader. Style can also reveal the writer's purpose and help you see and feel what the writer is describing.

Lesson 15: Literary Devices. You learned that writers can use a variety of literary or poetic devices to heighten the effects of language. Authors can make comparisons with **similes** or **metaphors**, and you learned how to find implied metaphors. **Alliteration** creates a pleasing sound, and **personification** paints an interesting picture. **Irony** can appear in a sentence or a situation, so pay close attention to double meanings.

In Section 1, you learned how to be an active reader, how to find the main idea, how to define unfamiliar words, and how to distinguish between fact and opinion. In Section 2, you learned about plot structure, chronological order, order of importance, comparison and contrast, cause and effect, and summaries and outlines.

If any of these terms or strategies are unfamiliar, take some time to review the term or strategy that is unclear.

Section 3 Practice

In these practice exercises, you'll combine your close reading skills with everything else you've learned so far in this book. Read each passage actively and carefully, then answer the questions that follow.

> **NOTE**
>
> If you come across unfamiliar words as you read these passages, do not look them up until after you've answered the questions.

Exercise 1

The passage that follows is an advertisement for Mercury Shoes.

Help your feet take flight! Mercury Shoes promises you high quality and can save you from the aches and pains that runners often suffer.

Running magazine has awarded Mercury Shoes its "High Quality" rating for our breakthrough in shoe technology! By studying the feet of track and field champions and ultra-marathoners, we have developed a revolutionary sole construction that offers complete support for dedicated runners. Our unique combination of gel and air cushioning provides greater stability and incredible comfort.

Three types of Mercury Shoes are now available:

Cheetahs: A racing shoe that combines light weight with real support.

Mountain Goats: A superior trail-running shoe with great traction and stability even on muddy or slick trails.

Gray Wolves: A shoe that gives maximum support in order to minimize common injuries caused by mile after mile of training runs on hard pavement.

Read the following questions. Circle the letter of the answer you think is correct.

1. The ad uses which point of view to refer to its readers?
   a. first person
   b. second person
   c. third person
   d. none of the above

2. The shoe names Cheetahs, Mountain Goats, and Gray Wolves reflect
   a. the personality of the shoe designer.
   b. the personality of the runner.
   c. the kind of running the shoe is designed for.
   d. the company's mascots.

3. Which of the following best describes the style of this passage?
   a. long sentences, lots of descriptive words
   b. lots of short, choppy, "bossy" sentences
   c. lots of similes and metaphors to create images
   d. slangy, informal words

4. Which of the following is presented as a *fact* in the ad?
   a. Mercury Shoes can save you from the aches and pains that runners often suffer.
   b. *Running* magazine has awarded Mercury Shoes its "High Quality" rating.
   c. Mercury Shoes has developed a revolutionary sole construction.
   d. Mountain Goats are superior trail-running shoes.

Exercise 2

This is the first stanza of a poem by Percy Shelley. The lines are numbered to help you answer the questions.

The Cloud
1 I bring fresh showers for the thirsting flowers,
2 From the seas and the streams;
3 I bear light shade for the leaves when laid
4 In their noonday dreams.
5 From my wings are shaken the dews that waken
6 The sweet buds every one,
7 When rocked to rest on their mother's breast,
8 As she dances about the sun.
9 I wield the flail of the lashing hail,
10 And whiten the green plains under,
11 And then again I dissolve it in rain,
12 And laugh as I pass in thunder.

5. What literary device is used to describe the cloud in this poem?
   a. metaphor
   b. alliteration
   c. personification
   d. irony

6. In the implied metaphor in line 7, what is being compared to a mother?
   a. the sky
   b. the earth
   c. a flower
   d. a storm

7. Which word best describes the tone of this stanza?
   a. gloomy
   b. hesitant
   c. angry
   d. confident

Exercise 3

You might recognize the first paragraph in the short story that follows.

A Day at the Nature Center

(1) Emma stared sadly out the window of the bus. Only 50 miles outside town was the farm. She thought about the farm all the time, remembering the breathtaking view from her bedroom window, the creaky wooden floors of the old farmhouse, and especially the animals.

(2) When Emma's parents sold their hundred-acre farm and moved to the nearby town of Carrville, Emma had been enthusiastic. But when she got to the new school, she felt overwhelmingly shy around so many strangers.

(3) With a sigh, Emma turned her attention back to the present. The bus came to a stop, and Emma climbed off with the rest of her Earth Studies classmates. "Welcome to the Leinweber Nature Center," her teacher, Mrs. Bowes, announced. "In a few minutes, a guide will give us a presentation about the area's native animals and habitat. After the presentation, you'll have a worksheet to complete while you explore the rest of the center. Now, I want everyone to find a partner."

(4) Emma looked around apprehensively as her classmates began to pair up. She didn't have any friends yet—who would be her partner? Emma hesitated for a moment and then approached Julia, a talkative and outgoing girl who sat near her in class. "Could I be your partner?" Emma asked tentatively.

(5) "Sure," said Julia warmly. "Let's go get the worksheet from Mrs. Bowes."

(6) Together, the girls walked into the Leinweber Nature Center. They listened to the guide talk about how the workers at the center cared for injured and orphaned animals and how the center tried to re-create the animals' natural habitats as much as possible. Emma

listened intently. She thought it would be wonderful to have a job that involved nurturing and caring for animals all day.

(7) After the presentation, the girls examined their worksheets. "Let's see," said Julia. "One of the things we're supposed to do is locate the rodent area and assist with feeding the baby squirrels. How big is a baby squirrel? Do you think we actually have to hold one? Maybe you should let me feed it while you watch." Julia was so excited that she fired off one question after another and didn't wait for a response from Emma.

(8) Emma and Julia walked into the rodent area and stood there, looking around at all the rats, mice, chipmunks, and squirrels. "Hi, there!" boomed an enthusiastic voice from behind them. "I'm Josh Headly, the keeper in charge of rodents. Did you come to see the squirrels?"

(9) "Yes," said Emma, turning around with an eager smile on her face. "Do we actually get to feed the babies?"

(10) "You sure do. Here—let me demonstrate the feeding procedure for you."

(11) Josh showed them how to wrap a baby squirrel in a towel and hold the bottle of warm milk. Emma settled back into a chair, enjoying the warmth of the tiny ball of fur nestled in her hand. She flashed a smile over at Julia, but Julia, who was suddenly silent, was focusing on her own baby squirrel.

(12) After the babies had finished eating, Josh asked, "Would you like to help feed the adult squirrels, too?"

(13) Emma was quick to volunteer, but when Josh opened the first cage, the squirrel inside leaped out. Julia shrieked and tried to jump out of the way. Emma maintained her composure, bent down, held out her hand, and made quiet, soothing sounds. The runaway squirrel cocked its head to one side and seemed to listen to her. Quickly, while the squirrel was

distracted by Emma, Josh reached over and scooped it up.

(14) He smiled appreciatively. "Good job, Emma! It's not easy to remain calm when a wild animal gets out of its cage. I'm impressed!"

(15) "Wow!" Julia chimed in. "You're always so quiet. I thought you were shy and scared of everything, but you're braver than I am if you can get close to a wild animal, even if it is just a squirrel."

(16) "I'm only shy around people, not animals. And I used to live on a farm, so I know that when animals are scared or excited, you have to stay calm—even when you don't feel calm—if you want to help them."

(17) Josh nodded in agreement. "You know," he began, "we've been taking applications for part-time volunteers to help out with the animals. Would you be interested in interviewing for a volunteer position here at the center?"

(18) "Interested? I would love to work here! What an opportunity! Where are the application forms? When could I start?" Now it was Emma who bubbled over with questions.

(19) That afternoon, in the bus on the way back to school, Emma sat next to Julia and they chatted back and forth. A rush of newfound contentedness washed over her. Not only had she found a place full of animals to help take care of, but she had also made a new friend.

Read the following questions. Circle the letter of the answer you think is correct.

8. In which of the following ways are Emma and Julia **alike**?
   a. They both are very outgoing and talkative.
   b. They both feel comfortable around animals.
   c. They both have a class called Earth Studies.
   d. They both live on farms outside Carrville.

9. Which words best describe how Emma feels when her classmates first begin to pair up?
   a. angry and disappointed
   b. anxious and uncertain
   c. enthusiastic and joyful
   d. jealous and hurt

10. Reread the following sentence from the story:

    Emma hesitated for a moment and then approached Julia, a talkative and outgoing girl who sat near her in class. "Could I be your partner?" Emma asked tentatively.

    As it is used in the story, what does the word *tentatively* mean?
    a. carelessly
    b. eagerly
    c. forcefully
    d. cautiously

11. The author presents Julia as someone who
    a. makes friends easily.
    b. is fun-loving but a poor student.
    c. knows a lot about animals.
    d. treats her friends badly.

12. Choose the correct sequence from the choices below.
    1. Julia and Emma sit together on the bus.
    2. A guide speaks about the nature center.
    3. Emma and Julia feed some baby squirrels.
    4. Josh introduces himself to the two girls.
    a. 3, 4, 2, 1
    b. 2, 4, 3, 1
    c. 2, 1, 4, 3
    d. 1, 4, 3, 2

13. Which word best describes Julia's tone in the following paragraph?

> "Wow!" Julia chimed in. "You're always so quiet. I thought you were shy and scared of everything, but you're braver than I am if you can get close to a wild animal, even if it is just a squirrel."

a. impressed
b. jealous
c. disbelieving
d. embarrassed

14. Reread Emma's reaction to Josh's offer.

> "Interested? I would love to work here! What an opportunity! Where are the application forms? When could I start?"

The *style* of Emma's response
a. helps create an excited tone.
b. is repetitive and dull.
c. shows that she is unsure what to do.
d. reflects her shy nature.

15. Emma is happy at the end of the story because
a. she is no longer shy.
b. she will be paid well for her work at the nature center.
c. she has a new job and a new friend.
d. squirrels are her favorite animals.

Answers

Exercise 1

1. b. In the first two sentences, the writers use the second person *you* to refer to readers. They use the first person *we* and *our* to refer to themselves in the second paragraph. If you missed this question, review Lesson 12.

2. c. The shoes are named for the kind of running they're designed for, based on the attributes of the animals they're named after. This is clear from each shoe's description. The Cheetahs (named after the fastest animal on earth) are "a racing shoe"; the Mountain Goats (named after these great climbers) are a "trail-running shoe." The Gray Wolves, meanwhile, are shoes designed for "training runs on hard pavement." If you missed this question, review Lessons 4 and 13.

3. a. Most of the sentences are long and full of descriptive words such as *high quality*, *revolutionary*, *complete*, *dedicated*, *unique*, *greater*, and *incredible*. Only two of the sentences are short, so this passage definitely does not have a choppy or "bossy" style (choice **b**). There are no similes or metaphors (though the first sentence is a form of **personification** that compares feet to a bird) so choice **c** is incorrect. Finally, there is no slang, so choice **d** is incorrect. If you missed this question, review Lesson 14.

4. b. Choices **a**, **c**, and **d** offer *opinions* about the quality and benefits of the shoes. Choices **c** and **d** use subjective, evaluative words—*revolutionary* and *superior*—to show they are stating an opinion. Choice **a** doesn't provide any evidence for this claim about the benefits of the shoes. Only choice **b** states a fact; this is the only statement here that is not debatable. If you missed this question, review Lesson 4.

Exercise 2

5. c. From the clue in the title, we know that the speaker in the poem is a cloud. The cloud is shown as a character who can do humanlike actions: "bring," "bear," "wield," and "laugh." This personification lets the reader see the cloud from a new perspective. If you missed this question, review Lesson 15.

6. b. The cloud is explaining how dew helps wake up the "sweet buds" (flowers) that are rocked "on their mother's breast, / As she dances about the sun." Flowers grow on the Earth, so the Earth is their mother. The second clue is that the mother travels around the sun, as Earth does. (Notice the personification of the Earth in these lines.) If you missed this question, review Lesson 15.

7. d. The best option for the tone here is *confident* because the cloud is explaining its actions in a straightforward, self-satisfied way. The poet's word choices don't suggest anything gloomy (**a**), hesitant (**b**), or angry (**c**). If you missed this question, review Lesson 14.

Exercise 3

8. c. Julia "sat near [Emma] in class," and they pair up to complete an assignment for their Earth Studies teacher, Mrs. Bowes (paragraphs 3 and 4). Choice **a** is incorrect because we are told from the beginning (paragraph 2) that Emma is new to the school and "overwhelmingly shy." Later in the story, we know that the adult squirrel frightens Julia, so choice **b** is incorrect. And in paragraph 2, we learn that Emma *moved* from the farm, so neither girl lives on a farm outside Carrville (choice **d**). If you missed this question, review Lesson 8.

9. b. The word choice in paragraph 4 provides the clues. Emma "looked around apprehensively." *Apprehensive* means feeling anxious or fearful. She also hesitates before she approaches Julia, which reflects her uncertainty. And she asks Julia *tentatively*, which means *hesitantly*. Even if you don't know what *apprehensively* and *tentatively* mean, you can assume that Emma would be anxious and uncertain because we are told she "felt overwhelmingly shy around so many strangers" when she arrived at her new school. Thus, she wouldn't feel choice **c**, enthusiastic and joyful. There's no evidence in the word choice or in Emma's personality that she'd feel choice **a**, angry and disappointed or choice **d**, jealous and hurt. These emotions would more likely come up if she'd been left out and couldn't find a partner. If you missed this question, review Lesson 13.

10. d. Emma's shyness suggests that she wouldn't approach Julia forcefully (choice **c**) or eagerly (choice **b**). Another clue is that she hesitates before she asks. She also looks around "apprehensively," which suggests she will proceed cautiously, not carelessly (choice **a**). If you missed this question, review Lesson 3.

11. a. Julia is described in paragraph 4 as "a talkative and outgoing girl," which suggests that she is someone who makes friends easily. We also see her making friends with Emma. She also responds to Emma "warmly." We know from her reaction to the adult squirrel that she does not know a lot about animals, so choice **c** is incorrect. She also treats Emma well, so choice **d** is incorrect. There is no evidence in the passage that Julia is a poor student, so choice **b** is also incorrect. If you missed this question, review Lesson 13.

12. b. The story is told in chronological order. First, we are told a guide makes a presentation (#2), then Josh introduces himself (#4) and shows them how to feed the squirrels (#3). The last event in the story is their ride home on the bus (#1). If you missed this question, review Lesson 7.

13. a. Julia is very impressed with Emma's composure. A big clue to this tone is the word "Wow!" Julia also says that Emma must be "braver than I am." If you missed this question, review Lesson 14.

14. a. Emma asks three questions and makes two statements, both with exclamation marks. All her questions and statements are short and seem to tumble one on top of the other, because Emma is too excited to wait for a response. If you missed this question, review Lesson 14.

15. c. Emma has a new friend at the end of the story, but that doesn't mean she is no longer shy (choice **a**). Josh uses the word "volunteer" twice, so we know she won't be paid for her work (choice **b**). Finally, while it's clear that Emma enjoyed nurturing the squirrels, there's no evidence that they are her favorite. (choice **d**). If you missed this question, review Lesson 4.

SKILL BUILDING UNTIL NEXT TIME

1. Review the Skill Building sections from Lessons 12 through 15. Try any Skill Builders you didn't do.

2. Write a few paragraphs about what you've learned so far. Begin each paragraph with a clear topic sentence. Here's an example: "Being observant will help me understand what I read." Then write several supporting sentences. Try to use at least one new word in your paragraphs.

S E C T I O N

4 ▶ READING BETWEEN THE LINES

Now that you've studied how writers use structure and language, and how to detect these features as a reader, it's time to put your knowledge to work on more difficult texts.

This week you'll look at passages that don't have a clear main idea. To understand this type of text, you need to look carefully for clues. You'll often need to *read between the lines* to see what the author means. Like Sherlock Holmes, and Sir Arthur Conan Doyle, you will really have to notice what you see.

By the end of this section, you should be able to:

- find an implied main idea (Lesson 17)
- identify the author's purpose (Lesson 18)
- identify an implied cause or effect (Lesson 19)
- analyze a fictional character (Lesson 20)

The skills you'll learn in this chapter will help you see how writers build strong characters, stories, and themes. The final lesson will then help you pull together everything you've learned from this section.

17 ▶ FINDING AN IMPLIED MAIN IDEA

LESSON SUMMARY

This lesson shows you how to find the main idea when there's no topic sentence or thesis statement to guide you. It also explains how to find a theme, the main idea in literature.

Oh, the power of suggestion! Advertisers know it well—ever see a fast food commercial that made you want some french fries so badly you could taste them?—and so do writers. They know they can get an idea across without saying it outright. They know that they don't always need a topic sentence because they can use structure and language to suggest their ideas (and they assume their readers will be attentive and engaged, like you are).

Think back to Lesson 2 for a moment. What is a **main idea**? It is a claim (an **assertion**) *about* the subject of the passage. It's also the thought that holds the whole passage together. Thus, it must be general enough to include all the ideas in the passage. Like a net, it holds everything together. Main ideas are often stated in topic sentences.

So far, most of the passages in this book have topic sentences. But you'll often come across passages (like the story "The Tryout" from Lesson 11) that *don't* have topic sentences. Writers often *imply* ideas instead of stating them directly. To *imply* means to hint or suggest. You'll need to use your powers of observation to determine (or infer) their message.

How to Find an Implied Main Idea

When there's no topic sentence, finding the implied main idea requires some good detective work. You know how to read carefully and find clues, and since you already know the importance of structure, word choice, style, and tone, these clues will help you figure out the main idea.

For example, take a look at the following paragraph:

> Fortunately, none of Toby's friends had ever seen the apartment where Toby lived with his mother and sister. Sandwiched between two burnt-out buildings, his two-story apartment building was by far the ugliest one on the block. It was a real eyesore: peeling orange paint (orange!), broken windows, crooked steps, crooked everything. He could just imagine what his friends would say if they ever saw this poor excuse for a building.

Which of the following expresses the main idea of this paragraph?
- **a.** Toby wishes he could move to a nicer building.
- **b.** Toby wishes his dad still lived with them.
- **c.** Toby is glad none of his friends know where he lives.
- **d.** Toby is sad because he doesn't have any friends.

From the description, we can safely assume that Toby doesn't like his apartment building and wishes he could move to a nicer building (choice **a**). But that idea isn't general enough to cover the whole paragraph, because it doesn't say anything about his friends. Sentence (choice **d**) isn't about his building, so it's not broad enough either. Besides, the first sentence states that Toby has friends. We know that Toby lives only with his mother and little sister, so we might assume that he wishes his dad still lived with them (choice **b**). But there's nothing in the paragraph to support that assumption, and this idea doesn't include the two main topics of the paragraph—Toby's building and Toby's friends.

What the paragraph adds up to is that Toby is terribly embarrassed about his building, and he's glad none of his friends have seen it (choice **c**). The paragraph opens with the word "fortunately," so we know that he thinks it's a good thing none of them have been there. Plus, look at the word choices. Notice how the building is described. It's "by far the ugliest on the block," which is saying a lot since it's stuck between two burnt-out buildings. The writer calls it an "eyesore," and repeats "orange" with an exclamation point to emphasize how ugly the color is. Everything's "crooked" in this "poor excuse for a building." Toby's ashamed of where he lives and worries about what his friends would think if they saw it.

Exercise 1

Read the following paragraphs and circle the letter of the answer you think is correct.

1. Day after day, Johnny chooses to sit at his computer instead of going outside with his friends. A few months ago, he'd get half a dozen phone calls from his friends every night. Now, he might get one or two a week. Used to be his friends would come over two, three days a week after school. Now, he spends his afternoons alone with his computer.

The main idea is:
- **a.** Johnny and his friends are all spending time with their computers instead of one another.
- **b.** Johnny's friends aren't very good friends.
- **c.** Johnny has alienated his friends by spending so much time on the computer.
- **d.** Johnny and his friends prefer to communicate by computer.

2. We've had Ginger since I was two years old. Every morning, she wakes me up by licking my cheek. That's her way of telling me she's hungry. When she wants attention, she'll weave in and out of my legs and meow until I pick her up and hold her. And I can always tell when Ginger wants to play. She'll bring me her toys and will keep dropping them (usually right on my homework!) until I stop what I'm doing and play with her for a while.

A good topic sentence for this paragraph would be:
a. I take excellent care of Ginger.
b. Ginger is a demanding pet.
c. Ginger and I have grown up together.
d. Ginger is good at telling me what she wants.

Casting a Net

When you're looking for an implied main idea, what you're really doing is searching for the right "net" to cast over the passage. What is the idea that encompasses all the other ideas in the passage? What holds it together? (Remember, a paragraph, by definition, is a group of sentences about the same idea.)

What if you're looking for the main idea of *several* paragraphs? Instead of determining the main idea of an individual paragraph, you're determining the overall main idea. Remember the comparison between a table and an essay? In an essay, the overall main idea is the tabletop, while the supporting ideas are the legs that support the table. Each of those legs might be paragraphs with their own main idea and supporting sentences.

Here's a very short essay with an implied main idea. Read it carefully. Can you see what the whole passage adds up to?

(1) When a lunar prospector took off in January 1998, it had been more than 25 years since the National Aeronautic and Space Administration (NASA) last sent a craft to land on the moon. The prospector launch was the first moon shot since astronauts last walked on the moon in 1972. This time, the moon-traveler is only a low-cost robot that will spend a year on the surface of the moon, collecting minerals and ice.

(2) Unlike the moon shots of the 1960s and 1970s, the lunar prospector did not carry a camera, so the American public would not get to see new pictures of the moon's surface. Instead, the prospector carried instruments to map the makeup of the entire surface of the moon.

(3) Scientists are anxious for the results of the entire mission and of one exploration in particular—that done by the neutron spectrometer. Using this instrument, the prospector examines the moon's poles, searching for signs of water ice. There has long been speculation that frozen water from comets may have accumulated in craters at one of the moon's poles and may still be there, as this pole is permanently shielded from the sun.

Which of the following statements seems to best express the overall main idea of this passage?
a. There is a great deal we can learn from studying the moon.
b. The prospector will collect surface data rather than take pictures.
c. NASA's newest moon-traveler is on an important mission.
d. Scientists hope the prospector will return with evidence of water on the moon.

If you remember that a main idea must be general enough to hold the whole passage together and that a main idea must also be an assertion about the subject, then it should be pretty easy to tell which is the correct answer. Choices **b** and **d** are too specific to be the main idea; they deal only with information in the second and third paragraphs, respectively. They only state facts; they don't make a claim about the subject. They can't be the overall main idea for this passage.

Choices **a** and **c**, on the other hand, both make assertions about the subject and are general. They both allow room for detailed support. But while choice **a** casts a wide enough net, it's not the right net for this passage—it's too general. The passage is about what NASA hopes to learn from this specific mission. "NASA's newest moon-traveler is on an important mission," however, casts a net that's just the right size, thus choice **c** is the correct answer.

Exercise 2

Read the following passage carefully and actively. Then circle the answers of the questions that follow.

(1) A healthy diet with proper nutrition is essential for maintaining good overall health. Since vitamins were discovered early in the twentieth century, people have routinely been taking vitamin supplements for this purpose. The Recommended Daily Allowance (RDA) is a frequently used nutritional standard for maintaining optimal health.

(2) The RDA specifies the recommended amount of a number of nutrients for people in many different age and gender groups. With RDA, consumers can see how much of those nutrients are offered in the products they buy and can better plan for a nutritious meal. But RDA values are based on the assumption that it is possible to accurately define nutritional requirements for a given group. In reality, individual nutritional requirements can vary widely within each group.

(3) The efficiency with which a person converts food into nutrients can also vary widely. Certain foods when eaten in combination actually prevent the absorption of nutrients. For example, spinach combined with milk reduces the amount of calcium available to the body from the milk, but this is not reflected in RDA values for either ingredient.

(4) The RDA approach also specifies a different dietary requirement for each age and gender, though it is clearly unrealistic to expect anyone to prepare a different menu for each family member.

1. Which of the following sentences best expresses the overall main idea of this passage?
   a. Although we cannot rely solely upon the RDA to ensure our overall long-term health, it can still be a useful guide.
   b. The RDA approach is problematic and should be avoided.
   c. It's important for consumers to monitor RDA levels carefully.
   d. After all, vitamins are the most important part of a healthy diet.

2. Where would this overall main idea make the most sense in the passage?
   a. at the beginning of the first paragraph
   b. at the end of the first paragraph
   c. at the beginning of the last paragraph
   d. at the end of the last paragraph

Main Ideas in Literature

Many people are intimidated by literature. It sounds like a big grand scholarly field when the truth is, it's just writing by writers who really enjoy languages and ideas. But finding the main idea or **theme** in literature isn't so different from finding the main idea in other texts. Once you've acquired a taste for finding clear meaning in what you read and thinking critically about that meaning, the literary world has miles and miles of stories to tell you, in poems, stories, essays, plays, and novels.

Theme

Theme is the overall message or idea that the writer wants to convey. Like a main idea, the theme is different from subject in that the theme *says something about* the subject. For example, take John Donne's poem "Death Be Not Proud." The *subject* of the poem is death. But the *theme* of the poem says something *about* death. The poem's message is that death is a gift for those who believe in God.

The main idea of a text is the thought that holds everything together. Likewise, the theme of a work of literature is the thought that holds together the characters and action. It's the idea that determines word choice, structure, and style.

Clues to Theme

You can find the theme in literature the same way you find it in other kinds of writing—by looking for clues in the action, in word choice, in style, and in structure. To practice, here's a poem by the American writer Stephen Crane. Read it actively, looking carefully at the action and the language (word choice, style, and tone) of the poem. Read it out loud at least once.

A Man Said to the Universe
A man said to the universe:
"Sir, I exist!"
"However," replied the universe,
"The fact has not created in me
A sense of obligation."

Look carefully at the language in the poem. What kinds of words has the poet chosen? Are they warm, friendly words, or are they cold, distancing words? Do they make you feel comfortable, welcome? Or uncomfortable, rejected? Are they specific or general? Do you feel like there's a personal relationship here? Or are things formal, official?

Read the poem again, then answer the questions in Exercise 3.

Exercise 3

Circle the letter of the answer you think is correct.

1. What is the tone of the poem?
   a. warm, caring
   b. hot, angry
   c. cold, uncaring

2. What is the theme of the poem?
   a. The universe is too big for humans.
   b. The universe is indifferent to humans.
   c. Humans have no obligation to the universe.

Summary

Writers often *suggest* their main idea without actually *saying* it. This is especially true in literature, where main ideas are called *themes*. Finding an implied main idea takes extra careful detective work. Look for clues in what the writer says and how he or she says it. Consider the structure, the point of view, word choice, style, and tone. What does the passage add up to? What assertion can you make that holds together all the ideas in that passage?

Answers

Exercise 1

1. **c.** By comparing and contrasting how things used to be with how they are now, we can see that Johnny's choice (to "sit at his computer instead of going outside with his friends") has created a distance between them. They don't call or come by as often as they used to. Choice **a** is incorrect because we don't know from the paragraph whether Johnny's friends are doing the same thing or not. It's possible, but remember, there must be evidence in the passage to support a main idea. There is no mention in this passage about how Johnny's friends spend their time, or that they prefer to communicate by computer, choice **d**. Choice **b** is also incorrect because it's clear that Johnny is choosing his computer over his friends. He's the one who's not being a good friend.

2. **d.** The writer may indeed take very good care of Ginger (choice **a**), but that's not the main idea here. Each specific example in this paragraph is about how Ginger communicates her desires to the writer. Choices **b**, **c**, and **d** are all true, but **d** is the best choice for main idea. The writer's tone tells you that she enjoys playing with Ginger, and demanding has a negative connotation. Choice **d** is the most positive.

Exercise 2

1. **a.** Each paragraph in this passage deals with the RDA and its values, so choice **d** is incorrect. You will rarely see a main idea that begins with "After all,"—this gesture usually signals a conclusion. Choice **b** is incorrect because the second paragraph mentions two specific benefits of RDA. Choice **c** is incorrect because it is too specific.

2. **d.** The best place for this overall main idea would be the very end of the passage. The passage explains what the RDA is, how it helps us, and why it is problematic. The writer should then conclude with this main idea—that while there are problems with the RDA, it's still a helpful guide.

Exercise 3

1. **c.** The words "sir," "fact," and "obligation" are cold and formal.

2. **b.** Crane's word choice helps convey his theme. The words "sir," "fact," and "obligation" are cold and formal. There's no sense of personal relationship between the man and the universe. This is heightened by the general nature of the poem. It's just "a man"—not anyone specific, not anyone you know. It's also written in the third-person point of view. The poem would have a different effect if it began, "*I* said to the universe." The universe says it does not feel an obligation and the tone is cold and uncaring. Further, the man also seems to be demanding attention from the universe. He yells, "Sir, I exist!" as if he wants the universe to pay attention to him. But the universe remains indifferent.

SKILL BUILDING UNTIL NEXT TIME

1. Listen carefully to people today. Do they sometimes suggest things without actually saying them? Are there times when you use suggestion to express your ideas? How do you do this?

2. Write a paragraph that does not have a topic sentence. Start with a clear main idea, but don't write that main idea down. Then, put in clues that will help readers figure out your main idea. For example, make a claim about yourself. What kind of person are you? Keep that main idea in your head. Next, write several sentences that support your assertion. Make sure those sentences lead your reader to your main idea. Then show your paragraph to others. Can they determine the main idea from what you've written?

3. Think about your favorite movies and books—are there common themes that draw you in? Flip it around—imagine you're holding a movie marathon. What would you show if the marathon theme was "Coming of Age," "Person Versus Society conflicts," or "Triumph of the Underdog"?

18 ▶ IDENTIFYING AN AUTHOR'S PURPOSE

LESSON SUMMARY

Writers always have a purpose in mind for their writing. This lesson shows you how to identify the author's purpose in many different types of writing.

On your way to lunch, your friend passes you a note in the hallway. What's the purpose of the note? Your friend might have written about a funny thing that happened to him last weekend. He might be telling you some details for your upcoming camping trip. Or maybe the note wants to convince you to see that new action film tomorrow night. Whatever the note contains, your friend has some *purpose* in writing to you.

Every writer has a goal in mind as she or he writes. Here are three simple ways to classify the author's purpose:

- to inform
- to persuade
- to entertain

Obviously there can be more nuanced or complicated versions, but these three categories are like umbrellas for more specific goals.

The purpose that the writer chooses will determine what kind of style, word choice, and structure he or she will use. If your friend wants to *inform* you about the upcoming camping trip, he'll probably include lots of specific details. If he's trying to *persuade* you to see that action film, he will try to build a convincing argument. And if he's sharing a story, he might use similes or other poetic language to make it interesting.

You can determine the author's purpose by—you guessed it!—watching the clues in word choice, style, tone, point of view, and structure.

Writing to Inform

Informative writing provides facts or instructions. You see this type of writing all the time. A recipe, for example, gives specific instructions for preparing food, and a bus schedule tells you the times and locations of the bus stops. When you read an instruction manual for your new camera, you expect the writer to tell you facts and details about how the camera works.

Most types of writing include facts *and* ideas, so you'll have to read carefully to identify the author's overall intent. This news article is a good example:

Greenville—On November 2, local resident Andrew Dixon was awarded the Lifetime Donor Award from St. Xavier Children's Hospital. This annual award recognizes community members who have made a long-term commitment to helping the hospital through charity drives or private funding. Dixon raised nearly $3 million for the hospital over the past 11 years by organizing an annual charity walk. "Andrew is one of the most generous, selfless people I have ever met," said Brian Benz, chairman of the hospital's Charity Division.

Most of this article presents facts that can't be argued with. The last sentence, however, gives an opinion: Andrew is generous and selfless. But notice that this isn't the *writer's* opinion. The statement appears inside quotations, so the author is quoting a source in order to show you someone else's opinion. The news story tells you what happened and why, but the writer does *not* tell you *what to think* about it.

Readers assume three things about texts written to inform:

1. Just the facts, please! The writer leaves out his or her personal opinions.
2. The writer knows what he or she is talking about and has authority on the topic.
3. The writing is **objective** and presents both sides of an issue.

Exercise 1

Read the text carefully and actively, and then answer the questions.

Organic farming is a carefully regulated industry. In order for foods to be considered organic, they must be grown without chemical fertilizers or pesticides. They must be processed without food additives. Foods such as meat or eggs must be from animals raised without hormones and fed a healthy diet. Foods that pass these requirements can be certified as organic. Traditionally, organic foods have been grown on small farms, but the growing market for organic goods at grocery stores around the world has boosted production in recent years.

1. What is the tone of this text?
   a. dismissive
   b. straightforward
   c. critical
   d. sympathetic

2. Which type of writing might include this excerpt?
   a. a novel about organic farming
   b. an editorial about organic farming
   c. an advertisement for organic farming
   d. a news article about organic farming

Writing to Persuade

Sometimes an author wants to *persuade* the reader to do or believe something. Common examples of this type of writing include bumper stickers, advertisements, and editorials. In Lesson 4 you practiced spotting facts and opinions, and in Lesson 14 we learned to listen for tone, and the same clues will help you identify the author's purpose. Compare these two fliers for a speech club.

1 The Mountain Junior High Speech Club meets Thursday afternoons at 4:45 P.M. in Classroom 40B. The club is led by sixth-grade science teacher Mr. Kimball. Currently there are 11 participating students, but new members are welcome. Interested students are invited to an information meeting this Thursday.

2 Do you want to be a better, more confident speaker? Try Speech Club! Weekly debate practice and easy speech exercises will build your skills in no time. The club meets Thursday afternoons at 4:45 P.M. in Classroom 40B. New members are welcome.

The first flier presents facts in every sentence, so we can safely assume that the author's purpose is to inform. It is written in third-person point of view and the tone is helpful and impartial. The second example includes some information about the club, but most of the sentences use *persuasive* language—the tone is enthusiastic and confident. The second-person point of view speaks directly to *you*, the reader. It tells you that speech club can make you a "better, more confident speaker" and "build your skills in no time." This is clearly the author's opinion. The purpose of the second flier is to persuade the reader to join the speech club.

Persuasive writing tries to convince the reader to agree with an opinion, but the author will probably use facts to build a strong argument. Part of being a good reader is noticing what the writer *doesn't* say and thinking critically about what they *do* say. If the author presents lots of facts, but they only inform you about one side of an issue, the purpose is probably to persuade. Try Exercise 2 to practice spotting an underlying opinion.

Exercise 2

Read the article to answer the questions below. The sentences are numbered for easy reference.

(1) Organic foods are grown by local farmers who use safe, sustainable farming methods. (2) One reason to eat organic is because these methods protect the earth. (3) Organic farming does not introduce dangerous chemicals into the soil, the crops, the air, or the ground water. (4) Organic foods are also better for our bodies than conventionally grown foods. (5) The long-term effects of genetically modified foods are still being studied, but pesticide residue is known to be poisonous to the human body. (6) Certified organic foods are minimally processed, and studies show that they can contain twice as many nutrients as conventionally processed foods.

1. Which statement from the text represents the author's opinion?
   a. Sentence 3
   b. Sentence 4
   c. Sentence 5
   d. Sentence 6

2. Which of the following titles would best introduce this text?
   a. Why Eat Organic?
   b. Organic Food Sales Are on the Rise
   c. Locally Grown Foods versus Organic Foods
   d. A History of Organic Farming

Writing to Entertain

Imagine you're packing for a weekend at your grandparents' house, and there's room in your suitcase for only one book. Would you rather bring your social studies textbook or a new novel by your favorite writer? Most of what we read (especially when reading for fun) is written to entertain. This type of writing includes fiction, such as mystery novels, creative nonfiction like essays or memoir, as well as plays, poems, short stories, and comic books.

Texts written to entertain will often include factual information, and they will often include the author's opinion or characters' opinions. But overall, the purpose is the reader's enjoyment. The next exercise tests your ability to distinguish between all three author's purposes: to inform, to persuade, and to entertain.

Exercise 3

Read each excerpt below and decide whether the purpose is to *inform* (I), *persuade* (P), or *entertain* (E). Write the corresponding letter on the line, as shown in the example.

Example

_P_ Chai tea is the best cure for the winter blues. A cup of chai, served warm or cold, will give you a boost of vitamins C and E to keep you feeling your best through the long winter season.

Remember, the difference between informative and persuasive has to do with facts versus opinions.

1. ___ Harriet Tubman was an African American abolitionist. She was born into slavery in 1820, but she escaped to Philadelphia in 1849.

2. ___ Cal stuffed a sandwich and his tackle box into his backpack. He perched anxiously on the couch, watching out the window for his father's car. It would be their first fishing trip this season, and he couldn't wait.

3. ___ Carrie quickly scribbled a sign for her bedroom door: *Keep out! Busy studying!* She wanted some quiet time to think, and her mother wouldn't pester her if she claimed to be studying.

4. ___ Requiring students to wear identification tags at all times will make it easier for school officials to identify security threats and protect students.

5. ___ More than 30 schools in southern Maryland introduced new policies about student identification tags this year. School officials say the policy has helped them to minimize security threats.

Author's Purpose and Genre

Genre is a way of classifying types of writing. Fiction genres include (among others) mysteries, love stories, and Westerns. Genre is often the biggest clue to the author's purpose in a text. An advertisement, for example, is always written to persuade. If you recognize the genre of a text, you can quickly identify the author's purpose. The chart below can help you remember the purpose of different writing genres.

GENRE	AUTHOR'S PURPOSE
News articles Textbooks Biographies Documentaries Book reports Instruction manuals Charts, graphs, tables, and maps	To inform (explain, illustrate, or give directions)
Advertisements Editorials Essays Campaign speeches	To persuade (convince readers to think/feel/act a certain way)
Novels Short stories Poetry Drama	To entertain (express a theme or story)

Summary

Recognizing the author's purpose is an important part of understanding the meaning of a text. By now you know where to look for clues: the style, tone, word choice, structure, and genre of a text will tell you whether the author intended the text to inform, persuade, or entertain the reader.

Answers

Exercise 1

1. b. The tone of this text is very straightforward and contains facts about organic farming; there's nothing dismissive (choice **a**), it doesn't criticize either farming or consumers (choice **c**), and while it doesn't seem unsympathetic, there's nothing in the text that seems like it's trying to persuade the reader of anything (choice **d**).

2. d. This choice is the best answer because of how objective and factual the passage is. If choice **a** were correct, the passage would likely have featured characters, a story, or a more distinctive voice. An editorial about organic farming (choice **b**) would have more evaluative or opinionated statements. An advertisement for organic farming (choice **c**) would probably be making claims about health benefits or encouraging the reader to buy a specific brand of produce.

Exercise 2

1. b. Sentence 4 is the only one of the answer options that expresses an outright opinion. The other statements (sentences 3, 5, and 6) might not be convincing, detailed evidence, but they are based in fact. In this example, the author tries to persuade the reader by presenting information about *one side of an issue*. It doesn't meet the objective and balanced test of informative writing because the intent is to sway the reader's opinion about the topic.

2. a. The title "Why Eat Organic" reflects the purpose of the passage. In contrast to the earlier excerpt, this text is trying to persuade readers that eating organic food has significant health benefits. No mention is made of food sales (choice **b**), there is no attempt to compare and contrast local food with organic foods (choice **c**), and the passage is not broad enough for a history of organic farming (choice **d**).

Exercise 3

1. I—These are neutral facts about Harriet Tubman's life.

2. E—This seems like the beginning of a story; the writer is trying to draw you into Cal's anticipation.

3. E—Like the previous one, this excerpt seems like the beginning of a specific character's story.

4. P—This excerpt hopes to convince you to agree with the writer's opinion about student ID tags; the word "easier" is a clue that it's an opinion (easier according to whom? By what standards?).

5. I—This is a fact-based accounting of student ID measures in progress; it cites school officials as an authority.

SKILL BUILDING UNTIL NEXT TIME

1. Find two newspaper articles that interest you, one from the news section and one from the opinion section. Read both articles and compare the style and word choice. What is the author's purpose for each article? How can you tell?

2. Choose one thing about eighth grade that you would want to tell a seventh grader about. (For example, how does eighth-grade science compare to seventh-grade science?) Write three short paragraphs about your topic: one paragraph to inform (for example, eighth-grade science includes two dissections and a unit on rocks), one paragraph to persuade (eighth-grade science is more fun than seventh-grade science), and one paragraph to entertain (a funny story about science class).

19 ▶ ASSUMING CAUSES AND PREDICTING EFFECTS

LESSON SUMMARY

Sometimes, writers don't directly explain a cause or effect. Instead, they *suggest* it. This lesson shows you how to "read between the lines" and find implied causes and effects.

Sometimes, we want to say something, but we don't want to just spell it out, whether to challenge or engage our readers. So, as writers, we use suggestion to get our point across. In the previous section, you saw how writers can use suggestion to convey their main idea. Suggestion works at all levels; supporting ideas and even specific details can be implied, too. This lesson focuses on two specific types of suggestion: implied cause and implied effect.

First, here's a quick review. A **cause** is a person or thing that makes something happen. An **effect** is the change created by an action or cause. Cause tells you why something happened; effect tells you what happened as a result of that action. The desired effect of an implication is called an inference—a text implies, the reader infers meaning.

Finding Implied Cause

Imagine that you have a classmate named Len. He walks into the room and looks upset. You know he has just met with the principal. You know that he's been late for school a lot lately and that he's been cutting classes. You also know that Len's parents would go crazy if they knew what Len was doing. When Len walks into the room, he doesn't say anything to you. Why would you guess he's upset?

a. He has to do extra assignments to make up for being late.

b. He is going to be transferred to another class.

c. He's just found out the principal has told his parents.

From what you know, it makes sense to conclude that Len is upset because choice **c**, the principal has reported Len's behavior to his parents. Len doesn't tell you this, but that's what the clues add up to. You used what you know about Len, his parents, and the principal to figure out the cause of Len's distress.

You can use the same process to determine an implied cause when you read. Here's how Len's problem might look in a reading passage:

Len was late for school for the ninth time in three weeks. In the last month, he'd cut Biology five times and Social Studies twelve times. His parents would ground him for life if they knew he'd been skipping classes. He looked nervous when he was called to the principal's office. A few minutes later, when he came back, he looked extremely upset. He walked past his classmates without saying a word and put his head down on the desk.

On a reading test, you might be asked to identify why Len is upset. This question asks you to identify the cause. Again, the clues add up to one thing: that Len's parents have been informed of his behavior.

Writers suggest cause in many ways. In the passage above, the clues are mostly action clues—what people said and did. Clues can also come in the form of details, word choice, and style. For example, look at the following passage:

Dennis was scared—really scared. His knees were weak and he tried to grip the rocky ground of the cliff with his toes. He looked down, 20 feet, to the water below. He looked up again, quickly. He tried to think of something else. He tried to reassure himself. "It's only 20 feet!" he said aloud. But that only made it sound worse. Twenty feet! He felt dizzy and hot.

This writer could have simply said, "Dennis was scared because he was afraid of heights." Instead, she *suggests* the cause of Dennis's fear by *showing* you how Dennis feels and where Dennis is. This way, you are able to see for yourself what Dennis is going through. And through these details, you can conclude that he is afraid of heights. The sentence structure is another clue. Notice that the sentences are short and choppy. In fact, they sound a little panicky. This helps us infer how Dennis feels.

Exercise 1

Here is an excerpt from a short story. Read the passage carefully, and then circle the answers of the questions that follow.

(1) Anne sat on the couch with her feet up on the coffee table, drinking a soda. She heard footsteps by the front door. Brenda was right on time, as usual. Never a minute early or late—for her, everything was very exact.

(2) Anne placed her feet on the floor, reached for the remote and turned off the television. She knew Brenda would demand her complete attention. She knew Brenda would hang up her coat in the closet by the door (third hanger from the left) and then head to the kitchen for her daily inspection (exactly seven steps). She knew this because they had been roommates for six months. Taking a deep breath, she thought about what she would say to Brenda. She waited and watched from her spot on the couch.

(3) A moment later, Brenda stepped into the kitchen and surveyed the scene. Anne looked at her expression, watched her eyes focus on the sink, and saw her face harden when she saw the dishes piled high. Looking at the dishes, Brenda said disappointedly, "I don't believe what I'm seeing. I thought we agreed to share the responsibilities. I thought it was your turn to clean the kitchen this week."

(4) "I haven't gotten to them yet," Anne replied. "I've been busy. Relax. I've got all night." She walked into the kitchen and added her empty glass to the top of the pile.

(5) Brenda fumed. "You know I'm having company tonight! Somehow I thought you would have done your share in the kitchen. If we want to remain roommates, things have to change."

(6) The phone rang, and Anne darted to answer it.

(7) Brenda said in the background, "Anne, please tell them to call back, we need to settle this now. I told you I'm having company soon."

(8) Anne tossed over her shoulder, "will you calm down? I'll get to it!" then spoke into the receiver, "Lucy! It's been ages, tell me everything!"

Circle the letter of the correct answer.

1. Why does Brenda get angry?
a. because Anne is unfriendly
b. because she had a bad day at work
c. because Anne didn't do the dishes
d. because Anne is lazy

2. Why didn't Anne do the dishes?
a. because she didn't have time to do them
b. because she wanted to start a fight
c. because she was too lazy
d. because she wants Brenda to get a new roommate

3. What does Anne do that shows she doesn't intend to shoulder her share of the responsibilities?
a. She turns off the television.
b. She begins to wash the dishes in the sink.
c. She always helps around the house.
d. She talks on the phone.

Finding Implied Effects

Just as writers can imply cause, they can also suggest effects. In the practice passage you just read, Anne clearly had a specific goal. She purposely decided not to do the dishes as an act of rebellion. Why? You know a little bit about Anne and Brenda from the passage. Use that knowledge to answer the following questions: What do you think Anne was hoping to achieve? What effect do you think she was looking for?

a. that Brenda would do the dishes herself for once
b. that Brenda would get a new roommate
c. that Brenda would stop being so neat and so regimented

How can you tell that choice **b** is the best answer? You have to look carefully at the passage. Anne deliberately disregards her roommate's request. Brenda says she is expecting company. Anne responds by ignoring her and answering the phone.

The passage doesn't directly say so, but from these clues, you can conclude that Anne clearly doesn't want to be Brenda's roommate much longer. That's why she didn't do the dishes and that's also why she gladly took a phone call.

But will she get the effect she hoped for? Take another look at the passage, paying close attention to the end. What do you think? Will Anne get her wish? Will Brenda move out? Why do you think so?

The end of the passage offers a strong clue. Brenda clearly wants to resolve the situation, but she doesn't have Anne's respect and probably won't put up with Anne's sloppiness much longer.

Exercise 2

Imagine that there has been a robbery in your apartment building. The victim is Mr. Ash, who lives a few doors down the hall. Below are two passages. One is a statement by the building manager, Mr. Billings. The other is a statement from Ms. Wilkins, who lives next door to Mr. Ash. Read their statements carefully and answer the question that follows. Use their statements to predict some effects. What will happen as a result of the robbery?

> **Mr. Billings (building manager):** This is the third robbery this month. Each time, thieves have gotten past building security. Each time, the thieves stole everything in the victim's apartment. Yet each time, the security officers claim they didn't see anything unusual.

> **Ms. Wilkins (Mr. Ash's neighbor):** Well, Mr. Ash is a carefree man. I knock on his door and he hollers, "Come in!" I just push the door open because it's never locked. He often forgets things, too. He forgets where he parked his car or where he put his keys. One time, I found him in the hall searching through his bags. He couldn't find his keys, but it didn't matter; the door was open anyway. And he left it open the day he was robbed. He's really shaken up by this. He says he can't trust anybody anymore.

Which of the following are likely to happen as a result of the robbery? What *effects* do these statements suggest? Circle the numbers of the correct answers.

1. Building security will be tightened.

2. Tenants will have to notify security before moving furniture out of the building.

3. The security officers will be fired.

4. The security officers will be thoroughly questioned.

5. Security cameras will be installed throughout the building.

6. Mr. Ash will get his things back.

7. Mr. Ash will be more careful with his keys.

8. Mr. Ash will get new locks on his door.

9. Mr. Ash will keep his door locked.

10. Some tenants will move out of the building.

Summary

Writers will often suggest causes and effects without explicitly stating them. You can use clues in the text to uncover these implied ideas. These clues can come in the form of action (what people say or do), specific details, word choice, tone, and style. Active readers look carefully at what people say and do and pay particular attention to details, word choice, and tone. By adding up these clues, they can determine implied cause and effect.

Answers

Exercise 1

1. c. Brenda's face "hardens" with anger when she sees the dishes in the sink. You can tell she expects the kitchen to be clean when she comes home. Anne waits for Brenda to begin her "daily inspection," and when she walks in, she looks around the kitchen as if she's inspecting it. Then she sees the dishes and her face hardens. She asks why the dishes are still in the sink. Further, she reminds Anne about the company she is expecting.

2. b. You can tell Anne is not interested in preventing Brenda's reaction because she is lazily watching television instead of cleaning the kitchen. She knows Brenda is going to check the kitchen and that Brenda is going to be angry about the dishes when she sees them. Instead of doing the dishes, Anne thinks about what she is going to say to Brenda.

3. d. Anne's actions speak loudly. She answers the phone and discontinues a conversation that is important if the two of them intend to remain roommates.

Exercise 2

1, 2, 4, 5, 7, and 9 are all logical predictions to make from these statements. Effect 3 is not likely; it's too extreme. The building manager's statement doesn't suggest that the security officers will be fired, but it *does* suggest that he plans to look into the problem. That's why 4 is a logical outcome. Nothing in either statement suggests that Mr. Ash will get his things back. In fact, there's no mention at all of what was stolen. Mr. Ash left the door open while he was robbed, so there's no need for him to get new locks. But you *can* conclude that Mr. Ash will be more careful because of how shaken up he is—he will probably be less trusting in the future. Finally, there's no suggestion that tenants plan to move. In fact, if they know security will be improved, they will be more likely to want to stay.

SKILL BUILDING UNTIL NEXT TIME

1. Watch people today and observe their behavior. See if you can guess the cause of their emotion or behavior. What clues can you uncover? Are they reading a letter? Talking with someone? Waiting for something? Why might they be acting this way? For example, if you see a man at a bus stop pacing back and forth and checking his watch every 30 seconds, you can infer that the bus is late or that he's late for an appointment.

2. Choose a news article that's about a current event like an election or a scientific discovery. What effects do you think this event will cause? Come up with at least three effects. Support your predictions with evidence from the article.

20 ▶ ANALYZING CHARACTERS

LESSON SUMMARY

Characters are a major part of every story, whether fiction or non-fiction; they experience the story's action and explore the story's themes. This lesson shows you how authors build characters and help you see behind the scenes of your favorite characters.

Who are your favorite fictional characters? Harry Potter, Batman, Katniss Everdeen, Wonder Woman, Charlie Brown—you could probably name 50 memorable characters from stories you have read or heard. Characters are the author's best tool for expressing the story's themes. Readers make stronger connections to a story's characters than to its setting, plot, or themes. If you think the main characters in a story are boring, you probably won't read very much of it!

As writers, we should work hard to create interesting, believable characters that will appeal to readers. In this lesson you'll learn how to analyze a character, understand his or her role in the story, and gain questions to ask yourself when you're developing characters of your own.

Understanding Characters

The first step of analyzing a character is looking at what the author (or speaker) says about the character. This usually includes details about **physical appearance**:

- species (human or animal)
- gender
- age
- height and weight
- color of hair/eyes/skin
- special abilities or disabilities
- health

Understanding the character's physical appearance will help you to make predictions about the character's role in the plot. If a character is particularly healthy, or ugly, or a fast runner, these traits might determine how the character acts in the rest of the story, how others react to them, or what decisions they make.

Personality Traits

The next step is to decide what the character is like. This requires more careful reading because authors usually *show* the character's personality rather than tell us right out. For example, we learn that Harry Potter is a good friend when he risks his life to save his friends. Personality traits are usually described using adjectives; here are some examples.

PERSONALITY TRAITS			
brave	greedy	kind	selfless
clever	helpful	outgoing	shy
cruel	humble	proud	stingy

A story might contain several different clues to the character's personality. First, you can look at how the author describes the character. Second, consider how the character perceives himself [or herself]. Does she think she's the best basketball player ever born? Is

he too shy to talk at school? Is he aware that his parents are proud of him?

Third, look for clues in the character's relationships. Actions speak louder than words, so watch how the character acts toward others. Personality traits are the best clues to how a character is going to act throughout the story. A cruel monster will likely cause conflict in the story, while a wise grandmother might help others or share good advice.

Another important trait to identify is a character's **motive**, the reason or intent behind his or her actions. Suppose Ben wants nothing more than to be the best football player at Wiley High. This idea will motivate his actions in the story. A character might have many motives, and she might develop different motives by the end of the story. For example, Bilbo, the beloved hero of J.R.R. Tolkien's *The Hobbit*, goes on an exciting adventure, but is motivated by thoughts of returning home to his quiet village life. On the journey, though, he discovers new motives—justice, friendship, and common purpose.

Round or Flat?

A writer might build original, complex, or he might use flat, undeveloped characters to help the stronger characters along—characters that serve this helping role are called foils. Most stories have a combination of both types. A rounded character has several motives or interests and a realistic personality. A flat character is one that the author doesn't develop with many details or a complex personality. Flat characters include stereotypes, such as a class clown, a wicked stepmother, or a beautiful princess.

In novels, the protagonist and other main characters are usually fully developed, but the minor characters are often flat. In traditional fairy tales, nearly all the characters are flat because they represent traits instead of having individual stories or personalities. Compare these two character introductions:

A. Once there lived a poor shepherd. He kept a small flock and one dog for company. On summer afternoons, he often sat near a clear brook, whistling pleasant melodies.

B. Isabel lay awake on her straw mat for hours into the night, trying to think of a way to help her father. She was too young to help the men in the fields, and although she did her best with the heavy pots, she wasn't much help in the kitchen, either. Still, she knew she could be useful to him somehow.

The first example introduces a character but doesn't go into detail about him. We don't even learn his name! This character is simple and straightforward, and probably has one motive. The author relies on the reader to visualize the physical details.

In the second example, the author has started to build a rounded character. Isabel has doubts, fears, and wishes. The reader gets to see inside the character's head to better understand her personality and motives. The reader is more likely to connect with this character as she develops and demonstrates her complexity.

Exercise 1

Here is an excerpt from Robert Louis Stevenson's pirate adventure novel *Treasure Island*. As you read it twice, look carefully for character clues to help you answer the questions that follow the excerpt.

From *Treasure Island*

(1) As I was waiting, a man came out of a side room, and at a glance I was sure he must be Long John [Silver]. His left leg was cut off close by the hip, and under the left shoulder he carried a crutch, which he managed with wonderful dexterity, hopping about upon it like a bird. He was very tall and strong, with a face as big as a ham—plain and pale, but intelligent and smiling. Indeed, he seemed in the most cheerful spirits, whistling as he moved about

among the tables, with a merry word or a slap on the shoulder for the more favored of his guests.

(2) Now, to tell you the truth, from the very first mention of Long John in Squire Trelawney's letter, I had taken a fear in my mind that he might prove to be the very one-legged sailor whom I had watched for so long at the old Benbow. But one look at the man before me was enough. I had seen the captain, and Black Dog, and the blind man Pew, and I thought I knew what a buccaneer* was like—a very different creature, according to me, from this clean and pleasant-tempered landlord.

buccaneer = pirate

1. What is Long John Silver's most striking physical characteristic?
   a. He has a broad, smiling face.
   b. He hops like a bird.
   c. He has one leg.
   d. He looks like a buccaneer.

2. What makes the narrator think that Long John is pleasant-tempered?
   a. He is talking cheerfully with the other people in the room.
   b. He has a plain, intelligent face.
   c. The narrator read in a letter that he is pleasant-tempered.
   d. The narrator believes that all buccaneers are pleasant-tempered.

3. The narrator is *surprised* at Long John's character. What sort of person was the narrator probably expecting?
   a. Strong and evil
   b. Dirty and corrupt
   c. Kind and nurturing
   d. Weak and fearful

Character and Plot

After you identify the character's physical and personality traits, you can look at how the character fits into the plot. In fiction, characters' motives and personalities drive the action, and their responses to the conflict build the author's theme. Even in nonfiction, people writing stories drawn from real life must turn the people they write about into developed characters.

Character and Conflict

Each character in the story is either a *major character* or a *minor character*. A major character has a big or important role in the plot. A minor character, by contrast, is not necessarily part of the conflict and its resolution. There are two special types of major characters. The **protagonist** is the hero, and the **antagonist** is usually the hero's enemy or opponent. Not every story has an antagonist, but most have a protagonist.

As explained in Lesson 6, the main character(s) will face conflict. This conflict might be beyond the character's control, such as trying to survive a dangerous sea voyage. Or the conflict might originate in the character's personality. (This is especially true in a character-versus-self conflict.) If Jeannie is jealous of her sister, her jealousy might cause the main action of the story. The characters and their relationships shape the story's action, and we learn about the characters by watching how they act.

Static or Dynamic?

You've seen how the character can affect the plot, but how does the plot affect the character? In many stories, the protagonist *learns* and *changes* during the story. A character who changes during the story is called **dynamic**. By contrast, a character who remains the same throughout the story is called **static**.

The key to being a dynamic character is *internal change*. If a character wins a million dollars, this external circumstance might affect her personality, or it might not. A static character, if she won a million dollars, would stay as generous or as cheap as she had always been. A dynamic character experiences a change in personality or perception. For example, Alexander, the boy who makes the choir in "The Tryout" (Lesson 11), is a dynamic character. In the beginning of the story he is unsure of himself, but as the story progresses Alexander gains confidence. In the story about roommates Anne and Brenda in Lesson 19, Anne is a static character. She is stubborn and lazy in the beginning, and the events of the story do not change her: she is stubborn and lazy at the end.

To decide whether a character has changed, compare his or her behavior at the start of the story to the behavior at the end. Ask yourself three questions:

1. Does the character have a new perspective on himself or herself?
2. Has the character started interacting with others in a different way?
3. Does the character have a new goal or motive?

Consider a few examples from popular stories. In Lewis Carroll's classic *Alice's Adventures in Wonderland*, Alice learns several lessons about how to survive in her strange environment. At the end of the story, she has learned to see things in a new way. The Cheshire Cat, on the other hand, remains just as enigmatic and strange from beginning to end.

In the *Harry Potter* books, the hero Harry Potter learns about his destiny; he becomes a wizard; he learns about friendship, compassion, and courage. Like most protagonists, he is definitely dynamic, as are his best friends, Ron and Hermione. Many of the minor characters in *Harry Potter*, though, are static. The villain Voldemort stays evil, though his external circumstances change as he regains power, for example. He doesn't change internally, and we count on him to be a "bad guy" in every scene.

Character and the Reader

You usually like the hero in a story and dislike the antagonist unless the author is being deliberately provocative or funny by making the villain entertaining and the hero boring, for example. Authors usually leave many clues to help you decide which characters to sympathize with. Compare the two character descriptions that follow.

> **A.** Morgan lifted the heavy pail from the floor and hoisted it onto his shoulder. "I'll be right back with water for your tea, Grandmother," he said, and rushed out into the cold morning. The ground was frosted, and he hoped there wouldn't be ice in their little well.

> **B.** Ezra was a thick stump of a boy, as cruel as he was stupid. Day and night he tormented other children, and when they outsmarted him, he turned ever more spiteful. His mother had a blind spot to his failings, and his father crowed over him no matter what he did.

Even in these short scenes, the reader can start to understand the character's personality and motives. Which character will you probably sympathize with? In example **A**, we see a boy working hard to help his grandmother. Helping others is a positive trait that earns Morgan our sympathy and respect.

Example **B**, on the other hand, shows a character who is "cruel," "stupid," and "spiteful." His physical description is not flattering, and he hurts other people. For these reasons, the reader doesn't want to like or trust him. The boy from the first example, Morgan, is a more likely protagonist because the reader wants him to succeed. And if we like the protagonist, we'll also be emotionally affected by the events that happen to him.

An author who wanted to make Ezra into a protagonist might show his development from a bully into a nice kid; he might have a change of heart or experience bullying himself. That writer wanted to teach readers about the dangers of bullying by selecting bullies as her audience.

Character and Theme

When a character learns a lesson, the reader usually learns a lesson, too. This is where the author's **theme** comes in. Remember from Lesson 17 that a theme is the main idea in literature. A theme might be "Don't trust first appearances" or "Friendship is more important than money." An author's themes are reflected through the main characters' experiences.

Let's return to the story of Goldilocks for an example. During her adventures at the home of the bears, Goldilocks upsets everything in their house before they find her and scare her away. Goldilocks is a dynamic protagonist, so she learns a lesson: Don't mess with the bears' stuff. But what theme does the *reader* explore through Goldilocks? The theme could be "Respect other people's things."

Exercise 2

One way to organize what you know about a character is to use a **character map**. This is a type of graphic organizer that shows some details and important traits of a character. There are many different ways to arrange a character map, but when you analyze a fictional character, you can draw your own map to include the most important information. Practice using the character map shown here, then create your own map for one of your favorite characters.

To practice, complete the following character map for Harry Potter (if you don't know much about Harry Potter, choose a different character that you are more familiar with). You could track his traits and description throughout the series, or just analyze his character at the very beginning of *The Sorcerer's Stone*.

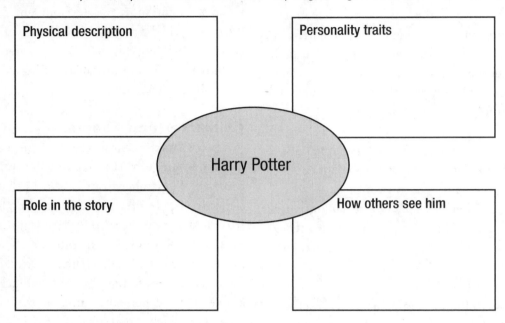

Physical description	Personality traits

Harry Potter

Role in the story	How others see him

Summary

Characters are the reader's window into a story; we can get involved in and experience the action and themes through them. Analyzing a character means understanding what makes the character tick and then closely watching the character's role in the plot. Some special words used to describe characters in literature include protagonist and antagonist, round and flat, and static and dynamic.

Even if you are writing about real people, you should make them vivid and engaging for the reader.

Answers

Exercise 1

1. c. A character's "most striking physical characteristic" is the most dramatic feature as recounted to us by the narrator. In this case it is Long John Silver's missing left leg. While he does have a broad, smiling face (choice **a**) and looks like a buccaneer (choice **d**), neither of those features is as striking as the missing limb. The fact that he hops like a bird (choice **b**) is an effect of missing a leg, so this is not the most correct answer.

2. a. In the first paragraph the narrator tells us Long John is socializing with patrons of the tavern. Long John's plain, intelligent face (choice **b**) is supporting evidence, but the most persuasive support is his actual manner of interacting with people. Read the second paragraph carefully—the letter the narrator received warned him about Long John (choice **c**). The way the narrator distinguishes what he thinks a buccaneer is like from the way he perceived Long John tells you choice **d** cannot be correct.

3. b. We know the narrator was expecting the opposite of "clean and pleasant-tempered." Dirty and corrupt is the best answer choice because it is the furthest from that expectation; we don't know from the passage whether the narrator expected Long John to be strong and evil (choice **a**); he couldn't have expected Long John to be kind and nurturing (choice **c**) because he's so surprised when he is pleasant; because the narrator was fearful about meeting Long John, he was probably not expecting that Long John would also be fearful (choice **d**); the narrator expected Long John to give him a reason to be afraid.

Exercise 2

Here is a sample character map for Harry Potter. You might have included slightly different details, but check to see that you included the correct type of information in each box.

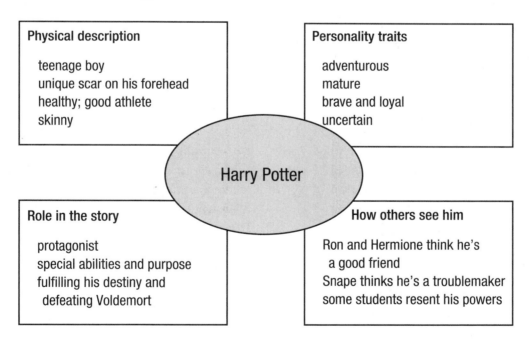

Physical description

- teenage boy
- unique scar on his forehead
- healthy; good athlete
- skinny

Personality traits

- adventurous
- mature
- brave and loyal
- uncertain

Harry Potter

Role in the story

- protagonist
- special abilities and purpose
- fulfilling his destiny and defeating Voldemort

How others see him

- Ron and Hermione think he's a good friend
- Snape thinks he's a troublemaker
- some students resent his powers

SKILL BUILDING UNTIL NEXT TIME

1. Write a quick analysis of your favorite fictional character. Answer these questions: Is the character rounded or flat? A protagonist or antagonist? What does the character look like? How does he or she act toward others? What are his or her motives at the beginning and end of the story? Does this character change during the story? What lesson does the reader learn through this character's experience?

2. Choose a novel or short story that you have read before. Look at the first chapter in which a major character is introduced. What words does the author use to describe him or her? Does the author *tell* you what the character is like, or *show* you through the character's actions? Is the reader supposed to like or dislike the character at first sight?

21 ▶ PUTTING IT ALL TOGETHER

LESSON SUMMARY

This lesson reviews Lessons 17 through 20 and combines the skills you've learned in this section. You'll use your powers of observation to recognize the theme, understand the author's purpose, predict effects, and analyze characters.

T his chapter briefly reviews Section 4 and then gives you two practice passages. These passages require you to use skills from each of the four sections you've read so far, so you'll have to think about the basics, structure, and language, as well as strategies for reading between the lines. Read each essay actively—you'll probably be surprised by how easy it is to use all these strategies at once. You started by building a strong foundation, and with each lesson, you've strengthened those basic skills and developed more advanced ones.

Review: What You've Learned

Here's a quick review of each lesson in this section.

Lesson 17: Finding an Implied Main Idea. You learned how to find the main idea in passages without topic sentences and the overall **theme**, or message, in literature. You used clues in word choice, style, point of view, tone, structure, and action to find the theme.

Lesson 18: Identifying an Author's Purpose. You learned that authors write for three main purposes: to inform, to persuade, and to entertain. You looked for clues to the purpose in the author's word choice, style, and structure.

Lesson 19: Assuming Causes and Predicting Effects. You learned to read between the lines to find implied causes and effects. You looked for clues in action, structure, language, and style.

Lesson 20: Analyzing Characters. You learned how to analyze and describe a character in literature. You saw how authors use characters to tell a story, and how readers connect to characters to experience the story's themes.

In Section 1, you learned how to be an active reader, how to find the main idea, how to define unfamiliar words, and how to distinguish between fact and opinion. In Section 2, you learned about plot structure, chronological order and order of importance, comparison and contrast, cause and effect, and summaries and outlines. In Section 3, you learned how writers use point of view, word choice, style, tone, and literary devices to help create meaning.

If any of these terms or strategies are unfamiliar, take some time to review the term or strategy that is unclear.

Section 4 Practice

Read these practice passages actively and carefully. Then answer the questions that follow.

> **Note:** If you come across unfamiliar words, do not look them up until *after* you've completed this practice exercise.

Exercise 1

For or Against?—That Is the Question

(1) Andy is the most unreasonable, pigheaded, subhuman life form in the entire galaxy, and he makes me so angry I could scream! Of course, I love him like a brother. I sort of have to because he *is* my brother. More than that, he's my twin! That's right. Andy and Amy (that's me) have the same curly hair and dark eyes and equally stubborn temperaments. Yet, though we may look alike, on most issues we usually take diametrically opposite positions. If I say day, you can count on Andy to say night.

(2) Just this week, the big buzz in school was all about the PTA's proposal to adopt a school dress code. Every student would be required to wear a uniform. Uniforms! Can you imagine? Oh, they won't be military-style uniforms, but the clothes would be uniform in color. The dress style would be sort of loose and liberal.

(3) Boys would wear white or blue button-down shirts, a school tie, blue or gray pants, and a navy blue blazer or cardigan sweater. Girls would wear white or blue blouses or sweaters, blue or gray pants or skirts, along with a navy blue blazer or cardigan sweater. Socks or tights could be black, gray, blue, or white. The teachers are divided: Some are in favor of the uniforms, others are opposed. The principal has asked the students to express their

opinions by voting on the issue before decisions are made. She will have the final word on the dress code.

(4) I think a dress code is a good idea. The reason is simple. School is tough enough without worrying about looking cool every single day. The fact is, the less I have to decide first thing in the morning, the better. I can't tell you how many mornings I look into my closet and just stare, unable to decide what to wear. Of course, there are other mornings when my room looks like a cyclone had hit it, with bits and pieces of a dozen different possible outfits on the bed, on the floor, or dangling from the lamps. I also wouldn't mind not having to see guys wearing oversized jeans and shirts so huge they would fit a sumo wrestler. And I certainly would welcome not seeing kids showing off designer-labeled clothes.

(5) Andy is appalled at my opinion. He says he can't believe that I would be willing to give up my all-American teenage birthright and trade in wearing whatever I want for the conformity of a uniform. Last night, he even dragged out Mom and Dad's high school photo albums. What a couple of peace-loving hippies they were!

(6) "Bruce Springsteen never wore a school uniform. Bob Dylan wouldn't have been caught dead in a school uniform!" he declared. Andy was now on his soapbox. "When I am feeling political, I want to be able to wear clothes made of natural, undyed fibers, sewn or assembled in countries that do not pollute the environment or exploit child labor. If I have to wear a uniform, I won't feel like me!"

(7) To which I replied, "So your personal heroes didn't wear school uniforms. Big deal! They went to high school about a million years ago! I feel sorry for you, brother dear. I had no idea that your ego is so fragile that it would be completely destroyed by gray or blue pants, a white or blue shirt, a tie, and a blazer."

(8) That really made him angry. Then he said, "You're just repeating what you hear that new music teacher saying because you have a crush on him!"

(9) "That is so not true. He's just a very good teacher, that's all," I said, raising my voice in what Mom would call "a very rude manner."

(10) "You have always been a stupid goody two-shoes, and you know it!" he snapped.

(11) "Is that so? Anyone who doesn't agree with you is automatically stupid. And that's the stupidest thing of all!" I said.

(12) Fortunately, the bell rang before we could do each other physical harm, and we went (thankfully) to our separate classes.

(13) The vote for or against uniforms took place later that day. The results of the vote and the principal's decision will be announced next week. I wonder what it will be. I know how I voted, and I'm pretty sure I know how Andy voted.

1. Amy and Andy fight because
   a. the school is forcing students to wear uniforms.
   b. they're both stubborn.
   c. they always take the opposite view on issues.
   d. they don't like each other very much.

2. You know that this selection is a personal narrative because the story is about a
   a. personal experience and is told in the first person.
   b. historical event and is told in the third person.
   c. conflict of opinions between two people.
   d. school policy decision that will affect many people.

3. What type of character is Amy?
   a. protagonist, rounded, dynamic
   b. protagonist, flat, static
   c. protagonist, rounded, static
   d. antagonist, flat, dynamic

4. Which of the following is the best statement of Andy's position on the issue presented in the story?
   a. School clothing should reflect parents' values.
   b. Wearing school uniforms means one less decision every morning.
   c. How one dresses should be an expression of one's personality.
   d. Teenagers should never follow the latest fads in dress.

5. What is the author's main purpose for this story?
   a. to inform
   b. to persuade
   c. to entertain
   d. to explain

6. Is there enough information in this story to predict an outcome? If so, what will probably happen next in the story?
   a. Yes. Students, teachers, and all staff members will begin wearing uniforms.
   b. Yes. Students will vote against uniforms, and the principal will agree with their decision.
   c. Yes. Students will vote against uniforms, and the principal will disagree with their decision.
   d. No. There is no way to determine what the outcome will be.

7. Read the following sentences from the story:
   Andy is appalled at my opinion. He says he can't believe that I would be willing to give up my all-American teenage birthright by dressing like—well, like a typical teenager.

   As it is used in these sentences, what does *appalled* mean?

   a. angry
   b. in denial
   c. supportive of
   d. horrified by

8. The overall organizing principle of this passage is
   a. chronological.
   b. order of importance.
   c. comparison and contrast.
   d. cause and effect.

9. Which of the following best expresses the main point Amy is trying to make in paragraph 7?
   a. Andy shouldn't look up to his heroes so much.
   b. Our clothes shouldn't determine how we feel about ourselves.
   c. Andy needs more modern heroes.
   d. Andy's lack of self-confidence is reflected in his clothing.

Exercise 2

Adapted from *Heidi* by Johanna Spyri
(1) From the little Swiss village of Mayenfeld, a footpath winds through green and shady meadows to the foot of the mountains, which look down from their stern and lofty heights upon the valley below. On a clear sunny morning in June, two figures slowly climbed the arduous, narrow mountain path; one, a tall girl, the other a child whom she was leading by the hand. The child's little cheeks were rosy with heat because, despite the hot June sun, she was dressed as if to keep off the bitterest frost. She

didn't look more than five years old, and her small feet, in thick mountain boots, laboriously plodded up in the heat.

(2) After an hour's walk, the two came to a small village. This had been the elder girl's home. Suddenly, a voice called. "Wait, Dettie. It's Barbel! If you're going up higher, I'll come with you."

(3) Dettie and Barbel walked ahead, while the child wandered behind them. "And where are you off to? Is that the child your sister left when she passed?" asked Barbel.

(4) "Yes," answered Dettie. "I'm taking her up to her grandfather, where she must stay."

(5) "You must be out of your mind, Dettie! The old man will soon send you and your charge packing!"

(6) "He can't. He's her grandfather and must do something for her. I've taken care of her till now, but have a chance for a better job. Her grandfather must now do his duty by her."

(7) "That would be fine if he were like other people," Barbel asserted. "But not a creature knows anything about the old man. He lives up on the mountain like a hermit, hardly ever allowing himself to be seen. When he does, the sight of him, with his bushy eyebrows and immense beard, is alarming!"

(8) "What of that?" said Dettie, in a defiant voice, "He's her grandfather all the same, and must look after her."

(9) At that point, Barbel turned back, but Dettie and Heidi continued to the top of the mountain. There, the grandfather's hut stood on a rocky ridge, overlooking the valley, exposed to the wind, but catching every ray of sunlight. Behind the hut stood three old fir trees with thick branches, and beyond them rose another wall of mountain. Next to the hut sat the grandfather. Heidi ran straight to the old man, put out her hand, and said, "Good-evening, Grandfather."

(10) "What's the meaning of this?" he asked gruffly. He stared at her from under bushy eyebrows, and Heidi stared back, for his long beard and thick eyebrows, growing together over his nose and looking like a bush, were so remarkable that she couldn't take her eyes off him!

(11) "I've brought you Tobias and Adelaide's child," said Dettie.

(12) "And what has the child to do with me?" asked the old man curtly.

(13) "She's here to remain with you," Dettie answered. "I've done my duty by her; now it's your turn."

(14) The grandfather rose and said in a commanding voice, "Be off, and don't let me see your face again!"

(15) Dettie didn't wait to be told twice. "Good-bye, Heidi," she called, as she hurried down the mountain.

(16) Meantime, Heidi's grandfather looked at her. "What is it you want?" he asked.

(17) "I want to see what you have inside the house," said Heidi, with sparkling inquisitive eyes the old man couldn't resist.

(18) Together, they walked into the hut. Thus starts the wonderful adventures of Heidi.

10. Which is the setting of this story?
a. a winter day in a German valley
b. a June day on a mountain in Sweden
c. a spring morning in a South American village
d. a summer day on a Swiss mountain

11. Which BEST describes Heidi's character?
a. a five-year-old orphan girl
b. a friend of Dettie's
c. a baby just learning to walk
d. Dettie's seven-year-old sister

12. What is the conflict at the beginning of this story?
   a. Dettie's external conflict with Barbel.
   b. Heidi's external conflict with Dettie.
   c. Dettie's internal conflict about losing her sister.
   d. Dettie's and Heidi's external conflict with the mountain.

13. Which is NOT one of Dettie's character traits?
   a. vain
   b. confused
   c. responsible
   d. hard-working

14. Why did Dettie need the grandfather to take over the care of Heidi?
   a. Dettie had a chance for a better job.
   b. Dettie was married and wanted children of her own.
   c. Heidi was sick and needed to be out in the mountain air.
   d. Heidi had grown up and was too much trouble for Dettie.

15. What is NOT a characteristic of the grandfather?
   a. mature
   b. lonely
   c. forceful
   d. adventurous

16. The following begins which section of the plot?
   "What's the meaning of this?" he asked gruffly.
   a. Climax
   b. Exposition
   c. Resolution
   d. Rising Action

Answers

Exercise 1

1. c. The narrator tells us in the first paragraph that she and Andy "usually take diametrically opposite positions. If I say day, you can count on Andy to say night." (If you don't know what *diametrically* means, you should be able to determine its meaning from context.) The rest of the story shows how they have completely opposite views. Choice **d** is incorrect because Amy tells us that she "love[s] him like a brother." It is true that the school isn't forcing a dress code—the PTA just introduced the issue for a vote (choice **a**) and that they're both stubborn (choice **b**), but neither of these are the reasons they fight.

2. a. This is the best choice because the story is told by Amy, who is describing a personal experience. Choice **b** is incorrect because the story is in the present; it is not an historical event, and it is not told in the third person. The fact that the selection reveals a conflict (choice **c**) does not make the selection a personal narrative. The fact that the selection involves a policy decision that will affect the students (choice **d**) does not make the selection a personal narrative.

3. c. Because Amy is narrating this story about her own experiences, we can eliminate the *antagonist* option, choice **d**. She may be antagonizing her brother, but for our purposes she's backing up her opinions with detailed support. Choice **b** is incorrect because the author has already given enough details about Amy to make her a rounded character, but she doesn't change her opinion over the course of the story.

4. c. This choice accurately states Andy's position on the issue of a school dress code. Choice **a** is incorrect because nothing in the narrative suggests that how students dress reflects their parents' views. Choice **b** is incorrect because it reflects Amy's views about the dress code, not Andy's. Choice **d** is incorrect because it does not reflect Andy's reasons for objecting to a dress code.

5. c. Like most fiction, this story is written to entertain the reader. It might also inform or persuade, but that idea is not emphasized enough to be its main goal.

6. d. At the end of the story, the reader does not know what the vote will be or what the principal will do, so we cannot effectively predict the outcome.

7. d. The best clue to the meaning is that Andy "can't believe" that Amy "would be willing to give up [her] all-American teenage birthright" to dress the way she pleases. He may be angry (choice **a**), but this passage tells us that he also is horrified. Choice **b** is incorrect because he does not deny Amy's opinion; he argues with it directly, which also rules out choice **c**.

8. a. This story is told in chronological order, from the PTA proposal to a day or so after the vote but before the announcement.

9. b. Although Amy uses ridicule to make her point, she does have a good point to make: that we shouldn't let our clothes determine how we feel. She tells Andy she feels sorry for him because his ego "would be completely destroyed" if he had to wear a uniform. In other words, she's upset that he'd let a uniform affect his sense of self.

Exercise 2

10. d. The author tells us in the opening, or exposition, that it's a hot summer (June) day on a Swiss mountain, and that Heidi is struggling in the heat. No mention was made of winter or Germany (choice **a**). Yes, it's a June day, and yes, it takes place on a mountain, but not one in Sweden (choice **b**). No mention was made of spring or South America (choice **c**). If you missed this question, review Lesson 6.

11. a. The author tells us Heidi is a five-year-old girl who has been living with her aunt because she lost her parents. Heidi has to walk up a steep mountain, not something a baby who's just learning to walk would do. She is Dettie's sister's *child*, not Dettie's friend (choice **b**). Dettie's been looking after Heidi since her mother, Dettie's sister, died (choice **c**). Barbel is Dettie's friend (choice **d**). If you missed this question, review Lesson 6.

12. d. Dettie and Heidi have a hard, long climb against the elements of nature: the heat of the day as they struggle to get to the top of the mountain. Dettie doesn't have a conflict with Barbel (choice **a**). The two have a discussion during the story to provide readers with information about the grandfather. Heidi has no conflict with Dettie, the child follows along and does what the older girl tells her to do (choice **b**). Dettie may have an inner conflict about taking her sister's child to the grandfather, but that's not the major conflict at the beginning of the story (choice **c**). If you missed this question, review Lesson 6.

13. b. Dettie is NOT confused; she knows exactly what she wants and will walk to the top of the mountain to get it. Dettie doesn't seem to be concerned with her appearance or overly proud (choice **a**). She shows that she IS responsible by taking care of her sister's child up to this point (choice **c**). She just needs the grandfather to help out now. Dettie is also hard-working because she had a job while taking care of her sister's child, and now will have another job when the grandfather takes Heidi (choice **d**). If you missed this question, review Lesson 20.

14. a. Dettie had a chance for a better job, so she wouldn't be able to take care of Heidi any longer. The author doesn't give any clues that would lead you to infer that she is married (choice **b**). The mountain air would be good for a child, sick or healthy, but the author doesn't give any clues to show that Heidi is sick (choice **c**). Heidi was only five, and she wasn't too much trouble because she did what Dettie told her to do (choice **d**). If you missed this question, review Lesson 21.

15. d. *Adventurous* means "daring or thrill-seeking," and the grandfather does *not* have this characteristic; he's a hermit who rarely leaves his home on top of the mountain. *Mature* (choice **a**) means "grown up or older," and grandfathers are definitely older. If he was lonely (choice **b**), he would have been happy to see Dettie and Heidi. The grandfather is forceful (choice **c**) in the way he commands Dettie to leave. If you missed this question, review Lesson 20.

16. a. This was the beginning of the turning point, the most exciting part of the story, when the story heads towards a resolution of the conflict. The exposition (choice **b**) gives background information and sets up the conflict. That was done earlier in the story, when readers learned who Dettie and Heidi were and what they were doing on the mountain. The resolution (choice **c**) is how everything turns out in the end, and that comes after this point in the story. The rising action (choice **d**) is what characters do to try to solve the conflict, leading to the high point, or climax. For example, Dettie and Heidi climbing the mountain is rising action. If you missed this question, review Lesson 21.

SECTION

5 ▶ INTERPRETING NON-LITERARY SOURCES

From movie reviews to textbooks, from editorials to cookbooks, there are many different types of written texts. Your active reading skills can apply to all of them, but some types of content require special skills. For example, writers might choose to convey information in pictures, graphs, or diagrams. These types of texts include words, but you'll need to read them differently than you would a poem.

In this section you will learn how to:

- follow instructions (Lesson 22)
- decode the argument in advertisements (Lesson 23)
- interpret graphs and charts (Lesson 24)
- use maps, illustrations, and diagrams (Lesson 25)

In each lesson you'll learn new strategies for reading and interpreting special sources. Then, in Lesson 26, you'll practice the skills you learned in this section, plus the skills you've learned in earlier lessons.

LESSON

22 ▶ INSTRUCTIONS

LESSON SUMMARY

The ability to follow directions is a key skill for test takers, and it is also useful in daily life. This lesson shows you how to interpret and follow instructions.

Suppose you want to fix the brakes on your bicycle. Your friend lends you a bicycle repair guide and says, "Good luck!"

How can you find the information you need? How will you know what all the steps mean? Instructions can be intimidating, but careful readers have a major advantage in successfully following directions. That's because good readers notice the key words in instructions (active readers even mark them!) and they use logic to follow the steps carefully. Good readers can also evaluate instructions to decide whether they make sense, because even professional writers sometimes make mistakes!

When you learn a new game, follow a recipe, or complete a homework assignment for class, you are already using many interpretive strategies. Directions on assignments and standardized tests can be particularly tricky (and misunderstandings can have significant consequences), so in this lesson you'll learn strategies to build your direction-following skills.

Why Read Instructions?

Suppose your teacher has just handed you a social studies exam. Should you skip the directions and spend your time writing answers, instead? We read instructions *to learn*.

The directions might tell you how long you have to complete the exam, or how many points each question is worth, or whether you can ask questions or use your notes. If you skip over the instructions, you might miss important information or waste time doing the exam incorrectly. Whether you want to learn how to make peanut butter cookies or how to put your bicycle back together, instructions give you the information to do it yourself. Even if you *think* you know what the instructions will say, it is important to read them closely, every time. It only takes a few seconds or minutes to read the instructions, but it could take a long time to realize you've made a mistake.

Read Ahead

Have you ever started to cook or bake something, only to realize that you're missing one or two necessary ingredients? Reading ahead can help you avoid careless mistakes and prepare you for what is coming next. Try this exercise:

1. Read all the directions first.
2. Think of your favorite fruit.
3. Focus on the first letter of that fruit.
4. Think of a person's name that starts with that letter.
5. Write that person's name on a piece of paper.
6. Fold the paper in half, then in half again.
7. Think of how many years you have known that person.
8. Write the number of years on the folded paper.
9. Do only step 2.

Did you follow the instructions correctly? You probably won't come across instructions like this in a real text, but it's a good reminder that if you don't read all the instructions, you only have part of the information. You could see instructions like this, however, on an exam:

> Read the article about deep-sea exploration. Underline the main idea in each paragraph. Use these main ideas to develop an outline of the author's argument.

If you only read the first sentence, you won't know to underline the main ideas. It will take extra time if you have to go back and do this step later. The third sentence tells you *why* you're underlining ideas—you'll need to use them to build an outline. Reading all the directions at once, before you start the test or project, can save you time in the long run. You'll know what's coming and how each step fits into the big picture.

Look Up Unfamiliar Words

In order to follow directions, you have to understand what the directions are telling you. Instructional texts, such as recipes, how-to articles, and user guides, often include lots of specialized terms. Look up any unfamiliar words *before* you start to follow the steps.

Read these directions from a user guide for a digital camera:

Taking Photos of Fireworks
Be sure to perform the following steps ahead of time so you won't miss the shot when the fireworks explode.
1. Set up your camera on a tripod. Aim the camera at a distant object that is at about the same location as the fireworks.
2. Press the shutter button halfway until the focus indication lights up.
3. Press the focus button to select manual focus.

4. When the fireworks appear, depress the shutter button fully to take the picture.

These instructions include a few specialized terms: *tripod shutter button*, *focus indication*, *manual focus*. If you don't know what these words mean, you won't be able to follow the directions, and you'll probably miss the photo opportunity.

Everything from board games to DVD players can have specialized terms, which might not be found in a dictionary. The instructions might have a **glossary** that explains uncommon words. You can also use **context clues** to help you figure out what the terms mean.

Knowing the exact meaning of words in instructions is even more important than understanding every word in a novel. Think of all the different ways you can cut up a potato: *chop*, *dice*, *shred*, *mash*. Each of these words is linked to a specific way of cutting, and if you misunderstand the word, you might perform the wrong action and wind up with a pile of french fries on top of your shepherd's pie.

Exercise 1

Read the instructions below for playing cricket. Then answer the questions that follow.

To play cricket, assemble two teams of 11 players each. The playing field is a flat grass field with a center strip called a pitch. First, place a wooden wicket at each end of the pitch to use as a target. Then, one bowler from the fielding team bowls a hard leather ball toward the opponent's wicket. To defend his wicket, the opponent's batsman uses a cricket bat to stop the ball.

1. What is *cricket*?
   a. a board game
   b. a classroom learning game
   c. an outdoor sport
   d. an indoor gym sport

2. What is the *pitch*?
   a. the center strip in the playing field
   b. a bat
   c. a wooden stick
   d. the action of the team's bowler

3. What is the purpose of a *wicket*?
   a. to hit the ball
   b. to protect the opponent's pitch
   c. to stop the ball
   d. to serve as a target

4. Which term describes the name of one *team*?
   a. bowler
   b. fielding
   c. batsman
   d. wicket

Follow the Sequence

Most instructions have multiple steps or procedures. In order to reach the end result, you have to follow the steps *in sequence*. Instructions might show the sequence in a numbered list, or they might use the sequence words and carryover clues you learned in Lesson 7.

For example, read the recipe below carefully and actively:

Briarcliff Blackberry Jam
Yield: 5 cups
8 cups crushed blackberries
5 cups sugar
2 tablespoons lemon juice

1. Mix all ingredients in a Dutch oven.
2. Heat to boiling over high heat, stirring frequently.
3. Boil uncovered, continuing to stir, until the mixture is translucent and thick—about 25 minutes.
4. Quickly skim off foam, as soon as the mixture thickens.

5. Immediately pour jam into hot, sterilized jars, leaving $\frac{1}{4}$ inch headspace.

6. Seal with canning-jar lids.

Notice how this recipe gives plenty of clues for proper sequencing. First, all the steps are numbered. Second, the writer provides carryover clues that link one step to another. In Step 3, for example, we are told to *continue to stir*. Thus, we can see that there was a previous step—Step 2—in which we were told to stir. In Step 4, we are told to skim off the foam *as soon as the mixture thickens*. Thus, we know that this step must come after Step 3, which tells us to stir "until the mixture is translucent and thick."

> Look for the logic in every set of instructions. This will not only make it easier to follow the steps, but you'll be able to catch a mistake if you accidentally skip a step. For example, if you get to the end of a recipe but you still haven't used two items from the ingredient list, you probably missed a step.

Instruction sequence is important on tests and assignments, too. Suppose you receive these instructions:

Select one story by Charles Dickens to read outside of class. Write a summary of the story's main events and characters. Then select a theme from the story that you will write an essay about. Propose your idea to Mrs. Phelps by Wednesday afternoon. Then find at least two reliable sources and write a two-page essay about your selected theme.

If you skip over any of these instructions, or if you do them in the wrong order, you probably won't get a very good grade on this assignment! If you don't read the story first, it will be hard to choose a theme. If you don't get your idea approved by the teacher, your essay might not meet her expectations.

Notice Key Words

You've seen how important it is to understand specialized words in instructions. On a test or assignment it is especially important to understand *what the instructions want you to do*. This means you have to pay attention to key words. Here are some sample multiple-choice questions, with the key words underlined:

1. All the choices below are <u>synonyms</u> for *viable* <u>except</u>
   a. valid
   b. possible
   c. incredible

2. Which sentence <u>best</u> explains why Kevin didn't make the choir in the story "The Tryout"?
   a. He was overly confident.
   b. He didn't have the right attitude.
   c. He sang too loud.

Do you see the key words in these two examples? Question 1 includes a specialized term—*synonym*. This means that some of the answer options will have *the same meaning as viable*. A second key word in this question is the last word, *except*. The question is asking, "Which answer option is <u>not</u> a synonym for *viable*?" If you read too quickly and skip the word *except*, you'll misunderstand the question and likely choose the wrong answer. If you read carefully, you'll know that the correct answer is choice **c**.

In Question 2, the word *best* tells us that *all* the answer options might seem plausible. Your job as the test taker is to find the *most* accurate or *most* complete of the answer options. Choice **a** might sound correct, but you'll have to read all three answer options to find the <u>best</u> answer. You may want to reread part of the story (in Lesson 11) to confirm that the answer is choice **b**. Kevin was very confident, and his voice was loud, but he didn't make the choir because he didn't have the right attitude.

KEY QUESTION WORDS

after	except
before	mainly
best	the main reason
difference	not
different from	the same as

Special Formatting

You might also see **boldface**, *italic*, or CAPITALIZED text in instructions. The writer uses these special formats to catch your attention. If text has special formatting, it is important!

Exercise 2

Underline the key word(s) in each test question.

1. Which word best describes how Crater is feeling?

2. What is the main reason that Sara's family moved to Dallas?

3. What does Mim do after Ryan hits a home run?

4. Which word means about the same as *hyperbolic*?

5. Which word is an antonym to *belligerent*?

6. What is the difference between copper and iron?

Verbs, Verbs, Verbs

Instructions on a test or an assignment might be as simple as "Answer the questions below." But if the directions are more specific, it's essential to read carefully so you'll know what to do. Here are some verbs you might see in an assignment or test question:

circle	explain	outline
compare	graph	research
contrast	identify	select
describe	list	summarize
draw	locate	underline
evaluate	name	write

Each of these verbs asks you to do something specific. On a test or an assignment, you'll only get the points if you follow the directions. If the instructions say, "List three inventions from the Industrial Revolution and describe the effects of each," you earn full credit by *listing* the inventions, then *describing* the effects of each one. If you list inventions but don't describe them, or if you *compare* the inventions instead, you will probably lose points on your answer. If any of these verbs are unfamiliar to you, look them up in a dictionary. These are important words and you'll likely see them again.

Evaluating Instructions

Not all instructions are easy to follow. A writer might assume that you already know about the subject and not include enough information. The writer might use confusing phrases, or even make an error in the directions. As a careful reader, you can evaluate instructions for completeness, clarity, and effectiveness.

To evaluate a set of directions, ask yourself a few questions:

- Are all needed ingredients, materials, or tools identified?
- Are the instructions for a beginner or for someone with advanced knowledge of the subject?

- Are the steps clear and easy to follow?
- Are there any diagrams or definitions to help you?
- What is the most complicated part of the instructions?
- What additional information do you need to complete the task?
- Would you recommend these instructions to a friend who wants to do the same task?

Exercise 3

Read the magician's instructions for doing a magic trick. Then answer the questions below. The sentences are numbered for easy reference.

Magic Bottle Trick

(**1**) Have a volunteer touch and examine the bottle to prove that it's normal. (**2**) Drop your magic wand into the bottle, saying, "Notice how easily it falls in." (**3**) Then secretly slip a piece of eraser into the bottle (don't let anyone see this part!). (**4**) Turn the bottle upside down slowly, pulling on the wand slightly when turning to wedge the eraser into the opening. (**5**) Your wand will be magically suspended in the bottle when you let go. (**6**) This simple trick will really impress your friends!

1. Are these instructions for a beginner or a professional magician? What makes you think so?

_____

_____

2. Which step sounds the most complicated?

_____

_____

3. What information could be added to make these instructions more helpful?

_____

_____

Exercise 4

Use what you've learned about effective instructions to write directions for how to make your favorite sandwich. Be sure to include all the necessary steps, and try to make the directions clear enough for a young friend to follow.

_____

_____

_____

_____

_____

_____

_____

_____

_____

Summary

There are many different types of instructions, but a careful reader can interpret their meaning by reading ahead, looking up unfamiliar words, following the sequence, and noticing key words and verbs. You can also evaluate instructions to determine whether they are clear, accurate, and easy to follow. Knowing how to interpret instructions will make it easier to follow directions, especially on homework and tests.

Being aware of what directions often leave out will help you communicate more clearly with others, too.

Answers

Exercise 1

1. **c.** You know you play cricket in a field, so you can eliminate choices **b** and **d**. The description of using a bat and ball eliminates **a**, so choice **c** is the correct answer.
2. **a.** The answer is in the second line.
3. **d.** The answer is in the fourth line.
4. **c.** The fielding team is the one whose turn it is to bowl.

Exercise 2

1. Which word <u>best</u> describes how Crater is feeling?
2. What is the <u>main</u> reason that Sara's family moved to Dallas?
3. What does Mim do <u>after</u> Ryan hits a home run?
4. Which word means about <u>the same as</u> *hyperbolic*?
5. Which word is an <u>antonym</u> to *belligerent*?
6. What is <u>the difference between</u> copper and iron?

Exercise 3

1. These instructions are probably for a beginner magician. The trick is something you can do at home with common items. Also, the last line of the instructions states, "This simple trick will really impress your friends!" so it is probably meant for showing your friends rather than performing on a stage.
2. Step 4 sounds the most complicated. The steps in sentences 1, 2, and 3 are easy to comprehend and probably easy actions to perform. Sentences 5 and 6 explain the outcome of the trick.
3. A diagram or picture might make it easier to follow the steps. The writer also forgot to include a list of materials needed. You know that you need a bottle, but what type of bottle? Is a dark glass bottle better than a clear water bottle? How big should the eraser be? How might you distract your audience so you can slip in the eraser? More details about the specific materials could improve your success with the trick.

Exercise 4

Your instructions should be specific to the type of sandwich you chose, but you will probably have some of these steps:

To make a sandwich, you'll need two pieces of bread. Any type of bread will work, but wheat bread is my favorite. Then find your ingredients. Peanut butter and peach jelly are a perfect combination. First, take a knife and spread the peanut butter completely on one piece of bread. Then spread the peach jelly on the second piece. Pick up the piece with the jelly and place it jelly-side down on top of the piece with the peanut butter, then cut your sandwich in half with a knife.

SKILL BUILDING UNTIL NEXT TIME

1. Use a book or the Internet to look up instructions for something you want to learn how to do, such as knit, ski, make waffles, or carve wood. Evaluate the instructions using the tips you've learned. Are the directions easy to follow? Are there unfamiliar words you need to look up? Do the diagrams or photos help you interpret the steps? Is any necessary information missing?
2. Write instructions for your favorite game. Be sure to include the list of materials, and make the directions as clear and precise as you can. Then use the instructions you wrote to teach the game to a friend or sibling.

23 ▶ ADVERTISEMENTS

LESSON SUMMARY

Advertisements use many techniques to persuade the reader. In this lesson you'll learn how to identify several advertising approaches. You'll also practice evaluating advertisements for logic, effectiveness, and hidden agendas.

Chances are, you're surrounded by advertising right now. The logo on your T-shirt, the label on your juice bottle, and the characters on your folders or notebooks are all sending you messages. You run into advertising every time you pick up a magazine, turn on the television, or walk down a city street.

It might seem like these advertisements are designed to give you information. But their true purpose is *to persuade* you to buy their product, order their service, or believe their message. They might tell you the whole truth, or part of the truth, or no truth at all! As a reader and viewer, how can you make sense of advertising?

First, you can learn the tricks and techniques of advertising. Then you'll be more prepared to interpret what you read and hear. Second, you can use the strategies you've already learned for interpreting arguments and persuasive writing. By reading carefully, you'll notice *how* the writer says things and *what effect* the advertisement is meant to have on you. Remember everything we've learned about opinions, facts, tone, motive, and purpose.

The World of Advertising

Can you name the product that's represented by a gecko? How about a polar bear, or a caveman, or an orange cheetah? Can you sing the jingle from the latest jewelry commercial, or repeat the slogan for a major insurance company? You'd be surprised at how many advertising slogans, mottoes, and jingles you know! Even when you're not paying attention to advertisements, they can affect how you think and act.

Where do advertisements come from? Companies that sell products or services generate the most advertisements. But political groups and politicians running for office also put promotional ads in the newspaper and on television. Religious groups might advertise in a radio commercial or in fliers and books. The military runs advertisements on the Internet and roadside billboards urging people to enlist or learn about its programs. Advertising is so widely used that you probably see more than 100 ads each day. It's important to know how to interpret this type of writing.

Advertisements work just like other types of persuasive writing, except that they might also use pictures or sounds to help convince you. All advertisements have a subject, a main argument, and supporting details. Because they are often very short, they use the fewest possible words to create the most powerful message. Rather than trying to communicate lots of *information*, advertisements often try to convey an *image* instead.

Building an Image

To help promote their goods, services, or ideas, advertisers try to build an image for the company. They're hoping that you'll like the image and buy their products. Advertisers have countless ways to build their image. For example, a soda company might use a cute, cuddly bear as a mascot. The bear doesn't make the soda, or drink the soda, or have anything to do

with the soda. But if *you* think the bear is cute, you will probably form a good impression of the company and may buy its products.

> Advertisements are often designed to build a persuasive image rather than give you information. A magazine advertisement for a chewing gum might show people doing extreme downhill skiing. The gum doesn't make them ski better or have more fun. But the advertiser is hoping that the next time you think about skiing, you'll remember the chewing gum, too.

Advertising Techniques

The persuasive argument in an advertisement might be logical or emotional. It might appeal to your ethics or your senses. Advertising writers have a whole bag of tricks, and they choose the technique that they think will work best for each product or service they want to sell. Ten of the most common techniques follow.

1. Bandwagon

"Everyone is doing it! Don't be left out!" This advertising approach shows or suggests that lots of people have already decided to use a product or service. If you don't join in, you'll be missing out on the fun, or you'll be stuck outside the group. Look for words that suggest huge popularity or ask you to join a major trend.

Example: Join the revolution! Millions of people are enjoying Space Age Satellite TV and you can too! Call today to join the era of Space Age luxury TODAY!

2. Ethics

"It's the right thing to do." This approach appeals to your sense of right and wrong, justice, or empathy. It suggests that if you are a good person, you will want to use this product or service. Look for words that inspire a strong emotional or ethical response.

> **Example:** Every hour, 400 children die of preventable diseases in the world's poorest nations. For the cost of just one cup of coffee, you can make a difference in the life of a child.

3. Fantasy

"The ideal can be yours." Superheroes, dramatic romance, wealth, and beautiful people are the staples of this appeal. By showing you something you might want to be, this type of advertising suggests that using the product or service will let you experience the fantasy. For example, if you use Shimmer Shampoo, your hair will be transformed (along with your body and your car). Look for miracle cures and dramatic scenarios that promise the reader something that the product cannot really provide.

> **Example:** Try Minty Fresh gum. Have the confidence to get close to the woman of your dreams.

4. Fear

"Don't be a victim, protect yourself and your loved ones." These appeals play on readers' fears. They might suggest that something is happening that you don't know about. Or they might insist that you need to act *right now* before the sale is over or the supplies run out. This is a type of *emotional* appeal. Look for words about time, immediate action, and frightening results.

> **Example:** Do you know where your teenagers are right now? Talk to your kids about drugs—before it's too late.

5. Humor

"If it's funny, you'll remember it." This appeal is one of the most popular in television commercials, and the humor often has nothing to do with the product being sold. But advertisers believe that if something makes you laugh, you'll feel good about it. Look for puns, jokes, funny clothing, or silly scenarios.

> **Example:** "Book with Rent-O-Trip and don't get left out in the cold!" accompanied by a family dressed for the beach shivering in a snowstorm outside the wrong hotel.

6. Nostalgia

"The old-fashioned way." Also called "plain folks," this appeal emphasizes a simple, old-fashioned ideal. Advertisements like these are often aimed at older adults. Look for phrases like "back to nature," "genuine family recipe," or "just like Grandpa used to do it." Also look for back-country slang and rural scenes.

> **Example:** Try Martha's pure, original honey. We've been making tummies happy for more than 80 years.

7. Sense Appeal

"You can't resist your senses." This appeal is especially useful for restaurants, grocery stores, perfume designers, clothing lines, headphones, and other companies that make products for your senses. How does the product smell? taste? feel? sound? What will it make *you* feel? Does it look fancy, or sharp, or clever, or cool? Look for descriptive words that cue your senses.

> **Example:** Bite into a sweet, creamy Choco-Pop, with its crunchy chocolate shell and strips of delicious caramel. Your mouth will thank you.

8. Snob Appeal

"Only the best for you." Most people like to feel special and unique. This appeal suggests that it knows the *perfect* choice for you. This is the opposite of the bandwagon appeal; it suggests that you can select something special or unique, to reflect how special—or clever, wealthy, or selective—you are. Look for words that compliment the reader or suggestions that the *usual* choice is a bad one.

> **Example:** This Mother's Day, don't buy cold, wilting grocery store flowers. Choose PortaFlora, where all the bouquets are cut and arranged by hand. Your mom deserves the very best.

9. Statistics

"The facts don't lie." Studies have shown that people are impressed by numbers, graphs, and charts, even if the data doesn't explain anything! Writers include statistics to convince you that lots of science or serious studies have been done on the product or service. But beware; data can be easily skewed or even made up, or the data an advertisement shows you might not have anything to do with the claim it is making. Be wary of charts, graphs, percentages, results of studies, or phrases like "4 out of 5 experts recommend—"

> **Example:** When you sprinkle FlowerGrow on your garden three times a month, 99% of weeds will be killed on contact, and your flowers will be five times larger and healthier.

10. Testimonial

"If a famous person likes it, you will too." If you recognize a famous person in the advertisement, it is probably a testimonial. There are celebrity endorsements (when a famous person is shown using a product), and there are expert endorsements (when a doctor, dentist, or other "expert" claims to approve the product). Advertisers expect that you will want to copy the celebrity or listen to the expert's advice. Look for famous people (or characters, like Big Bird) or claims from experts evaluating the product.

> **Example:** As a doctor, I take care of patients all day, but I have to take care of my own body, too. That's why I choose Pain Killer, the only medicine that stops my headaches as soon as they start.

Exercise 1

Read the advertisements below, and decide which type of appeal each one uses. Then write the type of appeal on the blank line after each advertisement.

1. Choose Milky premium dark chocolates when you want to send the very best.

   _____

2. Last year, 3 million parents couldn't afford to send their kids to college. How will you pay for your child's education? Start investing now.

   _____

3. Tuffie non-stick frying pans are the number one choice of celebrity chef Carly Calhoun.

   _____

4. Double-Fury for Gaming Machinez. Get yours.

   _____

5. Trust All-Insurance. We've been helping folks like you for four generations.

   _____

6. If you're spending your whole paycheck on the vending machines in the break room, it might be time to find a new job. Upload your resume to our Web site today. _____

7. The all-new Tundra Pony has a 6-point rotational system, a redesigned chassis for increased durability, and 250 horsepower to give you the performance you need.

_____

8. Every morning while you shower, brush your teeth, and make breakfast, you use nearly 28 gallons of water. That's enough to provide drinking water for ten children for a week. Do the right thing; conserve water whenever you can. _____

9. After a summer afternoon soccer game, kick back with a smooth, ice-cold Lava Juice. The sweet fruit flavor sends an icy blast to your insides. _____

10. Start your day with *Shimmer*, the new scent by Gabriel, and open the door to possibility.

_____

Exercise 2

Try to write your own advertisements using the techniques you've just learned. For each product, write two possible advertisements using the appeals shown below.

Example:
Product: bleach cleaning wipes

Statistics: Studies show that our bleach wipes kill 99.2% of household germs and viruses.

Ethics: Count on our germ-fighting bleach wipes to keep your family from getting the flu this season.

1. Product: organic applesauce

Nostalgia: _____

_____

_____

Testimonial: _____

_____

_____

2. Product: home landscaping service

Snob appeal: _____

_____

_____

Fantasy: _____

_____

_____

Being a Critical Reader

In general, people who write advertisements are hoping that you won't read or listen too closely. They're hoping that you won't question the information they're giving you. It can be a challenge to start evaluating advertisements because we see hundreds of them each day. But you can use your active reading skills to see how advertisements work. And with a bit of practice, you'll be able to spot misleading information, weak arguments, and hidden agendas.

Check the Logic

Any persuasive argument should build evidence to support an opinion. But the argument in an advertisement might have gaps in its logic. It might also present lots of unsupported conclusions. The fantasy appeal is especially guilty of this. If you have your hair cut at Nolan's Salon, will the most popular boy in school really ask you to the prom? Advertisements might seem to present a *cause and effect* relationship, but there isn't always a logical link between them. As you read, look carefully at the causes and effects that the advertisement promises.

Too Good to Be True

You've probably heard the saying, "You can't get something for nothing," or "If it sounds too good to be true, it probably is." These sayings are popular in our culture because we need the reminder! Advertisements often promise things that sound like an amazing opportunity. For example, "Call in the next five minutes, and we'll send you ten issues of the magazine for free!" But after you call, you'll discover that the free issues are in exchange for signing up for a paid membership. You can avoid these pitfalls by reading closely. Always read the fine print, and look for the catch.

Hidden Agendas

As you learned in the lesson about implied main ideas and themes, a writer might bury the true message. In advertisements you might notice hidden agendas, too. For example, you might see a preview for the latest Superman movie, which will only be sold on Blu-ray discs. The advertisement seems to promote a movie, but is also subtly promoting another product, the Blu-ray disc player.

Propaganda

Propaganda is a special type of advertising that only shows one side of an issue. Instead of selling you a product or service, propaganda wants to sell you an *idea*. Governments and political parties, especially controversial ones like the Nazi Party, can use propaganda to convince people of their ideas. Even documentaries and news reports can be propaganda if they have very unbalanced coverage of an issue.

To spot propaganda, be critical and skeptical:

- What idea does the writer want me to believe?
- Has the writer shown both sides of the issue?
- Did the writer ignore other important points?
- What might be a valid objection or opposing perspective?

Propaganda is a dangerous type of advertising because ideas are more powerful and more important than dish soap or video games. If you read actively and critically, you won't be fooled by propaganda.

Exercise 3

Use your active, critical reading skills to analyze this longer advertisement. The sentences are numbered to help you answer the questions below.

(1) Have you been waiting for the perfect cure? (2) Your wait is over! (3) Try the new and improved *BetterX*, the latest product from CyberStuff. (4) Everyone is raving about *BetterX*. (5) "This is the product I've been waiting for," says Shirly McCloud from Denver. (6) "Once you try *BetterX*, you'll never go back to your old remedies!" (7) Other products cost up to $200 or more, but you can try *BetterX* today for just $64.99. (8) If you call in the next five minutes, we'll send you a month's supply of *BetterX* completely free! (9) Supplies are disappearing quickly, so don't miss your opportunity.

1. Which advertising technique is used in sentence 4?
   a. snob appeal
   b. bandwagon
   c. statistics
   d. ethics

2. Which advertising technique is used in sentence 5?
   a. testimonial
   b. nostalgia
   c. fantasy
   d. statistics

3. Which sentence promises something that is probably too good to be true?
   a. Sentence 3
   b. Sentence 6
   c. Sentence 7
   d. Sentence 8

4. What does *BetterX* do?
   a. cures headaches
   b. balances your finances
   c. prevents insomnia
   d. the advertisement doesn't tell us

Summary

Advertisements are a special type of persuasive writing. They are meant to sell you a product, a service, or an idea. By reading actively, you can spot the techniques behind the ad's argument. You can also evaluate the message to decide whether it is straightforward or misleading, logical or illogical. Now you know how to spot hidden agendas and propaganda, which makes you a smarter consumer.

Answers

Exercise 1

1. **Snob appeal:** The "premium" adjective tells you this is meant to appeal to a reader's love of luxurious things.
2. **Fear:** The large number of kids, the ominous specter of paying for expensive higher education, this advertisement is using fear to motivate parents to invest.
3. **Testimonial:** the celebrity chef endorsement of a specific product makes this one a testimonial.
4. **Bandwagon:** "Get yours" implies everyone else is getting theirs, and if you don't move quickly you might miss out.
5. **Nostalgia:** The approachable language of "folks," the "four generations" message; this ad is designed to earn your trust and capitalize off your love of family and security.
6. **Humor:** The implication of spending your paycheck in the break room is that they're basically paying you in quarters; the advertiser is promising their job hunting site will help change your luck. If this got a chuckle out of you, you already know it's humor.
7. **Statistics:** Car companies are especially notorious for rattling off specifications of the car being sold, the implication being that if you know enough to be impressed by those numbers, you're the right kind of person to buy that car.
8. **Ethics:** The number of gallons you waste plus the number of children you could be helping with it indicate this is designed to play on your sense of ethics and spread the message of conservation.
9. **Sense appeal:** Setting the ad in a "summer afternoon," taking the time to describe the "smooth, ice-cold" juice; this ad wants you to suddenly be very thirsty and think "hey, that fruit juice sounds pretty good right about now."
10. **Fantasy:** The tagline for this fragrance promises an attractive, exciting life for you, provided you smell like Gabriel.

Exercise 2

Answers will vary, but they might resemble these responses.

1. **Nostalgia:** Our organic applesauce is made from apples and sunshine. That's a recipe grandma would approve of.
   Testimonial: I've been feeding my children organic applesauce for years. It's the only applesauce I trust.
2. **Snob appeal:** Call us for all your home landscaping needs. We tailor every job to your exact needs to give you the best-looking lawn in the neighborhood.
   Fantasy: Trust our landscaping service to make a good impression. Because you never know who might drop by [the president, a celebrity, etc.].

Exercise 3

1. **b.** Sentence 4 is a classic example of "everybody's doing it."
2. **a.** Although this person is not a celebrity or an expert, it is still a testimonial. Testimonies from average people are effective for advertising because people tend to trust the recommendations of others. If your best friend says a new video game is really amazing, you are likely to believe it. In advertising, though, remember that the company ignores all the bad reviews of its product and only shows the good reviews. Testimonials might also be totally made up.

3. d. Sentence 8 promises a free supply of the product, which is very unlikely to be true. In any promise of something for nothing, there is bound to be a catch.

4. d. Sometimes advertisements focus on persuading you to like their *image* and don't even explain what they are selling. A critical reader will think, "What are they trying to sell me? Is it something I really need?"

SKILL BUILDING UNTIL NEXT TIME

1. Find two advertisements from different sources today (television, magazines, Internet, radio, billboard). Read or listen to each one carefully. What kind of appeal does each advertisement use? Is there a hidden agenda? Is the argument logical? Does it sound too good to be true?

2. Use a book or the Internet to look at some examples of propaganda. These might be pictures, videos, or text. What idea does the propaganda promote? What kind of arguments are used to persuade you? Are you convinced by the propaganda?

24 ▶ GRAPHS

LESSON SUMMARY

Writers can use graphs and charts to communicate information. In this lesson you learn how to interpret three types of graphs: bar graphs, line graphs, and pie graphs.

Have you ever noticed that your math and science textbooks include a lot more graphs and charts than your language arts textbooks? Graphs can be a very useful tool for conveying information, especially numbers, percentages, and other data. Scientists and mathematicians often use graphs to show the results of studies or experiments. A graph gives the reader a *picture* to interpret. That can be a lot more efficient (and interesting!) than pages and pages explaining the data.

Graphs can seem intimidating, but reading a graph is a lot like reading a story. The graph has a title, a main idea, and supporting details. You can use your active reading skills to analyze and understand graphs just like any other text. First, let's look at the parts of a graph.

The Parts of a Graph

Most graphs have a few basic parts:

- a caption or introduction paragraph
- a title
- a legend or key
- labeled axes

An active reader looks at each part of the graph *before* trying to interpret the data. Legends and labels are instructions for reading the data correctly.

Caption or Introduction

Before you even look at the graph, you'll want to look for clues to its significance. If the graph is shown in the middle of a paragraph, read the text before it. It will probably introduce the topic and suggest the author's purpose in including a graph. What point is the author trying to illustrate? Is the graph being used to prove the writer's point or strengthen an argument?

If the graph is off to the side of the text, look for a *caption* underneath. Captions will usually tell you where the data came from (for example, a scientific study of 400 African elephants from 1980 to 2005). Captions usually summarize the author's main point as well, which is the reason for including the graph.

Title

The title is very important. It tells you the *main idea* of the graph by stating what kind of information is being shown. A graph might have the title, "NASA program spending from 2002 to 2008." You can already guess that the graph will show some different NASA programs, some years, and some monetary amounts. Just by reading the title, you can start to make predictions about the data and prepare your brain to interpret the graph.

Legend

A **legend**, also called a key, is a guide to the symbols and colors used in the graph. It tells you what is being measured on the graph. You can't make sense of the graph without first looking at the legend. Here are some examples:

●	6th graders
●	7th graders
●	8th graders

🌲	Picnic table upgrades
💧	Swimming pool upgrades
⛺	Camping site upgrades

Not every graph will require a legend, but if the graph shows multiple colors, solid and dotted lines, or symbols or icons, be sure to look for the legend. Then you'll understand what data are shown and how the data are organized.

Labeled Axes

Many graphs, including bar graphs and line graphs, have two axes that form a corner. Usually these axes are the left side and the bottom of the graph. Each axis will always have a label. The **label** tells you what each axis measures. Look at these examples:

Expenses (dollars)

Month

U.S. population (millions)

Year

In the first example, the bottom axis, called the **x-axis**, shows time in months. The vertical axis, or the **y-axis**, shows the amount of money spent. According to the text in parentheses, the y-axis is measured in *dollars*. Thus, dollars are the **unit of measurement** for this graph. The second example uses years as the unit of measurement for one axis, and millions of people for the other axis. Notice the word *millions* in parentheses. The graph might *seem* to show about "300 people" in the year 2008, but the units tell you to read it as "300 million people."

The units on each axis won't always start at 0, but they will follow a consistent interval. For example, a graph that measures the U.S. population might start at 50 million if there are always at least 50 million people in the data. A graph that tracks monthly expenses might show 5, 10, 15, 20, 25 on the y-axis, an interval of $5. This makes the graph easier to read, and you can still plot other numbers, like 18, by placing them in the correct spot, in this case about halfway between 15 and 20.

Bar Graphs

Now that you know the basic parts of graphs, let's look at some specific types. A **bar graph** has two axes and uses bars to show amounts. Here's a basic bar graph with vertical bars:

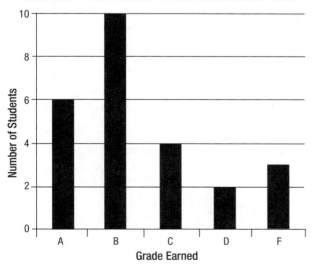

Student Performance on Social Studies Quiz

In this graph, we see that the x-axis shows grades that students earned, and the y-axis shows how many students earned each grade. You can see that 6 students earned an A because the bar for A stretches up to 6 on the vertical measurement. There is a lot of information we can get from a simple graph like this. Try to answer these questions:

1. Which grade did the most students earn?
2. How many students passed the quiz with a grade of C or better?
3. How many students took the quiz?

The bar for a B grade is the tallest, so the most students earned that grade. To find out how many students earned a C or better, add up the number of students who earned an A (6), B (10), *or* C (4). Therefore, the total number of students who earned a C or better is 20. To find the total number of students who took the quiz, just add all the grades together, for a total of 25 students.

Some bar graphs will measure more than one set of data. Be sure to check the graph's legend to see how the data are presented. Now let's look at a more complex bar graph:

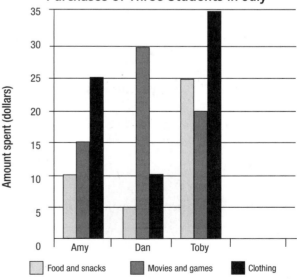

Purchases of Three Students in July

First, look at the title. This graph will show the purchases of three students during one month. It might focus on how much money they spent or what they bought. In fact, the graph shows both. The bottom axis lists three different students: Amy, Dan, and Toby. Each student has three bars of data. The legend shows us what each bar means. And the y-axis shows how much was spent. Dan, for example, spent $5 on food and snacks.

Now that you know how to read the graph, try Exercise 1 to answer some questions about it.

Exercise 1

1. According to the graph, how much money did Toby spend on movies and games?
   a. $20
   b. $25
   c. $30

2. Which student spent the most on food and snacks?
   a. Amy
   b. Dan
   c. Toby

3. What is the total amount that Amy spent?
   a. $45
   b. $50
   c. $65

4. How much did all three students spend on clothing?
   a. $70
   b. $80
   c. $85

5. What did Dan spend the majority of his money on?
   a. food and snacks
   b. movies and games
   c. clothing

Line Graphs

A **line graph** looks similar to a bar graph, but instead of bars, it plots points and connects them with a line. It has the same parts as a bar graph—two labeled axes—and can be read the same way. To read a line graph, it's important to focus on the *points of intersection* rather than the line segments between the points. This type of graph is most commonly used to show how something changes over time. One axis will often show a unit of time, such as years, months, or hours. Here is a graph that charts how far a bird flies during the first five days of its spring migration:

The Pipit's Spring Migration

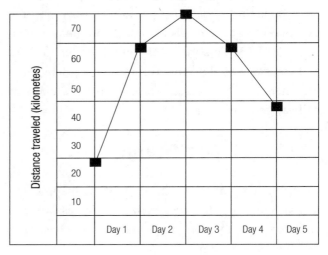

The unit of measurement for the x-axis is days. The unit of measurement for the y-axis is kilometers. Thus we can see that, on the first day, the pipit flew 20 kilometers. The line segment goes up between Day 1 and Day 2, which means that the bird flew *farther* on Day 2. If the line segment angled down, as between Day 4 and Day 5, it would mean that the bird flew *fewer kilometers* than the day before. This line graph is a quick, visual way to tell the reader about the bird's migration.

Double Line Graph

Just like a bar graph, a line graph can show more than one set of data. Two (or more) sets of data are graphed to help the reader *compare* the data. The lines might be different colors or types, such as dotted, dashed, and solid lines. Again, be sure to read the legend so you know how to read the graph. Try the next exercise to interpret a double line graph.

Exercise 2

This double line graph shows two sets of data. Look carefully at the title, legend, and axes to decide how the graph organizes the information. Then answer the questions that follow.

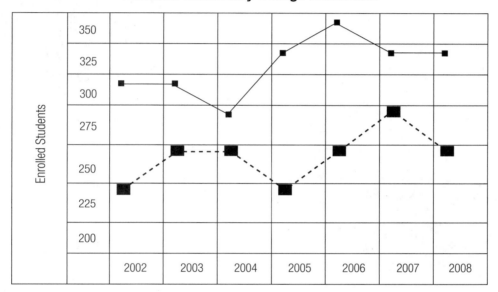

Midland Community College Enrollment

1. In 2002, how many full-time students were enrolled at the college?_____

2. In which year was part-time student enrollment at its highest?_____

3. In 2005, how many more full-time students enrolled than part-time students? _____

4. How many total students were enrolled in 2007? _____

5. From 2004 to 2006, did the enrollment of full-time students increase or decrease? _____

Pie Graphs

A typical **pie graph** (also called a **pie chart**) looks like a circular pie or pizza. The circle is divided into sections, and each section represents a fraction of the data. (Unlike a bar graph or line graph, a pie graph only shows one set of data.) These graphs are commonly used to show percentages; the whole pie represents 100 percent, so each piece is a fraction of the whole.

A pie graph might include a legend, or it might use icons or labels within each slice. This pie graph shows one month's expenses.

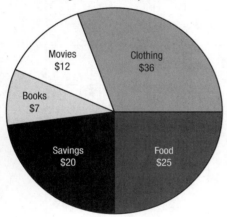

Amy's June Expenses

Food $25
Movies $12
Clothing $36
Savings $20
Books $7

The pie graph shows us different categories for Amy's expenses. You can quickly determine that Amy spent more on movies than books. How much did Amy spend on food and clothing combined? By adding $25 and $36, you see that Amy spent $61 on these two categories. How much did Amy spend total? By adding all the amounts, you discover that Amy spent $100 total.

Exercise 3

Look at the next pie graph and try to answer the questions below.

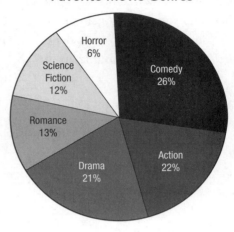

Favorite Movie Genres

Comedy 26%
Romance 13%
Science Fiction 12%
Action 22%
Drama 21%
Horror 6%

1. Do more people like drama or comedy? _____

2. Which two genres are the least popular? _____

3. Which is more popular—action, or romance *and* science fiction? _____

4. What percentage of people like *your* favorite movie genre? _____

5. What information is missing that might make this graph more meaningful?

_____

_____

Tips for Reading Graphs

As you read a graph, there are a few strategies you can use to be sure you interpret it correctly. First, as you look at the data on the graph, check your understanding. Ask, "Does this make sense?" Suppose the graph shows the U.S. population. If you read the 2002 U.S. population as 280 but you know that there are more than 280 people in the United States, you'll quickly realize that you've misread the data. A graph is a scientific way of showing data, so the graph should seem logical to the reader.

Second, as you look at the graphed data, check for *patterns* and *groups*. Does the amount increase every year? Is there a sharp decrease at one point on the graph? Also keep an eye out for *differences*. This is especially important when more than one set of data is being graphed.

Finally, if you are trying to answer questions about a graph, be sure you know what information you're trying to find. If you understand what the question is asking, you'll have a much better chance of answering it correctly. To answer the question "How many people were counted in 2003?" you're looking for a number, while the question "In what year was the U.S. population at its lowest?" should be answered with a year.

Summary

Three common types of graphs are bar graphs, line graphs, and pie graphs. To interpret a graph, you can use your active reading skills to examine the introductory text, title, legend, and axes. Once you've identified the main idea of the graph, you're ready to interpret the data.

Answers

Exercise 1

1. **a.** To read this graph, first isolate the column for Toby's purchases, then read the key to figure out which shaded column corresponds with movies and games. Look across to the Amount Spent measures on the Y-axis to find the answer.

2. **c.** First, look for the tallest light-shaded bar, then figure out which student it belongs to by following it downward.

3. **b.** Use the Amount Spent axis to determine that Amy spent $10 on Food and snacks, $15 on Movies and games, and $25 on Clothing. Add it up to get $50.

4. **a.** Add up the three dark-shaded columns. Amy spent $25, Dan spent $10, and Toby spent $35, for a total of $70.

5. **b.** The tallest column attributed to Dan is the medium-shaded bar; he spent $30 on Movies and games.

Exercise 2

1. 300
2. 2007
3. 100
4. 600
5. increase

Exercise 3

1. Comedy (26%) is more popular than drama (21%).
2. Horror (6%) and science fiction (12%) are the least popular genres.
3. Romance and science fiction combined (25%) are more popular than action (22%).

4. Answers will vary according to your favorite movie genre.
5. It would make this graph more meaningful to know how many people were surveyed, what their demographics are, how the genres are defined, or when the survey was conducted.

SKILL BUILDING UNTIL NEXT TIME

1. Find a graph in your math or science textbook. Does the graph have a title and caption? Can you tell what the graph is about without reading the surrounding paragraphs? What is the main idea of the graph?
2. Write down a list of all the friends you can think of who (1) walk to school; (2) bike to school; or (3) ride the bus to school. Then draw a bar graph to show this data. On the x-axis (bottom axis), write *walk*, *bike*, and *bus*. The y-axis should show the number of students. Then put it in a pie chart. If you have access to a computer with Excel or any spreadsheet data processing program, play around with making tables of data you can collect yourself, then graph it in various ways.

25 ▶ VISUAL AIDS

LESSON SUMMARY

Writers can use more than just text to get a point across. Diagrams, maps, tables, illustrations, and timelines can all be used to convey information to the reader. This lesson shows you how to interpret several types of visual aids.

You have probably heard the saying "A picture is worth a thousand words." When you look at an image, your brain interprets it in an instant, while it might take you five minutes to read a page of dense text. Images and other visual aids are efficient ways to organize lots of information in a small space. Just think how much easier it is to look at a map of your city than to read a paragraph explaining where all the roads are located.

When you were young, most of your books had pictures on every page. Illustrations help children understand the text. As you get older, your books aren't always illustrated, but writers still use images and diagrams to help the reader visualize the information.

Maps

A **map** is a visual representation of an area. There are many types of maps, and they can be used to present a wide variety of information. Maps often include the names of continents, countries, and cities. They might also show elevation, the shapes of landforms, or the view of the land from a satellite. Maps can also be used to show data, such as the population density of major cities or the main crops of several countries.

To read a map, remember the steps you learned in the previous lesson for interpreting a graph. First, look at the introductory text or caption to determine *why* the map has been included. What idea or topic is it trying to illustrate? Second, look at the title. This will tell you what the map is supposed to show. Keep using your active reading techniques to annotate important features.

A map of basic landforms and place names might not include a legend. But if the map shows special data, such as the sheep population of Europe, the legend will explain the symbols or colors used. Here's a map showing a bird migration range:

Range of the American Robin

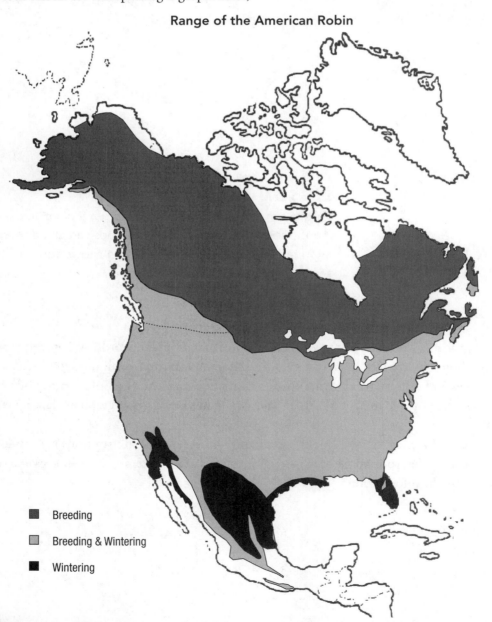

- ■ Breeding
- ■ Breeding & Wintering
- ■ Wintering

The map's title tells you that the main idea of the map is where the American Robin lives. The legend explains the different markings on the map. Notice that the states and cities are *not* labeled, because the writer assumes that you will recognize the geographic location.

Illustrations

An **illustration** might be a photograph or a drawing. It could be simple or complicated, realistic or cartoonish. It might represent information, strengthen an argument, or tell a joke. A comic is a self-contained illustration with no accompanying text. Other illustrations are linked to written content though there may be text in speech or thought bubbles.

When you come across an illustration in a book or on a test, there are a few things to check:

- **context:** If the illustration has an accompanying article or story, be sure you read that first.
- **title:** This is an easy clue to the main idea of the illustration.
- **caption:** This can provide an important explanation of what the illustration shows or what idea the illustration helps to prove.
- **figure number:** Books or articles that have more than one illustration often number the images to help the reader identify them. Illustrations might be numbered with whole numbers (1, 2, 3, and so forth). They might also be numbered by chapter; the third picture in Chapter 4 could be called 4.3, 4-3, or 4c. When you read a book or article that includes illustrations, check to see how the illustrations are identified; then you'll be able to match the illustration to the related content in the text. This is especially important when the illustrations are on a different page than the related text.

- **labels:** Within the illustration there might be words or symbols. These labels explain the parts of the illustration and help the reader understand its meaning. Here's an example of an illustration with labels:

Parts of a Flower

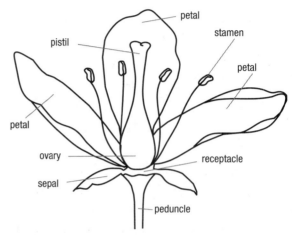

All flowers share several basic parts. Each begins growing at the end of a branch called a peduncle, which enlarges to become a receptacle. Sepals protect the flower's ovary, and petals surround the stamen and pistil.

Exercise 1
Examine the flower illustration above to answer the questions.

1. What is the stem of the flower called?
   a. a peduncle
   b. a receptacle
   c. an ovary

2. What does a sepal do?
   a. protects the stamen
   b. protects the ovary
   c. attracts insects

3. How many different parts are labeled on this diagram?

    a. five

    b. seven

    c. eight

4. Which types of flowers have the parts shown in the diagram?

    a. roses and lilies

    b. only lilies

    c. all flowers

Tables

A **table** is an organized grid of words or symbols. The information is arranged in columns and rows. Tables are an efficient way for writers to show lots of numbers or percentages that would be confusing in sentence form. Sentences with nothing but statistics are usually boring and unmemorable anyway. A table usually has labels across the top, or the side, or both. Before you look at the table, read the labels to see what is being measured and what units are used.

You see tables on the back of every cereal box and candy wrapper—nutrition labels are a type of table. Here's an example of a nutrition table for corn chips.

NUTRITION FACTS	
AMOUNT PER SERVING	% DAILY VALUE
Calories 140	7
Fat 7 g	11
Cholesterol 0 mg	0
Sodium 150 mg	6
Carbohydrate 17 g	6
Fiber 1 g	4

Because you see nutrition labels all the time, the table is probably familiar to you. In this table, the identifying labels are along the top row. The first column shows the amount per serving. There is no unit of measurement listed beside the label because the rows in the column don't share a common unit. For example, fat is measured in grams, while sodium is measured in milligrams. The second column is labeled "% Daily Value," and all the numbers in this column are shown as percentages.

> The key to interpreting tables is to read the labels carefully. When you understand how a table is organized, you'll be ready to understand the information, draw conclusions, make comparisons, or answer questions about the table.

Exercise 2

Look at the price comparison table and examine the labels and units. Then answer the questions.

GROCERY STORE PRICE COMPARISON			
PRODUCT	GIANT	WHOLE FOODS	COSTCO
Dish soap	$2.22	$4.13	$3.57
Corn chips	1.62	1.80	2.85
Deli turkey	4.99	4.19	5.75
Mustard	2.25	2.58	2.10
Lemonade	0.85	1.09	0.99
Napkins	0.99	1.99	1.45

1. What is the purpose of this table? _____

_____

_____

2. How many grocery stores are being compared?

_____

3. Which store offers corn chips at the lowest price? _____

4. Which store charges the most for mustard?___

_____

5. How much does deli turkey cost at Costco?

_____

6. What is the cheapest product listed in the table? _____

_____

Timelines

You probably remember the date of your birth, the years that your siblings or friends were born, and other important events in your life. But do you know when the yo-yo was invented, when the Mexican War ended, or when the French Impressionist movement began? Dates can be tough to keep track of, so writers sometimes use a **timeline**. A timeline shows events organized by date.

Timelines cannot show every possible date, so they show a range of dates. The units are usually years, but they could also be months. The **interval** between the dates could be one year, ten years, 100 years, or more. Here are some examples of possible date ranges:

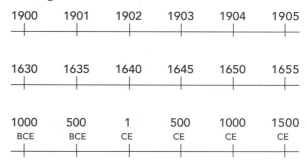

The interval in the first timeline is every year, and the interval in the second timeline is every five years. The third example starts in 1000 BCE and counts up to 1500 CE with intervals of 500 years. The date units are included in the third timeline to make it easier for the reader to interpret. The important thing to notice is that the interval is consistent. It doesn't jump from one year to five years within the same timeline.

The text in a timeline usually shows a specific date and the name of an event. Timelines often use sentence fragments, rather than full sentences, to save space. In Section 1 you read about the history of bicycles. Those events can also be shown in a timeline.

THE HISTORY OF THE BICYCLE							
1810	1820	1830	1840	1850	1860	1870	1880
1818 First bicycle invented in Germany		**1839** Macmillan improves tire and crank design			**1861** Michaux brothers improve the crank mechanism	**1871** Starley adds gears and spokes	**1874** Lawson builds first modern bicycle with equal-sized wheels

Exercise 3

Read the timeline to answer the questions about the history of bicycles.

1. What date interval is used in this timeline?

_____

2. How many events are shown in the timeline?

_____

3. In what year were spokes first added to the bicycle?_____

4. Who built a bicycle with equal-sized wheels?

_____

5. How many years passed between the first bicycle and Macmillan's design improvements?

_____

Venn Diagrams

A **Venn diagram** is made of two overlapping circles. It is used to show that two or more sets of data have something in common. Here's an example of a Venn diagram that represents the hobbies of two friends, Maria and Stanley:

Maria & Stanley's Hobbies

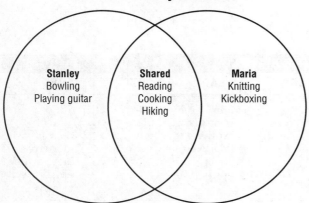

Each circle includes its own set of data. Stanley's hobbies are bowling, playing guitar, reading, cooking, and hiking. Maria's hobbies are knitting, kickboxing, reading, cooking, and hiking. The activities they have in common can be shown in the middle where the circles overlap—these activities apply to both. If something is not in the overlapping part, it is not shared. You can see that Stanley doesn't kickbox or knit, and Maria doesn't care for bowling or playing guitar.

Exercise 4

This diagram tells you which flowers bloom in each season. Examine the diagram carefully to answer the questions that follow.

Seasonal Flowers

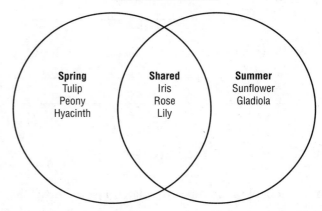

1. Which flower blooms only in spring?
   a. iris
   b. tulip
   c. daisy

2. How many flowers bloom in both spring and summer?
   a. three
   b. six
   c. nine

3. If you want to buy fresh flowers in August, which type will not be in season?
   a. iris
   b. gladiola
   c. peony

Summary

Writers have many options for presenting information. Maps, illustrations, tables, time lines, and Venn diagrams are all visual ways to show information. If they are included in a book or article, they might be used as evidence and support for the author's argument. If you encounter a map or diagram by itself, you can use your active reading skills to interpret its meaning. The title, caption, labels, and unit of measurement are key clues to help you understand how the data is organized.

Answers

Exercise 1

1. a. The text beneath the illustration calls the stem a "branch," but by looking at the image itself you should be able to identify the stem as the "peduncle."

2. b. You know this is the correct answer from reading the caption.

3. b. All three petals are labeled, but they are only one part of the flower.

4. c. No specific flowers are mentioned; though the image appears to be a lily, the caption says "all flowers."

Exercise 2

1. The table's purpose is to compare the prices of several products at different grocery stores.

2. Three grocery stores are being compared.

3. Giant offers corn chips at the lowest price. To find the answer, go to the row labeled corn chips and find the lowest price, then move up the column to see the store name.

4. Whole Foods charges the most for mustard.

5. Deli turkey costs $5.75 at Costco.

6. The cheapest product listed in the table is lemonade ($0.85).

Exercise 3

1. An interval of ten years is used in the timeline.

2. Five events are described in the timeline.

3. Spokes were first added in 1871.

4. Lawson was the first to build a bicycle with equal-sized wheels.

5. Twenty-one years passed between the first German bicycle and Macmillan's new design.

Exercise 4

1. **b.** The tulip is the only one of the answer choices that appears in the Spring side of the Venn diagram.

2. **a.** Three flowers bloom in both spring and summer—they're in the middle of the Venn Diagram.

3. **c.** Since August is a summer month, the flower that will *not* be available is the peony. It is the only answer choice that does not appear in the Summer or in the Shared part of the Venn diagram.

SKILL BUILDING UNTIL NEXT TIME

1. Make a timeline of events in your life. Remember to use a consistent interval (two years, for example) and to include short descriptions of each event.

2. Write a list of your five favorite things to do. Then think of your best friend or sibling. Write five things that he or she likes to do. What activities do you have in common? What activities are unique to you? Draw a two-circle Venn diagram to illustrate. For practice, look online at three stores that sell the same kinds of items—electronics, clothes, or videogames. Make a table and pick four items to compare which store has the best value.

26 ▶ PUTTING IT ALL TOGETHER

SECTION SUMMARY

This lesson reviews Lessons 22 through 25 and combines the skills you've learned in this section. You'll use your skills to interpret special texts, including instructions, advertisements, graphs, and other visual aids.

This chapter briefly reviews Section 5 and then gives you three practice passages. These passages will require you to use skills from each of the five sections you've read so far, so you'll have to apply your active reading skills to interpret information from many types of texts. Remember to read actively, look for clues, and examine the parts and organization of any visual aids.

Review: What You've Learned

Here's a quick review of each lesson in this section.

Lesson 22: Instructions. You learned how to understand and follow directions by looking up unfamiliar words, following the sequence, and noticing key words. You learned to pay careful attention to the verbs used in instructions. You also practiced evaluating instructions for clarity and completeness.

Lesson 23: Advertisements. You learned how to recognize ten different advertising techniques: bandwagon, ethics, fantasy, fear, humor, nostalgia, sense appeal, snob appeal, statistics, and testimonial. You also saw how to evaluate an advertisement for logic, hidden agendas, and propaganda.

Lesson 24: Graphs. You learned to identify and interpret the parts of a graph: the caption, title, legend, and labeled axes. You practiced reading three common types of graphs: the bar graph, line graph, and pie graph.

Lesson 25: Visual Aids. You examined several visual aids that writers use to present information with minimal text: maps, illustrations, tables, time lines, and Venn diagrams.

In Section 1, you learned how to be an active reader, find the main idea, define unfamiliar words, and distinguish between fact and opinion. In Section 2, you learned about plot structure, chronological order and order of importance, comparison and contrast, cause and effect, and summaries and outlines. In Section 3, you learned how writers use point of view, word choice, style, tone, and literary devices to help create meaning. In Section 4, you learned how to read between the lines to find implied ideas, themes, causes, and effects.

If any of these terms or strategies are unfamiliar, take some time to review the term or strategy that is unclear.

Section 5 Practice

Read these practice passages actively and carefully. Then answer the questions that follow.

> **Note:** If you come across unfamiliar words, do not look them up until *after* you've completed this practice exercise.

Exercise 1

Planting Flowers in a Container

(1) If you want to have a garden but don't have lots of space, you can plant flowers in a container. Follow these simple steps for a foolproof container garden.

> Materials:
> a container of your choice (such as a
>   pot, basket, wheelbarrow, tire, or
>   boot)
> a drill
> a broken shard of pottery
> woodchips
> potting soil
> fertilizer
> plants or flowers

(2) If your container doesn't already have holes in the bottom, use the drill to make at least one drainage hole. Inside the container, place the piece of broken pottery over the drainage hole. This facilitates consistent, steady draining. It also prevents the dirt from washing out the bottom of the container.

(3) As you fill your container, it is important to add materials in the right order. First, fill the container halfway with woodchips. Then add the potting soil up to three inches from the top of the container. Sprinkle a layer of fertilizer on top of the potting soil. Organic Vermicompost is the best fertilizer product available.

Layers of Soil in Flower Pot

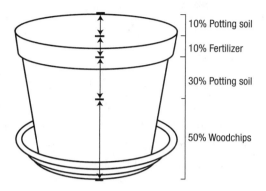

10% Potting soil

10% Fertilizer

30% Potting soil

50% Woodchips

(4) Now you're ready to add your plants to the container. Position them carefully so the roots will have room to grow. When your plants are in position, add more potting soil to keep them in place.

(5) When you water your plants for the first time, add water until it starts to drain out of the bottom. Then water your plants every time the soil feels very dry. Sun dries container plants very quickly, so be sure to water your container plants in the morning.

1. What is *Vermicompost*?
  a. a type of container
  b. a type of fertilizer
  c. a type of potting soil
  d. a type of flower

2. What is the second step in constructing your container planter?
  a. Fill the container with woodchips.
  b. Place the plant in the container.
  c. Cover the drainage hole with a pottery shard.
  d. Drill holes in the container.

3. What explanation does the writer give for using a pottery shard?
  a. it prevents the water from draining out
  b. it prevents the soil from draining out
  c. it fertilizes the plants
  d. it keeps the soil dry

4. Which statement from the text is an example of an *opinion*?
  a. place the piece of pottery over the drainage hole
  b. fill the container halfway with woodchips
  c. organic Vermicompost is the best fertilizer product available
  d. sun dries container plants very quickly

5. Which potting material fills the majority of the container?
  a. woodchips
  b. fertilizer
  c. potting soil
  d. water

Exercise 2

Refresh Yourself with the Vacation of a Lifetime

(1) Give your family a chance to experience the fun and relaxation of a cruise with SunSkipper Cruise Line. Escape to the location of your dreams—perhaps a tropical beach in Mexico, or maybe the bustling ports of Spain. We have more than 60 destinations to choose from, and special tours that take you to the world's most beautiful spots.

(2) SunSkipper offers first-rate entertainment for both children and adults. Spend an afternoon at one of our five swimming pools. Relax in the sauna or enjoy spa treatments. See a play or join in the nightly ballroom dancing. The movie lounge offers large-screen movie viewings, and the children's lounge features

toys, crafts, and other projects to keep your kids entertained. On a SunSkipper cruise, you'll never be bored.

(3) There are many more great reasons to choose SunSkipper. Our ships offer extra-large cabin rooms and a lounge on each deck. You can try new delicacies each day at our nine restaurants. With plenty of luxuries to enjoy, we promise you'll receive the pampering you deserve.

(4) Remember, it's not the destination but the journey that counts. Choose SunSkipper for your family's next vacation, and make memories to last a lifetime. Call 1-800-SunSkipper to start planning today.

6. What is the author's purpose in this text?
   a. to inform
   b. to persuade
   c. to entertain
   d. to advertise

7. Which advertising technique does the writer use overall?
   a. fantasy
   b. bandwagon
   c. statistics
   d. testimonial

8. What is the tone of the advertisement?
   a. friendly
   b. inviting
   c. aggressive
   d. passionate

Exercise 3

Reintroducing the Gray Wolf

(1) After years of heated debate, gray wolves were reintroduced to Yellowstone National Park in 1995. Fourteen wolves were captured in Canada and transported to the park. By 2007, the Yellowstone wolf population had grown to more than 170 wolves. The wolves live in 11 packs, and each pack maintains a specific territory, as shown in the figure.

(2) Gray wolves once roamed the Yellowstone area and much of the continental United States. But they were gradually displaced by human development, and hunted by farmers and ranchers for preying on livestock. By the 1920s, wolves had practically disappeared from the Yellowstone area. They migrated farther north into the deep forests of Canada, where there was less contact with humans.

(3) The disappearance of the wolves had many consequences. Deer and elk populations—major food sources for the wolf—grew rapidly without their usual predator. These animals consumed large amounts of vegetation, which reduced plant diversity in the park. In the absence of wolves, coyote populations also grew quickly. The coyotes killed a large percentage of the park's red foxes, and completely eliminated the park's beavers.

(4) As early as 1966, biologists asked the government to consider reintroducing wolves to Yellowstone Park. They hoped that wolves would be able to control the elk and coyote problems. Many ranchers and farmers opposed the plan because they feared that wolves would kill their livestock or pets. Other people feared that the wolves would not be well protected in Yellowstone anymore.

2007 Yellowstone Wolf Pack Territories

Source: http://www.nps.gov/yell/naturescience/wolves.htm

(5) The government spent nearly 30 years coming up with a plan to reintroduce the wolves. They included many compromises to help people accept the wolves' presence. For instance, although the wolves are technically an endangered species, Yellowstone's wolves were classified as an "experimental" population. This allowed the government more control over the wolf packs. They also pledged to pay ranchers for livestock killed by wolves.

(6) The U.S. Fish and Wildlife Service carefully monitors and manages the wolf packs in Yellowstone. Certain wolves wear special collars to help biologists gather information about how the wolves live, hunt, and breed. Each year the wolf population is counted. The 2007 population of the major packs is shown in the table.

2007 YELLOWSTONE WOLF COUNTS		
PACK	ADULTS	PUPS
Agate	8	9
Bechler	8	3
Cougar	3	4
Druid	9	7
Gibbon Meadows	11	6
Hayden	1	3
Leopold	13	3
Mollie's	9	5
Oxbow	8	8
Slough	7	9
Yellowstone Delta	16	6

Source: "Yellowstone Wolf Project Annual Report: 2007"
www.nps.gov/yell/naturescience/wolves.htm

Today, the debate continues over how well the gray wolf is fitting in at Yellowstone. Elk, deer, and coyote populations are down, while beavers and red foxes have made a comeback. The Yellowstone wolf project has been a valuable experiment to help biologists decide whether to reintroduce wolves to other parts of the country as well.

9. What is the main idea of the second paragraph?
   a. Gray wolves were gradually reintroduced to Yellowstone.
   b. Canada provided a better habitat for gray wolves.
   c. Gray wolves were displaced from their original homes by humans.
   d. Gray wolves were a threat to ranchers.

10. Why did biologists ask the government to reintroduce wolves in Yellowstone?
   a. to control the elk and coyote populations
   b. to restore the park's plant diversity
   c. to control the local livestock
   d. to protect the wolves from extinction

11. Reread this sentence from the text:

   For instance, although the wolves are technically an endangered species, Yellowstone's wolves were classified as an "experimental" population.

   In the preceding sentence, why does the writer include the word *technically*?
   a. to emphasize the legal definition of *endangered*
   b. to show that the government controls the wolves' status
   c. to explain why the wolves are endangered
   d. to highlight that the Yellowstone wolves are a special population

12. What point of view is used in the article?
  a. first-person
  b. second-person
  c. third-person
  d. both first-person and third-person

13. What is the organizing principle of the third paragraph?
  a. compare and contrast
  b. cause and effect
  c. chronological order
  d. order of importance

14. In 2007, which wolf pack had the *fewest* members?
  a. the Hayden pack
  b. the Druid pack
  c. the Yellowstone Delta pack
  d. the Cougar pack

15. What is the implied main idea of the article?
  a. Yellowstone's wolf program was a mistake.
  b. The government is responsible for reintroducing wolves.
  c. Wolves are an important part of our national parks.
  d. Yellowstone's wolf program has been beneficial for the wolves and the park.

Answers

Exercise 1

1. b. The context of the word suggests that it is a type of fertilizer. If you planned to follow these directions, you would probably want to research this (and other types of) fertilizer to make your own informed decision about the product. If you missed this question, refer to Lessons 3 and 22.

2. c. In constructing your container planter, the second step is to place a pottery shard over the hole (the first step is to drill a drainage hole). Note that step 3—adding materials to the container—has its own sequence. In step 3 the writer uses sequencing clues and carryover clues. But don't confuse the overall sequence with the sequence in step 3. If you missed this question, refer to Lessons 7 and 22.

3. b. The first paragraph tells you to add the pottery shard to the container because it "facilitates consistent, steady draining" and "prevents the dirt from washing out." If you missed this question, refer to Lesson 19.

4. c. The author is recommending a certain product, which reflects his or her opinion. The other options are matter-of-fact instructions. If you missed this question, refer to Lesson 4.

5. a. The instruction to add woodchips says to fill the container halfway, so 50% of the container holds wood chips. The other 50% holds a combination of potting soil and fertilizer, so neither of those can be the largest ingredient. Water is only added at the end and is intended to drain out of the container. You could come to the same conclusion by reading the text or by looking carefully at the diagram. If you missed this question, refer to Lesson 25.

Exercise 2

6. b. As you learned in Lesson 18, the author's purpose can be to inform, persuade, or entertain. An advertisement is a type of persuasive text. If you missed this question, refer to Lesson 18.

7. a. Fantasy is the best description of the advertising technique used in this passage. The text paints images of escape, excitement, beautiful places, relaxing activities, and good family memories. This appeals to the reader's imagination more than to his or her senses, logic, or ethics. If you missed this question, refer to Lesson 23.

8. b. Inviting is the best option to describe the tone of this advertisement because it is encouraging the reader to become interested and take action. It is somewhat friendly (choice **a**) but has a strong persuasive purpose. Many advertisements are aggressive (choice **b**), but this example is not overly pushy. There are no phrases that suggest a passionate (choice **d**) tone. If you missed this question, refer to Lesson 14.

Exercise 3

9. c. This paragraph explains that wolves used to live in the Yellowstone area until conflict with humans caused them to disappear. The wolves moved to Canada (choice **b**), and were a threat to ranchers (choice **d**), but these choices are too narrow and do not reflect the main idea of the paragraph. You can eliminate choice **a** because it's the main idea of the first paragraph. If you missed this question, refer to Lesson 2.

10. a. Biologists hoped that wolves would help balance the elk and coyote populations. Restoring the park's plant diversity (choice **b**) was a factor, but not the main motive. Ranchers and farmers objected to the wolves killing their livestock, so choice **c** can't be the reason for reintroduction. And although the wolves are technically extinct, the Yellowstone wolves are governed by special, looser rules, so choice **d** can be eliminated. If you missed this question, refer to Lesson 19.

11. d. The phrase "although the wolves are technically an endangered species" suggests that the Yellowstone wolves are going to be an exception. More specifically, the word *technically* tells us that the exception will be to their endangered status. It only suggests the legal definition of *endangered* (choice **a**) but does not explain it. Choice **b**, that the government controls the wolves' status, is a true statement, but it is not the best answer to the question. The statement also does not explain why the wolves are endangered (choice **c**). If you missed this question, refer to Lesson 13.

12. c. Because the purpose of the article is to inform, the author chooses a third-person point of view to seem impartial and balanced. If you missed this question, refer to Lesson 12.

13. b. Paragraph 3 shows the outcome of the wolf's disappearance. Although the events occur in chronological order (choice **c**), they are organized to show cause and effect. If you missed this question, refer to Lesson 7.

14. a. According to the table, the Hayden pack had only one adult and three pups, for a total of four wolves. This small family unit forms the smallest of Yellowstone's packs. If you missed this question, refer to Lesson 25.

15. d. The author concludes the article by listing some of the positive effects of the wolf's return: beaver and red fox populations are being restored, and elk and coyote populations are balancing to normal levels. Thus the author must not believe that the program was a mistake (choice **a**). Choice **b** is not broad enough to encompass the main idea of the whole passage. Choice **c**, on the other hand, is too general, because the article only discusses Yellowstone Park and does not comment on the wolf's role in other national parks. If you missed this question, refer to Lesson 17.

SECTION

6 ▶ WRITING SKILLS

Whether you want to write a note to your best friend, an article for the school newspaper, or an essay for history class, communicating effectively requires the same basic skills. People who read often and actively make the best writers, because these skills overlap. First you learn to recognize literary devices, then you begin to use them in your own writing. By reading actively, you'll be able to add new tools to your writer's toolbox, helping you become a strong writer as well.

In this section you will learn how to:

- get organized *before* writing (Lesson 27)
- structure an informative, persuasive, or narrative essay (Lesson 28)
- create focused, clear writing (Lesson 29)
- review and revise your writing (Lesson 30)

In each lesson you'll learn tips to improve your writing. Then, in Lesson 31, you'll practice the skills you learned in this section, plus the skills you've learned throughout the book.

PREWRITING

Think of your favorite book. Did the author sit down and write the whole book in a day, or even a week? Writing is a *process*—because it isn't just one step. Writers spend lots of time *thinking* before they even start writing. That's because the purpose of writing is to communicate ideas, so the first step to good writing is to have strong, clear ideas to convey.

Prewriting is the first step in the writing process; it helps you to come up with ideas about the topic you've chosen. There are many ways to prewrite, and you can experiment with the method that works best for you. When your ideas are clear, you'll be ready to organize them and start writing.

Why Prewrite?

Suppose you plunge right into writing an essay about your summer vacation. You write about the new bike you got and the tree house you built with your best friend. As you reread your essay, though, you might realize that your first paragraph sounds silly, or that you left out the story about your trip to your grandparents' house. You might have forgotten lots of interesting details, or strayed too far from the original topic.

You probably have lots to say about your summer vacation, but it could be harder to come up with ideas for an essay about politics or history. (Plus you'd need to research facts and dates you don't have memorized yet.) By prewriting, you can write down all the ideas you think of, and then pick the best ones to include in your writing. You'll also be able to see whether you need more information about the topic. This can save you lots of time in the long run!

There are many ways to prewrite. This lesson shows you several simple methods to get your ideas flowing.

Brainstorming

Brainstorming means coming up with many ideas that are related to a topic. You can brainstorm by yourself, with a friend, or with a teacher or parent. In fact, talking with another person about your topic and ideas can be quite useful, because he or she might have a different perspective. Brainstorming with someone else can help you see connections and ideas that you might not have thought of before.

When you brainstorm, be sure to notes on paper. You'll want to remember all the great ideas you come up with—and be able to trace your thinking back to see how you instinctively organized your ideas. You can start by writing down the topic. What does the topic make you think of? Do you associate it with a particular person, event, or experience? If it's tough to make your own connections, try to think of it from another person's perspective. How would your grandparents respond to the topic? If a student from another country were going to read your essay, what information would she find really interesting?

Suppose you're assigned to write an essay about American culture in the 1920s. Your brainstorming notes might look like this:

The 1920s
"Roaring Twenties"
jazz
prosperity
modernist art and literature
flappers
prohibition
Babe Ruth

From the list, you'll be able to pick a specific direction for your essay. You can draw connections between ideas, or eliminate the ideas that won't work well for the assignment. If you already have a pretty good idea of what you want to write about, try brainstorming for specific details. You might think of a specific story to tell, or identify strong words or images to include.

Remember, when you are brainstorming, there are no wrong answers. Just write down all the ideas you have, to encourage your brain to think creatively. Later, when you start to organize your essay, you'll be able to choose only the best ideas and ignore the rest.

Exercise 1
Read the topic, and then brainstorm related ideas. Consider the season, foods, colors, people, decorations, and events you associate with it.

Topic: What does you favorite holiday mean to you?

Holiday: _____

Brainstorming ideas: _____

_____

_____

_____

Freewriting

Freewriting, also called **journaling**, is an exercise to help you start writing and connecting ideas. There are no rules for this type of prewriting. Just grab a pen and a notebook and start writing. A paragraph might be enough to get your creativity flowing, but a few paragraphs or pages will give you more ideas to work with.

Every few minutes, look back at the original topic. Try to keep focused on the topic, but experiment with many ways of looking at it. Like brainstorming, there are no right or wrong ideas in freewriting. Don't worry about your spelling, grammar, or organization. Don't revise or correct your sentences. Just write!

When you have finished freewriting, read what you've written. Which sentences contain the most interesting ideas? Can you expand on any of the ideas with more details? Are any of the ideas boring or predictable? Use a highlighter or marker to highlight the ideas that seem the most promising. Copy your best ideas onto another piece of paper, where you can start more specific brainstorming or outlining.

Listing Ideas

A **list**, like the brainstorming example, is a very basic way to show information. Lists can be especially useful when you're ready to organize information in a certain order. You can use more than one list, or write two lists side by side to compare ideas. For example, this prewriting uses lists to compare and contrast two perspectives.

Topic: What are the advantages and disadvantages of year-round school?

YEAR-ROUND SCHOOL

Advantages
1. Several breaks evenly spaced
2. Easier to remember information between semesters
3. See friends year-round

Disadvantages
1. No extended vacation
2. No long break from studying
3. Can't do summer camp

The list in this example is already pretty well organized. Each list has three ideas, and each advantage has a matching disadvantage. Writing these ideas down as a list can help you see where there are holes or weak spots in your plan. If you intend to do research about your topic, you can also make a list of things you want to know, as in this example:

Topic: NASA's newest spacecraft, *Orion*.

Details to research
In what year was it built?
Has it been launched yet?
What is the design based on?
Is it manned or unmanned?
Where will NASA send it?

Lists are a useful way to prepare for your writing because they can help you stay organized and focused on the topic. Lists are also easy to revise or reorganize when you are ready to select your best ideas for writing.

Exercise 2
Suppose your school has given the eighth grade a choice between a trip to the zoo or an end-of-the-year party. Your teacher has asked everyone to write an essay explaining his or her preference. Use the lines

to complete a prewriting list. In each column, try to list at least one advantage and one disadvantage.

Zoo trip

_____

_____

_____

_____

_____

School party

_____

_____

_____

_____

_____

Using Graphic Organizers

A **graphic organizer** can take many different forms, but one common graphic organizer is the cluster diagram. A **cluster diagram** looks like a spider web. To make a cluster diagram, start by writing the topic in the center of your paper. Draw a circle around the topic. Then draw a short line from the circle toward each corner of the paper. At the end of each line, write a more specific topic or idea, and circle those. Continue to branch out from each idea until you can include specific details.

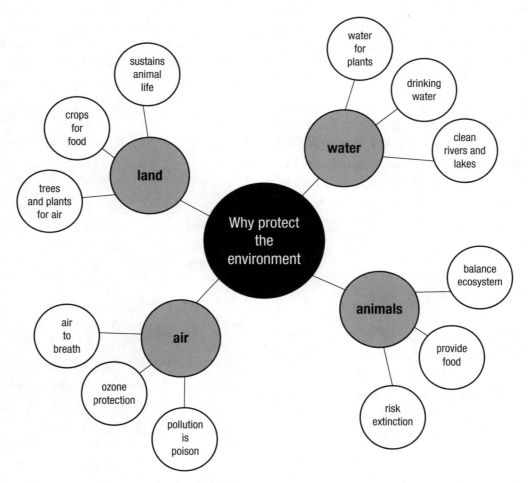

Above is an example of a cluster diagram for the topic, "Why is it important to protect the environment?"

In this example, the writer has branched out into four smaller sections: *land*, *water*, *air*, and *animals*. Now she can brainstorm on each subtopic individually. This helps the writer to brainstorm in a focused, organized way. He or she may eventually decide to write only about air and water, or just focus on animals. But by prewriting in a cluster diagram, the writer is able to arrange and rearrange ideas in a visual way.

The biggest advantage of using a graphic organizer for your prewriting is that you can create a picture or map for your writing and you can see connections laid out on the page. For people who like to learn from diagrams, graphic organizers are often the best way to brainstorm.

Outlining

As you saw in Lesson 10, outlines are great for taking notes from your readings, but they are also one of the easiest ways to organize your thoughts before you write a story or essay. First, write down your topic and one or two main ideas, and then add the supporting details to your outline.

An outline can be general or specific. Each line can include a single word, a complete sentence, or a blank space to serve as a placeholder. Include as much information as you need to get your thoughts organized. For example, look at this outline for a student's essay about the bombing of Pearl Harbor:

Attack on Pearl Harbor
I. Events leading to the attack
  A. United States halted trade with Japan (1940)
  B. Japan invaded French Indochina (1940)
  C. United States halted oil exports to Japan (1941)
II. Damage caused
  A. Naval equipment and ships
  B. Injuries and casualties
    1. Military personnel
    2. Civilians
III. Results of attack
  A. United States enters WWII

There are many correct ways to reorganize these ideas, and it is much easier to change the order before you start writing your essay. Seeing your ideas arranged as an outline can help you identify the points that need more support. It can also help you make sure that the ideas follow a logical order.

Exercise 3

The outline below shows another way to brainstorm for the topic "Why is it important to protect the environment?" Use the cluster diagram you read previously or your own ideas to complete the outline. One entry has been completed for you.

Why Protect the Environment?
I. The importance of land
  A. Humans rely on crops and other plants for food.
  B.
  C.
II. The importance of water
  A.
  B.
  C.
III. The importance of air
  A.
  B.
  C.
IV. The importance of animals
  A.
  B.
  C.

Review Your Prewriting

When you've completed your prewriting, read it over carefully. Circle, highlight, or put a star next to the ideas that seem most promising. Ignore or cross out the ideas that you don't plan to include in your writing. If you wrote a list of ideas, and then picked one or two, try making a cluster diagram with those ideas to develop them further. You could also share your prewriting with a friend, parent, or teacher to get their feedback and additional ideas. The more planning you do, the easier it will be to write.

Even after you start writing, don't throw your prewriting notes away. They can be a useful reference when you get stuck or start to stray off topic.

Summary

Spend some time prewriting before you start writing. There are many ways to prewrite: brainstorming, freewriting, lists, graphic organizers, and outlines. Choose the prewriting method that works best for the topic, and don't be afraid to experiment with new methods. These prewriting notes will be a *plan* for your essay, helping you to focus your ideas and write with confidence.

Answers

Exercise 1
Answers will vary. Here is one possibility:

Holiday: Easter
Brainstorming ideas: egg hunt, painting eggs, filling baskets, hiding candy from my brother, pancake breakfast, visiting aunt and uncle for dinner, Grandma's bunny cookies, fifth grade pink bunny costume

Exercise 2
Answers will vary. One possibility is shown here. Notice that the first three items in each list are advantages, and the last item is a possible disadvantage of that option.

Zoo trip
spend the day away from school
fun to see the animals
eat a picnic lunch
visited the zoo last month with my family

School party
everyone will be there
fun to decorate the school
teachers will order pizza
no break from being at school

Exercise 3

If you completed the outline with your own ideas, answers will vary slightly. If you used the ideas from the previous cluster diagram, your outline should look similar to this:

Why Protect the Environment?

I. The importance of land
 A. Humans rely on crops and other plants for food.
 B. Land sustains animal and human life.
 C. All animals need trees and plants to produce oxygen.

II. The importance of water
 A. We need clean drinking water to survive.
 B. Clean rivers, lakes, and oceans support marine life.
 C. Rain and groundwater allow plants to grow.

III. The importance of air
 A. All plants and animals need clean air to breathe.
 B. The ozone protects us from harmful radiation.
 C. Air pollution leads to acid rain and poisons humans, animals, and plants.

IV. The importance of animals
 A. Animals provide food and companionship for people.
 B. Animals balance ecosystems and affect the survival of plants and humans.
 C. Many species are in danger of extinction if humans don't protect them.

SKILL BUILDING UNTIL NEXT TIME

1. Read a magazine or newspaper article that interests you. What kind of prewriting might the author have done? If you were assigned to write an article about the same topic, what type of prewriting would you choose?

2. Think of your favorite park or building in town. Imagine that the city has proposed to tear it down to make room for a new skyscraper. You decide to write a letter to the mayor about it. Do a freewrite or make a cluster diagram to brainstorm reasons why your park or building should be saved.

3. Spend some time thinking about how your brain organizes ideas and processes information, then play around with arranging them visually on the page. Everyone's brain is different, and the better you understand yours, the more clearly you can communicate with others.

28 ▶ ORGANIZING IDEAS

LESSON SUMMARY

Writers have many options for organizing their ideas. You'll learn about writing academic essays and how to select the best organization for each essay type. This lesson will also show you how to use the organizing principles you learned in Lesson 7.

Most people's brains organize thoughts like a spider web rather than a straight line. For example, maybe the thought of your dog makes you think of his favorite toy, which makes you think of the park, and then you remember your last trip to the park with your grandfather, which reminds you that he promised to take you out for ice cream, which makes you think of how much your dog loves ice cream. Wow!

Although those ideas might be connected in your mind, a reader could have trouble making sense of them. That's why organization is so important. In this lesson you'll learn how to put the organizing principles you've learned about into action in your own writing.

The Essay

In previous lessons you've learned about many different types of writing: news articles, novels, editorials, poetry, and advertisements, to name a few. In school, the most common type of writing you'll do is essays. An **essay** is a type of literary composition. Its purpose is to *analyze* ideas or information. To *analyze* means that the author includes *perspective* and *reflection*.

Essays can be written about thousands of different topics, but each essay maintains a specific focus on one idea. The essay usually includes a **thesis statement** that narrows the topic to a specific point or perspective. The rest of the essay uses supporting details to build the argument. Essays use the general standards of writing and language, as well as the literary devices of literature and poetry, such as metaphors and foreshadowing. An essay might be a single page or more than 100 pages long.

There are three basic types of essays that match the three author's purposes you learned about previously—information, entertainment, and persuasion. As you brainstorm and prepare to write, it's important to decide which type of essay you are writing. Each type of essay has unique organization options.

The Informative Essay

The author's purpose in an informative essay, also called an **expository essay**, is to inform the reader. This type of essay presents information, description, and details. It explains or describes a topic. It generally does *not* include the writer's personal feelings or reactions. Nevertheless, the informative essay also needs to show some *analysis* or reflection. You can show your analysis through the thesis of your writing and the details you include. Choosing the **thesis**—what you want to say *about* the topic—can be the trickiest part of writing informative essays. As you read this paragraph from an informative essay, try to identify the author's thesis.

Read actively and make notes if you need to.

The Ducks Fly Again

In recent years, the local minor league baseball team, the Dowshire Ducks, has become standard weekend entertainment for hundreds of families. On summer afternoons, the bleachers in Hulldown Stadium are crowded with cheering fans. But it wasn't always so. Even ten years ago, ticket sales were limited, and the team was largely ignored. The Ducks rarely won games or placed well in regional tournaments. The arrival of coach Duncan Brin in 2004, however, started a new era of success and fame for the Ducks.

The topic for this essay is the Dowshire Ducks baseball team. Details about the team are introduced and explained through comparison and contrast. In the last sentence of the paragraph, though, the author launches the *thesis*: coach Duncan Brin improved the team's status. This qualifies as a thesis (the main idea of the whole essay) because it expresses an idea or assertion that will be proven throughout the essay.

Organizing an Informative Essay

Informative essays are often organized by comparing and contrasting, or by cause and effect. These patterns allow the writer to include lots of details and show a balanced objective view of the topic. Organizing by cause and effect also emphasizes logic and evidence rather than the author's opinion. Not all topics will fit well into these two organizational patterns, but they are good options to consider when you're writing this type of essay.

The Narrative Essay

A **narrative essay**'s purpose is to entertain. Narrative is another word for story. Essays are a nonfiction genre, so a narrative essay tells a *true* story. Generally authors choose a short, specific story that can be fully told in a single essay. The story should show the writer's feelings and reactions to the events. The narrative essay has a thesis. The author has something to say *about* the story, such as a lesson he learned from the experience.

This paragraph is from a narrative essay. As you read, notice how its style and organization are different from the informative essay example.

Baseball at Hulldown

When I was seven years old, my father took me to see the Dowshire Ducks play minor league baseball at Hulldown Stadium. From the first moment I stepped into the stadium, I was captivated. Long rows of scuffed metal benches stretched like giant arms embracing the field. Peanut shells and popcorn littered the floor, filling the air with a salty, dusty scent no seven-year-old can resist. The stands were practically empty—it was a Thursday afternoon—but the shouting grownups and sticky-fingered children sitting around us seemed like the happiest people I'd ever met. I felt as though I had stumbled on a secret world.

In this essay introduction, the reader learns that the author is going to tell about an experience she had, using a personal voice and the pronoun "I." This tells you that it's a narrative essay. The setting is a baseball stadium, and the characters are the author at age seven and her father. The author gives us details about the sights, smells, and sounds, and how they affected her. You can also begin to guess at the author's thesis. The baseball stadium seems to have been a strongly, positive experience that probably sparked a lifelong love of baseball.

Organizing a Narrative Essay

Narrative essays are usually organized chronologically, because that is often the easiest way to tell a story. Even though a narrative essay tells a true story, all the rules of good fiction storytelling apply. The people in the story should be introduced and described to the reader. Many sensory details—sights, smells, sounds—should be included to help the reader picture the scene. The story should have a beginning, middle, and end. The plot, though, is less

important than the author's reflection or analysis. After telling the story, the writer concludes with the point of the story, such as what changed, the lesson learned, or the long-term effects of the experience.

Skilled, experienced writers can take liberties with flashbacks or a disjointed narrative, but make sure you master the basics before attempting something experimental.

The Persuasive Essay

The purpose of a **persuasive essay** is to persuade the reader to do something or believe something. The basis for the essay is a strong *opinion* supported by facts or other details. As a critical reader, you've learned how writers use persuasive language in editorials and advertisements. Now you can use those same skills to write your own convincing essays. Here's an example of an introduction to a persuasive essay.

Protect Hulldown Stadium

Last month, the Dowshire Planning Commission announced that Hulldown Stadium, home of the Dowshire Ducks minor league baseball team, will close in November. According to the Commission's statement, the stadium is old and in need of major repairs. They believe that it would be cheaper to tear down the stadium and build a new one across town. But Hulldown Stadium is a local landmark. It has been the home of the Ducks for three generations. Thousands of children spend their summers sipping root beers and eating soft pretzels in Hulldown's green metal bleachers. The stadium is more than a building; it's a symbol of our community spirit and our common love of baseball. Whatever the cost, the stadium must be saved.

The writer begins the article with facts, and then begins to introduce opinions. There are many clues in the word choice, style, and tone that reveal the author's perspective. For example, in describing the commission's reasoning for tearing down the stadium, the writer includes the phrase *they believe*. This phrase casts doubt on whether it really *is* cheaper to build a new stadium, and suggests that the writer disagrees with this plan.

The writer also moved from citing an authority ("the Commission's statment") to evoking a sense of nostalgia ("thousands of children") and lands on a strong assertion ("it must be saved") that the reader is more likely to agree with, thanks to the supporting details.

When you are writing a persuasive essay, try to look at your essay from the perspective of a critical reader. Have you included enough information to build a convincing argument? Are your facts distinct from your opinions, and clear to the reader?

Organizing a Persuasive Essay

One way to organize a persuasive essay is by order of importance. You might start with the most important point and end with the least important, or start with the least important and build to the most important. This strategy allows you to build a strong, convincing argument, as you have seen in earlier exercises.

Another common organizational pattern, as demonstrated in the preceding example, is to start by explaining the *opposing* point of view. In the essay, the author introduces the topic by listing the city's reasons for tearing down the stadium. By laying out the opposing opinion first, the author acknowledges that she recognizes and understands those ideas, but still disagrees with them. This strategy strengthens your argument because it shows the reader that you are well informed and aware of other opinions. A reader is more likely to be convinced by a writer who sounds informed and thoughtful than by someone who can see only one side of the issue.

Exercise 1

Read each excerpt and decide whether it belongs in an informative essay (I), narrative essay (N), or per-

suasive essay (P). Write the letter of your answer on the blank line.

1. ___ When the Bridgeville skating rink opened in 2005, my mother signed me up for ice skating lessons. My first instructor, Lauren, was a former professional skater, and she had won awards in national competitions.

2. ___ The Bridgeville skating rink has been a major success. Nearly every night, there is an event at the rink. Wednesdays are reserved for lessons, the high school ice hockey team practices on Thursdays, Friday nights are open to teenagers only, and Saturdays are crowded with families.

3. ___ The Bridgeville skating rink was the site of my first kiss. Cleveland Hunter had taken me to get ice cream, even though it was freezing in January! My best friend, Sallie, came too, because my mother wouldn't let me go alone.

4. ___ Bridgeville's skating rink is a dangerous place that needs more police monitoring. Bullies and gangs hang out there, making it scary for other kids who want to skate.

The Five-Paragraph Essay

For whatever type of essay you plan to write, the most common structure is a **five-paragraph essay**. As you can probably guess, this structure includes (at least!) five paragraphs:

1. Introduction to the topic, ending with a thesis statement
2. First supporting detail and explanation
3. Second supporting detail and explanation
4. Third supporting detail and explanation
5. Conclusion

The Introduction

An introduction paragraph can be depicted as an upside-down pyramid. The first sentence introduces the general topic. The next few sentences explain the topic or issue. The last sentence is the thesis.

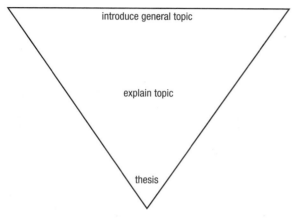

introduce general topic

explain topic

thesis

A thesis is the main idea of the whole essay. It is an **assertion**—a statement that includes the author's judgment or opinion. The rest of the essay will include details to support or prove the thesis statement. Thus, the thesis should be something that a writer can successfully argue within an essay. Try to select the best thesis statement from these three options:

a. Mike Morrissey played baseball for 19 years.
b. Mike Morrissey was the best player Dowshire has ever had.
c. Mike Morrissey experienced success both on and off the baseball field.

The first statement is a fact. It does not leave anything for the writer to *prove* in the rest of the essay. A fact alone cannot be a thesis. The second option is an opinion. Mike Morrissey may or may not be the best player the team has ever had. However, this type of assertion will be very difficult to prove in an essay, unless you go on to specify "has the best hitting record" (which is a fact) or a similar measurable statistic. Some readers will always disagree with such a simplistic opinion. Choice **c** is the best thesis statement for this essay because it makes a reasonable assertion that can be proven with supporting details.

Exercise 2

Read the pairs of statements below, and circle the best thesis statement in each pair.

1. a. It is in the best interest of students to have open-campus during lunch.
   b. Students deserve to have open-campus during lunch.

2. a. The new math curriculum has been used in six classrooms this year.
   b. The new math curriculum has helped students to succeed on state tests.

3. a. Mrs. Sprout is the best teacher at Rigby Junior High.
   b. Mrs. Sprout is the best teacher at Rigby Junior High because she is fair, fun, and creative.

The Supporting Details

Essays usually include three paragraphs of details to support the thesis. These details or ideas are needed to convincingly argue your thesis. In these middle paragraphs, you'll use the organization that's best for the type of essay you're writing. For example, if you're writing a narrative essay, these middle paragraphs will tell the story, probably in chronological order. Each paragraph might explain one event or episode in the story. You might explain the outcome or lesson learned within each paragraph, or wait until the concluding paragraph to discuss what changed.

For an informative essay, you might choose to organize by cause and effect. You could include one cause and effect pair for each paragraph (ABAB), or describe the cause in the first paragraph (AA) and the effects in the second and third paragraphs (BB BB). There are infinite ways to organize your supporting details, and the topic will help you determine which method of organization is the best for that essay.

You might organize a persuasive essay by order of importance. If you decide to go from least important to most important, building your argument to a big conclusion, you will put the least convincing details in the first paragraph. The second paragraph will contain more important details than in the first paragraph. This pattern will continue until the final paragraph, where you will place the evidence most critical to your argument.

The Conclusion

In the conclusion paragraph, the writer summarizes the thesis to remind the reader what has been asserted in the essay. The rest of the paragraph "zooms out" from the thesis, returning to the general topic. It can be an opportunity to tie up loose ends in the essay, or to explain how the topic fits into a bigger picture.

Often, conclusion paragraphs mention how the topic will continue beyond the essay. An essay about declining wolf populations, for example, might conclude with the statement "If humans don't intervene to help wolves, they could be extinct within 20 years." This sort of statement gives the reader something to think about after the essay is over.

> A conclusion paragraph can be depicted as an upright triangle, the opposite of the introduction paragraph. The conclusion starts with the most specific assertion and ends by talking about the general topic once again.

Exercise 3

An essay has been outlined for you. Use the ideas from the outline to write a conclusion paragraph on the lines below.

Thesis: The library offers more opportunities to learn than just books.

Detail 1: It offers films, records, and movies.
Detail 2: It hosts concerts and lectures.
Detail 3: Librarians can make recommendations and help you find special resources.

Exercise 3

Conclusion:

_____

_____

_____

_____

_____

_____

_____

_____

_____

_____

_____

_____

_____

_____

Summary

Essays are a useful way for writers to explore a topic. There are three major types of essays: informative (or expository), narrative, and persuasive. Each type of essay has several options for organizing the argument, but all essays follow the same basic structure. The first paragraph introduces the topic and the author's thesis. The middle paragraphs explain details to support the thesis. The final paragraph summarizes the thesis once more and concludes the topic.

Answers

Exercise 1

1. N. This essay would likely tell the story of the writer's early experiences with skating lessons. The first-person perspective tells you that it will be a personal narrative story.

2. I. The first sentence asserts that the skating rink has been "a major success." The next sentences try to prove this with information and details. The third-person point of view and the lack of a strong opinion or suggested action tell you that it must be an informative essay.

3. N. The use of first-person point of view is your first clue to narrative perspective. This narrative will tell the story of the writer's first kiss.

4. P. In this excerpt the writer presents a strong opinion and suggests a course of action that should be taken to resolve a problem.

Exercise 2

1. a. This statement makes a clear assertion that the writer will be able to prove in the rest of the essay. The supporting details will show how open-campus during lunch is "in the best interest of students." Choice **b**, on the other hand, uses the phrase "students deserve." This phrase represents a stronger opinion that is hard to measure, and it will be harder to argue with rational reasons.

2. b. This statement is the best thesis because it makes an assertion. Choice **a** is a fact, so it doesn't leave anything for the essay to prove.

3. b. The second option makes a better thesis because it includes specific reasons behind the assertion. The rest of the essay would likely explain how the writer knows that Mrs. Sprout is "fair, fun, and creative," and why these three qualities qualify her as the best teacher. Choice **a** is an opinion that is too simplistic to be provable.

Exercise 3

Answers will vary, but here is one possible conclusion.

> The library offers many learning opportunities that are often overlooked. The next time you have a free afternoon, consider spending it at the library. You'll be sure to find something there to interest you.

Make sure yours contains a recap and a closing line that leaves the reader with something to think about.

SKILL BUILDING UNTIL NEXT TIME

1. Many well-known writers, including novelists and poets, have also published books of essays. Find an essay to read today. What is the topic of the essay? What is the author's thesis? How many paragraphs of supporting details does the author include? Is it a narrative, informative, or persuasive essay?
2. Choose a topic that interests you, such as your favorite athlete, teacher, or activity. If you needed to write a narrative essay about this topic, what would your thesis be? Write it down. Then write possible thesis statements for an informative essay and a persuasive essay about the same topic. Which essay would be the most interesting to write?

LESSON 29 ▶ WRITING WITH FOCUS AND CLARITY

LESSON SUMMARY

The same techniques of style, tone, and word choice that you recognized as a reader can be used to strengthen your own writing. This lesson shows you how to stay focused on the topic and develop supported ideas in your writing.

You've done your prewriting, identified the type of writing you'll do, and decided on the writing's purpose. You have notes, a story to tell, and details to back it up. Take a walk, take a shower, have a snack, then it's time to sit down and write. As you start writing, there are a few strategies that will help you communicate effectively.

Focusing on the Topic

We write to communicate an idea, story, or feeling to our readers. An important part of being a good writer is the ability to focus on a main idea. An essay that lacks focus will be confusing to a reader who might finish reading a piece and still not know what it was about! Whether you are writing a story, a report, or even an advertisement, you need to establish a clear main idea and make sure that everything in your piece of writing relates to that topic.

For example, an essay that begins, "My dog, Gabe, is an important member of the family," but goes on to talk about baseball and the movies, lacks focus. When this happens, the writer has failed to communicate. A better essay would follow the topic sentence "My dog, Gabe, is an important member of the family" with several statements about Gabe and why he is important, such as, "Gabe's been with us for eight years," "He exercises with my dad," "He makes people feel better when they're upset," and "He protects our house."

Writing a Thesis Statement

The first thing you should do to develop the focus of your writing is to construct a strong topic sentence (for a single paragraph) or thesis statement (for an entire essay). As discussed in Lesson 28, the topic sentence or thesis statement should be broad enough to apply to the other ideas in the passage, and also should take a position that you will support throughout the rest of the passage. In writing an essay, make sure that your thesis statement directly addresses the topic you are given.

Your thesis statement can usually help you outline the rest of your essay (see Lesson 10). This can help you organize your writing, and it also helps your reader to understand your argument. For example, you could extend the topic sentence

"My dog, Gabe, is an important member of the family."

to become the thesis statement

"My dog, Gabe, is important to my family because he's lived with us for a long time, he helps us get exercise, he brings us joy, and he keeps us safe."

The first sentence is a good paragraph starter, but the second helps to focus an entire essay and give it structure. It also lays the groundwork for a narrative essay made up of specific, meaningful experiences you can explore in an in-depth way.

Exercise 1

Read the following essay topics and choose the best thesis statement for each one.

1. **Topic:** What I did over summer vacation
   a. Summer vacation is really fun.
   b. This summer I went on trips, joined the swim team, and hung out with friends.
   c. Summer vacation is okay, but my favorite vacation is spring break.
   d. This summer my grandma gave me a pony.

2. **Topic:** Is the space program important?
   a. Space travel is dangerous and expensive.
   b. I want to be an astronaut because I think it would be fun, challenging, and exciting.
   c. The space program is not important.
   d. Scientists in the space program conduct essential research about earth and the universe.

3. **Topic:** Should we protect the environment?
   a. Global warming is a major problem.
   b. We should try to save the rain forests.
   c. There is no such thing as global warming.
   d. We should take care of the Earth because it is our only natural habitat.

Choosing Relevant Details

When you do your prewriting, you'll generate lots of ideas or details, but not all will be equally useful for your writing. Use your best, careful judgment to decide which details to include. See if you can spot the unnecessary details in this paragraph:

Last winter my family took a trip to Big Bear Mountain in British Columbia for a ski weekend. It was the coolest ski trip we've ever taken. Big Bear has a huge lodge with a hotel, restaurant, and beautiful views. We had room

322. The first day, my sister and I started on the bunny slopes. We felt brave enough to try the bigger routes, but our parents insisted. By the second day, though, I found an awesome run called the Hopper, and I tried it at least six times. It had a few tricky spots with sharp curves, but I only fell once. My sister liked the Lobster route.

The topic for this paragraph is a ski trip to Big Bear Mountain, and the main idea is that it was a cool trip. Details that support this main idea should be included, but details that don't help prove a larger point can be left out. There are two unnecessary details in this paragraph: the sentence "We had room 322" and the last sentence, "My sister liked the Lobster route." These details are dead ends. They don't relate to a larger theme or lead to analysis. Dead-end details distract the reader from the main idea, so they should be left out.

Developing Depth

In writing, *depth* means thoroughly exploring an issue or idea. It means that the writer looks at the idea from many perspectives and analyzes it critically. Analytical writing such as essays needs depth to fully explore the idea.

To develop depth in your own writing, follow these three strategies:

1. Support your assertions with details.
2. Show, rather than tell.
3. Include more than one perspective.

Remember that a thesis (in an essay) is an **assertion**. An assertion includes the author's judgment or perspective on a topic, so in order to convince the reader that the assertion is valid, the author has to include supporting details. Supporting details are most effective when they show the reader something and let her make her own conclusions. For example, in an essay about why Rigby Junior High should have a new cafeteria menu, a detailed description of the cafeteria's food will make a stronger impression on the reader than simply stating "Students don't like the food."

Which of the following paragraphs is more convincing?

A. Sharon is the rudest girl in class. I don't like her. She never talks to me.
B. Sharon is the rudest girl in class. She interrupts the teachers without raising her hand. She always jumps to the front of the lunch line instead of waiting her turn. Once, she pushed Sally Markov out of the way so she could be first out the door.

Both paragraphs start with the same assertion: Sharon is rude. Paragraph A supports this assertion with two details, and neither is very convincing (or interesting) to the reader. These details *tell* the author's opinion, rather than *showing* the reader why the assertion is true. Paragraph B, on the other hand, includes three details. Each detail shows one instance of Sharon's rude behavior. This allows the reader to come to the same conclusion as the writer; Sharon *must* be rude if she acts like that!

A third strategy for developing depth in your writing is to include multiple perspectives. This shows the reader that you are well informed; you've done research or thought deeply about the topic. In informative or narrative writing, this allows your writing to be balanced and trustworthy. In persuasive writing, you can describe several ways of looking at the topic but still argue that one way is better than the others. A rational, balanced argument is more persuasive than an illogical, narrow-minded one!

Exercise 2

Write one paragraph about a trip you took recently (or a place or person you visited). Focus on only one location so you can describe it in depth. Use descriptive details to *show* the reader your experience.

Use the lines below, or a notebook, or a computer.

_____

_____

_____

_____

_____

_____

_____

_____

_____

Style and Tone

As you learned in earlier lessons, writers have many options when building a style and tone for their writing. Choose the style and tone that works best for your topic and the type of writing you are doing. There are several guidelines that will make your selection easier.

Know Your Audience

If you are writing an essay for class, you will probably choose a very different style than you would for a letter to a friend. Writers must consider their audiences because there is a relationship between the writing and the reader. An article in your school newspaper is meant for students and teachers, so it might casually mention people or locations that all the readers will recognize. If that same article were published in a national newspaper, though, it would need more details and explanation to help the new audience understand it.

Your audience might be a friend or classmate, a teacher or other adult, or a young child. It might be someone who knows a lot about your topic or who has never heard of the topic before. For persuasive writing, you might write to an audience that already agrees with you, or readers who are trying to make up their minds, or readers who totally disagree with your perspective. Each of these audiences will require a slightly different use of style, tone, and word choice.

Point of View

On school assignments, your teacher might tell you whether to use first-person, second-person, or third-person point of view. Otherwise, you are free to choose the point of view that is most appropriate.

- Informative writing usually uses third-person point of view.
- Narrative writing usually uses first-person point of view.
- Persuasive writing could use first-person or second-person point of view, but third-person usually creates the most balanced, rational tone.

The most important part of point of view is to be consistent throughout your essay. If you start with third person, you can't suddenly switch to first person in the next paragraph. (Imagine how odd it would seem if this book suddenly switched to saying, "The student will complete this exercise" or "I will tell you how to use point of view"!)

Tone

A calm, rational, professional tone is acceptable for almost any type of writing. When writing for class or a test, try to avoid sarcasm, jokes, or an overly personal tone. If you are writing for a humor contest, you'll want it to be lighthearted and funny. If you're writing an essay about the Civil War, the tone will be much more serious. Be aware of the genre in which you're writing and of the audience you're writing for; use a tone that will communicate most effectively.

Word Choice

One important rule of diction is to use words that you know; even if you use a thesaurus to prompt you, pick a word you recognize. A big word used incorrectly won't impress your readers. It might even distract them from the point of the sentence or make the writing seem less reliable.

To create a smooth rhythm in your writing, remember to vary the length of your sentences. Short sentences let the reader pause and think or provide emphasis. Long sentences provide extended description or details.

Your audience will also determine the words you use. When writing for your peers or classmates, they'll probably share your vocabulary. You might need to choose different words when you're writing a letter to your grandparents. If you use specialized words, such as snowboarding terms, consider whether your audience will be familiar with the terms. If not, you'll need to include some explanation for unfamiliar words.

Exercise 3

Read the two writing excerpts, and then answer the questions.

A. I've been trying to think of something fun to do this summer. Dad wants me to go to soccer camp, and Mom wants me to stay home and watch my little brother. But I secretly want to go to art camp. There's a program up in Minnesota where you camp in the forest and then study art all day. It sounds awesome! Do you think it's a good idea?

B. I would like to participate in the Summer Art Days program. I have always been interested in art, in school and at home. I have experimented with watercolors, oil paints, and pencil drawings and have undertaken several projects by myself. My favorite thing to draw is rockets, but I would like to learn how to draw other things as well. I am excited to learn new skills at your art camp.

1. The audience for Paragraph A is probably
   a. the writer's parents.
   b. the writer's friend.
   c. the writer's school principal.

2. The style of Paragraph A is
   a. relaxed, funny.
   b. formal, serious.
   c. informal, honest.

3. The audience for Paragraph B is probably
   a. the art program director.
   b. the writer's friend.
   c. the writer's teacher.

4. Compared to Paragraph A, the style of Paragraph B is
   a. more formal.
   b. more detailed.
   c. more personal.

Summary

To communicate effectively, your writing must be clear and focused. Construct a strong thesis statement. Include relevant details to stay focused on your main idea. Develop depth and explore ideas fully by supporting your assertions, using details that *show* rather than tell the reader something, and including multiple perspectives. Select a style and tone that is appropriate for your type of writing. Writing takes lots of practice, but your skills will improve every time you write!

Answers

Exercise 1

1. b. This is the strongest thesis because it is focused on the topic, takes a position, and outlines how the essay will answer the question. Choices **a** and **c** do not directly address the prompt, which suggests that the essay will lack focus. Choice **d** hints that the author will talk about playing with the new pony over the summer, which would address the prompt, but it is less clear and direct than choice **b**. Choice **d** would be a good essay opener, but a poor thesis statement.

2. d. This thesis directly addresses the prompt, clearly states the author's position (notice the clue word *essential*), and focuses the structure of the essay. Choice **a** takes a position and suggests an outline for the following argument, but does not quite address the question of the space program's importance. choice **b** does not address the prompt. Choice **c** directly addresses the prompt and takes a position, but does not provide any detail about how the author will proceed. It is an acceptable thesis, but not the best one, because it doesn't help the reader know *why* the space program is unimportant.

3. d. This thesis clearly answers the prompt and takes a position that can be supported through the rest of the essay. choice **a** makes a strong statement, but does not quite address the question. The author's view on whether we should do anything about global warming is vague. Choice **b** is too specific and does not offer a reason for saving the rain forest. Choice **c** does not directly address the prompt.

Exercise 2

Answers will vary, but here is one possible paragraph:

> Two weeks ago, my family drove to Mattawa to visit my cousins. My Aunt Shirley and Uncle Joe have three kids—Joel, Maggie, and Simon—and their house is the most fun to visit. They live in a big blue house on a hill and have a large backyard. Joel, the oldest, has a real motorbike, and he let me ride it all over their giant yard. They also have two Newfoundland dogs, the biggest dogs I have ever seen! Inside the house, there are stacks of board games and walls of books. And Aunt Shirley is always cooking something delicious.

Is your thesis clear? Are your details accurate, persuasive, or relevant?

Exercise 3

1. **b.** The audience can't be the writer's parents (choice **a**) because they are mentioned in the text. The style is too informal to be written for a school principal (choice **c**), so it must be written for a friend.

2. **c.** The style is definitely informal, so choice **b** can't be correct, and the writer is presenting a secret interest and a genuine question, so choice **a** can't be correct.

3. **a.** The formal style and tone tells you that it must be intended for an adult, and the paragraph concludes "I am excited to learn new skills at *your* art camp," so the audience must be the art program director.

4. **a.** The paragraphs have about the same amount of detail (choice **b**), and Paragraph A is more personal (choice **c**) than Paragraph B, so the answer must be choice **a**, more formal.

SKILL BUILDING UNTIL NEXT TIME

1. Read a news article or short essay today. What is the author's main idea? Who is the intended audience for the text? Is the tone detached and serious, silly, lighthearted, or something else? If you planned to write about this same topic, would you select the same audience, style, and point of view?

2. Find an essay or paper you recently wrote for a class, and evaluate your writing. Does the essay stay focused on the main idea? Are there any dead-end details? Are your assertions (or thesis) supported with descriptive details? Who is the audience for the text? What point of view did you use? If you could revise the essay now, what are two things you would do differently?

3. Use one of the essays from practices 1 or 2 and rewrite for a different audience, with a different tone. Notice how you select different words or reorganize your ideas.

30 ▶ REVIEWING AND REVISING

LESSON SUMMARY

The final step in the writing process is to review and revise your writing. This lesson shows you how to look critically at your writing and make changes to improve its clarity, focus, and quality.

When a sculptor begins a new sculpture, she starts with a big piece of wood or stone. The first step is to decide what to carve. The next step is to sketch the design from multiple angles. Then cut away the big pieces and get a rough outline of the final shape. Finally, the sculptor is ready to begin polishing and fine-tuning the sculpture to create a detailed, finished work of art.

Writing, like sculpture, is a complicated art that requires many steps. First, you plan what to write. Then you research to find out what else you need to know. Then you write a rough draft. Now you're ready to polish and perfect your writing. This process is called editing, and even professional writers spend lots of time on this stage of the writing process.

Why Review Your Writing?

There are thousands and thousands of people who want to be writers. What separates the dreamers from the ones who achieve their writing ambitions is the drive to write, to tell stories, to make something new, and then the focus to spend hours revising, finessing, reconsidering, and improving a piece of writing. Make sure your writing is as sharp and honed as you can make it—it may be the factor that sets you apart from the next eager writer.

Every professional writer was once a student who liked putting words together—or maybe a student who struggled with reading or editing. There are always going to be setbacks, frustrations, and rejections along the way, but please don't let yourself get discouraged.

In your writing, you might decide to stop after a rough draft. But then you'll never know how good the story or essay could have been! Every time you look over your text and make changes, the passage improves. By spending a few minutes reviewing your essay on a test, or an hour reviewing a long story you've written, you'll be developing a stronger, more effective final product and the editorial muscles that make every stage of your writing more efficient.

Editing Techniques

When you have the time to do a really good edit, you should rethink everything in your essay, as well as check for errors in grammar and punctuation. Ask yourself questions like "Is this thesis statement strong enough?" "Is this opinion supported by facts?" "Is my assertion something I can measure?" "Does the structure I've chosen accomplish my goal for the essay?" "Is this word spelled correctly?" "Will my audience understand what I'm trying to say?" Editing may sound like a pain, but you'll be surprised how much your writing improves when you take the time to review it thoroughly.

There are several techniques to keep in mind when editing. These include adding information, removing unnecessary details, rearranging ideas, replacing words, and catching mistakes. You may go sentence by sentence to fix multiple errors at once, or it may make more sense to go all the way through checking first for ideas, then for clarity of structure, then for spelling and grammar. Using these techniques will help you look critically at your own work and result in a more polished product. Your friends might even notice your writing skills and ask you to help them edit their essays!

Add Information

One thing to look for after you have written an essay or a story is whether you may have left out important details. Missing information can be very confusing to readers, and will weaken an otherwise strong essay. For example, imagine you are writing an essay on your favorite season and come up with this thesis statement: "My favorite season of the year is fall because it's nice outside, school starts, and I get to play soccer." When you review your essay, you realize you forgot to write the section on school starting. This will be a problem, because your reader, especially a teacher, is expecting you to discuss school and will notice its absence. By editing, you'll find the missing information so that you can fix it (either by adding a school section or deleting the reference to the start of school).

Missing information can also be a problem when your reader does not know as much about your subject as you do. For example, if you write a story about turning an amazing triple play in baseball, but don't tell your reader that triple plays are really rare, the reader may not realize what an accomplishment your feat was. You also need to be careful to explain technical terms that a reader may not understand (a triple play involves getting all three outs on one ball in play). When you're editing, think as a reader, and look for this kind of missing information—adding a sentence here or there can make a big difference in the quality of your essay!

Remove Unnecessary Details

Another important step in editing is to look for and remove unnecessary details. This was discussed in the previous lesson in the section "Focusing on the Topic." Dead-end details don't link to the main idea and can be distracting for the reader. Also watch for pointless repetition. Occasionally, in a long essay or story, you might repeat some piece of information if it is very important that the reader remember that detail to understand what you are going to say next. Sometimes, however, you might forget you have already mentioned something. Unnecessary details and repetition make an essay seem disorganized and can confuse readers. Editing will help you weed out these statements and make your essay stronger.

Rearrange Ideas

When you edit your essay, read it all the way through and consider whether your argument is logical, and whether you have chosen the best kind of structure. A logical argument will have a strong thesis and *relevant* supporting details. For example, if your thesis asserts "Cats are really smart," and then you tell a story about the time your cat ate a bag of cotton balls, your argument will not be logical. Make sure your argument makes sense.

You should also make sure your structure fits the kind of essay you are writing. For example, your essay about cats would likely benefit from an "order of importance" structure, while a story about your swimming career would work best with a chronological structure. Restructuring an essay isn't too hard, and it can make a big difference in the long run. Don't be afraid to move whole paragraphs around, as long as you proofread carefully afterwards.

Replace Words

Another way to polish your writing is to think about your word choices. When you read your essay, does a certain word catch your attention? Maybe it's because that word doesn't quite fit, or maybe you notice you're using the same word over and over. A thesaurus can help you find just the right word to help your reader understand what you're trying to say, but don't use a $10 word when a 10 cent one will do. Also watch for clichés. A cliché is an expression or phrase that is overused. For example, "as white as snow" is a cliché; if you need to describe something white, try to think of your own comparison. Your reader has heard "as white as snow" before, and will appreciate your creativity.

Catch Mistakes

One of the most important things you can do in editing is to catch mistakes. Everyone makes mistakes, like spelling errors, typos, or grammar errors, when they write, and careful writers catch those mistakes before anyone else sees them. When you edit, keep your eyes open for these types of errors. When you're writing on the computer, a spell checker will help, but it won't find everything. For example, the spell checker won't know whether you have used *to*, *too*, and *two* correctly. It also may not recognize if you have double-typed a word. These kinds of mistakes can not only cause confusion, but also make your writing look sloppy. Reading your work or asking a friend to look it over before you turn it in will help you catch many of these mistakes.

Exercise 1

Read the letter from a student to a store owner, and then answer the questions.

> Dear Mr. Halifax,
>
> (1) Last week I bought a fish tank at you're store, Pet World. (2) It is bluue glass with green trim. (3) It holds 50 gallons. (4) How many fish can I put in it? (5) Please reply to this letter with any recommendations. (6) In my old tank, I have seven tropical fish and one turtle.

1. What is the error in Sentence 1?
   a. *you're* should be *your*
   b. *bought* should be *brought*
   c. *Pet World* should be lowercase

2. Which sentence contains unnecessary details?
   a. Sentence 1
   b. Sentence 2
   c. Sentence 6

3. Which sentence contains a spelling error?
   a. Sentence 1
   b. Sentence 2
   c. Sentence 5

4. Which sentence would make a better final sentence?
   a. Sentence 4
   b. Sentence 5
   c. Sentence 1

Editing Symbols

When you edit your work, it can be hard to fit all your changes in the margins of the paper. Editors invented a set of symbols to make it clear which changes need to be made and where they should go. Editing on a computer is different, but for editing on paper, try using these symbols. Most of these symbols go underneath the word or letter they refer to, then you annotate in the margin what symbols you've used, next to the line where they appear.

DESCRIPTION	SYMBOL	DESCRIPTION	SYMBOL
Capitalize	≡	Delete	ℐ
Lowercase	/	Delete and closeup	ℐ̶
Insert	∧	Indent	⌐

Exercise 2

Use the symbols you've learned to mark errors in the passage below. If you're borrowing this book from the library, either make a copy of the page, or practice writing the symbols on a separate piece of paper. (The sentences are numbered for use in the answer key.)

The Tryout

(1) A lark—that's what Alexanders family called him because he sang all the time. (2) Personally, Alexander believed he sounded more like acrow, but it didn't concern him. (3) He simply liked singing

(4) He sang in the shower he sang while he did his homework, and he sang while he walked to school.

(5) He couldnt have cared less what he sounded like, until Kevin started talking about the tryouts for the City Boys' Choir.

(6) "Yeah, I'm attending the tryouts this weekend, he heard Kevin bragging one day in class. (7) "With my voice, I'm pretty much guaranteeed a spot. I imagine they'll want me to perform lots of solos, to."

(8) Every one around school knew that Kevin had a fantastic singing voice. (9) Normally, alexander just ignored him, but whille he was walking home from school (singing as usual), he kept imagining himself as a member of the boys' chor. (10) Wouldn't it be fun, he thought, to sing cooperatively with other kids and have someone actually teach him about singing

(11) Bright and early saturday morning, Alexander's mom dropped him off at the Auditorium where the tryouts were being held. (12) Alexander took a deep breath, walked into the building, registered at a large table, and then joined the other boys who were all chattering nervously in the hallway (13) The only one who didnt look nervous was Kevin. (14) And why should he be? (15) Kevin had been taking lessons years and had won numerous competitions. (16) Alexander, on the other hand, had never taken a music lesson in his life, muchless performed for an audience.

Reviewing a Passage

One way that we learn how to be better writers is by reading other people's writing. When you read work written by very good writers, you should pay attention to how they use language to communicate effectively. First, you can find their thesis statements to see how they will focus their work. Then you can read on to observe the ways in which they maintain the focus of the essay or story by using relevant statements. By following their example, you will improve your own writing.

Another way to improve your writing is by helping other people improve theirs. This is sometimes called *reviewing*. When you review your friend's work, look for mistakes she may have made in grammar, spelling, or general structure. You should also check for focus errors. Sometimes a writer gets carried away with one section of the essay and forgets what the original question was! When you review for focus, make sure that the passage has a strong thesis statement. Then, as you read, ask yourself whether each statement addresses the topic and supports the thesis. You can suggest that weak thesis statements be rewritten, and delete or alter sentences that do not focus on the main idea.

You also can offer specific or general suggestions to improve her writing. And, don't forget, when you're good at reviewing other people's writing, you'll be better at reviewing your own, too!

Exercise 3

Read and review the following essay. Keep your eyes open for grammatical errors, spelling irregularities, and structural problems, and pay especially close attention to the essay's focus.

Buying a Computer

(1) There are two basic ways to buy a computer: buying a premade one, or buying it piece-by-pieces. (2) There are advantages and disadvantiges for both methods. (3) Buying a premade computer is the easiest method—the consumer can just go to the store, pick out a computer that seems good, and take it home. (4) Of course, computers (both as a premade package and as individual parts) can also be purchased online from a variety of retailers. (5) One such online retailer, Newegg.com, was founded by a Taiwanese immigrant named Fred Chang. (6) The problem, however, is that premade computers may not have everything a person wants (e.g., it may have a large hard drive, but not enough RAM, or a huge monitor, but a poor video card.). (7) Also, sometimes prices are higher for premade computers.

(8) On the other hand, buying a computer piece-by-piece is great because it allows a consumer to get exactly what he or she wants. (9) Nevertheless, buying individual components can add a lot of installation time, and, if not done correctly, can result in a non-functioning computer! (10) Choosing which method to use is one of the most important decisions you can make when buying a computer and can make it a satisfying purchase or one that generate headaches. (11) Likewise, choosing whether to rent or buy a car is also a very important decision.

1. Which sentence contains a spelling error?
   a. Sentence 2
   b. Sentence 5
   c. Sentence 8
   d. Sentence 11

2. Which *two* sentences are off-topic and do not belong in this essay?
   a. Sentences 1 and 5
   b. Sentences 5 and 11
   c. Sentences 8 and 9
   d. Sentences 2 and 4

3. What is the error in Sentence 1?
  a. The colon is misused.
  b. It should say, "There **is** two basic ways to buy a computer. . . ."
  c. It should say "piece-by-piece."
  d. "Buy" should be spelled "by."

4. What is the grammar error in Sentence 10?
  a. It should say "generates."
  b. It should say "Choosing **what** method to use. . . ."
  c. The sentence is too long.
  d. The word "generate" is used incorrectly.

5. Which sentence is the thesis statement?
  a. Sentence 1
  b. Sentence 2
  c. Sentence 8
  d. Sentence 11

Summary

Reviewing and revising are very important parts of the writing process. When you take the time to review your work, you will probably find things you need to revise. There might be simple mistakes, such as spelling errors, that you'll want to clean up so that your work doesn't look careless or sloppy. In some cases, there may be larger issues you'd like to work on, such as adding information, removing unnecessary details, rearranging ideas, or improving your choice of words. Now that you know some editing symbols, reviewing and revising should be a little easier! You also can use your new skills to help your friends improve their writing.

Answers

Exercise 1
1. a. "You're" is the contraction of "you are;" "your" is the possessive form of "you."
2. c. The details about the old aquarium's inhabitants aren't relevant to the pet store owner receiving the letter.
3. b. There should only be one "u" in "blue."
4. b. Sentence 5 is a firm, friendly request for a reply that the recipient can easily understand and respond to.

Exercise 2
You should have used the editing symbols to mark the errors shown in bold.

Sentence 1 (1 error)
Sentence 2 (1 error)
Sentence 3 (1 error)
Sentence 4 (1 error)
Sentence 5 (1 error)
Sentence 6 (2 errors)
Sentence 7 (2 errors)
Sentence 8 (1 error)
Sentence 9 (3 errors)
Sentence 10 (1 error)
Sentence 11 (2 errors)
Sentence 12 (1 error)
Sentence 13 (1 error)
Sentence 14 (0 errors)
Sentence 15 (1 error)
Sentence 16 (1 error)

The Tryout

(1) A lark—that's what **Alexanders** family called him because he sang all the time. (2) Personally, Alexander believed he sounded more like a crow, but it didn't concern him. (3) He simply liked singing

(4) He sang in the shower he sang while he did his homework, and he sang while he walked to school.

(5) He **couldnt** have cared less what he sounded like, until Kevin started talking about the tryouts for the City Boys' Choir.

(6) "Yeah, I'm attending the tryouts this weekend, he heard Kevin bragging one day in class. (7) "With my voice, I'm pretty much **guaranteed** a spot. I imagine they'll want me to perform lots of solos, to."

(8) **Every one** around school knew that Kevin had a fantastic singing voice. (9) Normally, **alexander** just ignored him, but **whille** he was walking home from school (singing as usual), he kept imagining himself as a member of the boys' **chor**. (10) Wouldn't it be fun, he thought, to sing competitively with other kids and have someone actually teach him about singing

(11) Bright and early **saturday** morning, Alexander's mom dropped him off at the **Auditorium** where the tryouts were being held. (12) Alexander took a deep breath, walked into the building, registered at a large table, and then joined the other boys who were all chattering nervously in the hallway

(13) The only one who **didnt** look nervous was Kevin. (14) And why should he be? (15) Kevin had been taking lessons years and had won numerous competitions. (16) Alexander, on the other hand, had never taken a music lesson in his life, **much less** performed for an audience.

Exercise 3

1. **a.** The word *disadvantiges* should be spelled *disadvantages*.

2. **b.** Sentences 5 and 11 are not focused on the topic, how to buy a computer. Sentence 5 mentions the founder of an online company, and Sentence 11 introduces an entirely new idea at the end of the essay. Sentence 11 should be cut to improve the essay's focus. Sentence 5 could either be deleted or refocused: for example, "One online retailer, Newegg.com, actually gives you a choice of which way to buy your computer."

3. **c.** The phrase is *piece-by-piece*.

4. **a.** The singular, and correct in this case, form of the verb is *generates*.

5. **a.** Sentence 1 is the thesis. It focuses the essay and outlines its structure.

SKILL BUILDING UNTIL NEXT TIME

1. Find one of your old essays and review it, using the editing symbols to mark errors or changes you'd like to make. Revise the essay; see whether you can improve it using some of the strategies in this lesson. Can you use better words? Would a different structure help your argument? Is your argument logical? Then bring a copy of your old essay and a copy the new and improved version to a parent, sibling, or friend and ask them which version they think is better. Chances are, they'll choose the essay you took the time to revise!

2. Look for an interesting article in a newspaper or magazine, or online. Read it critically and think about how you would have completed that assignment. Did the author make any mistakes? Would you have used the same structure? How would a different word here or there change the article's tone or meaning? Thinking critically about other people's writing will make you a better writer!

31 ▶ PUTTING IT ALL TOGETHER

SECTION SUMMARY
This lesson reviews Lessons 27 through 30 and combines the skills you've learned in this section. You'll use your active reading skills to critically analyze writing samples.

This chapter briefly reviews Section 6 and then gives you three practice passages. These passages will require you to use skills from each of the five sections you've read so far, so you'll have to apply your active reading skills to interpreting information from many types of texts. Remember to read actively, look for clues, and examine the parts and organization of any visual aids.

Review: What You've Learned

Here's a quick review of each lesson in this section:

Lesson 27: Prewriting. You learned that prewriting is the first step in the writing process. You discovered several ways to prewrite, including brainstorming, freewriting, lists, graphic organizers, and outlines.

Lesson 28: Organizing Ideas. You learned about three types of essays: informative, narrative, and persuasive essays. You also learned the basic structure of a five-paragraph essay.

Lesson 29: Writing with Focus and Clarity. You used your critical reading skills to become a more effective writer. You practiced focusing on the main idea with clear thesis statements and relevant details. You learned how to develop depth in your writing, and you practiced selecting an appropriate audience, style, and tone for each piece of writing.

Lesson 30: Reviewing and Revising. You learned why it is important to edit and revise your writing. You practiced several strategies for revision, including adding and removing information, rearranging ideas, replacing words, and catching simple mistakes. You also saw some basic editing symbols to use when editing with pen and paper.

In Section 1, you learned how to be an active reader, find the main idea, define unfamiliar words, and how to distinguish between fact and opinion. In Section 2, you learned about plot structure, chronological order and order of importance, comparison and contrast, cause and effect, and summaries and outlines. In Section 3, you learned how writers use point of view, word choice, style, tone, and literary devices to help create meaning. In Section 4, you learned how to read between the lines to find implied ideas, themes, causes, and effects. In Section 5, you learned how to analyze special texts, including instructions, advertisements, graphs, and other visual aids.

If any of these terms or strategies are unfamiliar, take some time to review the term or strategy that is unclear.

Section 6 Practice

Read these practice passages actively and carefully. Then answer the questions that follow.

Note: If you come across unfamiliar words, do not look them up until *after* you've completed this practice exercise.

Exercise 1

Dear Shinto,

(1) Thanks so much for the letter and photos you sent me last month. The picture of the monkeys in your backyard was my favorite!

(2) Since I last wrote too you, two exciting things have happened. First, we had Spring Break. That means we get a week off of school. My best friend went on a trip with her parents to Ocean World. My family didn't go on a trip, but my mother took a day off of work to take me to the zoo!

(3) We went on a Thursday. We saw hundreds of animals: lions, giraffes, lemurs, hippopotamuses, you name it! My favorite animal is the red panda. There were three of them at the zoo, and they were all sleeping in trees. My mother's favorite animals were the gazelles. Do you have gazelles in Japan?

(4) The second exciting thing that happened was the eighth grade started to prepare for our Spring Performance. Every spring, the eighth grade performs a show with musical instruments, dancing, and costumes. All the parents and siblings come watch. This year, the theme is Mythology. I get to dress up like Hera, the queen of the Greek gods!

(5) I can't wait for our performance next month. I'll send you pictures of my costume when it's ready. Does your school do any musical or theater performances?

Write back soon!
Maya

1. What is the main idea of the letter?
  a. Maya loves the zoo.
  b. Maya misses her friend Shinto.
  c. Two exciting things have happened to Maya.
  d. Maya wants to visit Shinto's school.

2. What error appears in the first sentence of Paragraph 2?
  a. *since* should be *after*
  b. *too* should be *to*
  c. *two* should be *too*
  d. *have* should be *has*

3. Which of the statements below is an unnecessary dead-end detail?
  a. My family didn't go on a trip.
  b. We went on a Thursday.
  c. My mother's favorite animals were the gazelles.
  d. I can't wait for our performance next month.

4. Which organizing principle is used in the letter?
  a. comparison and contrast
  b. cause and effect
  c. order of importance
  d. chronological

5. Clues in the letter tell you that Shinto is probably
  a. Maya's teacher
  b. Maya's American friend
  c. Maya's Japanese pen pal
  d. Maya's newest friend

Exercise 2

New Opportunities at Summer Camp

(1) Students have many options for how to spend their summer vacation. Some students stay home with their siblings and friends. Some students get a part-time job helping a parent or relative. Others get involved with volunteer programs. But many students choose to participate in a summer camp. There are many types of summer camps, and each camp has unique opportunities. Whether the camp lasts one week or three months, summer camp is a valuable experience that can enrich a student's life.

(2) The first advantage of summer camp is that you get to meet new people. For some students, it will seem scary or challenging to make new friends. Students become comfortable with their school friends and want to spend time with them. But at summer camp, all the students have something in common! If it is an art camp, you'll be able to find new friends who love art. At a music camp, or a theater camp, or an outdoor adventure camp, the students will all have a shared interest. Summer camp is an opportunity to meet kids from different schools, or even different states, who share your interests.

(3) Another advantage of summer camp is that you get to learn in unusual ways. In school, the teachers have to teach certain subjects, such as history and math. But students can choose a summer camp that focuses on the subject they find most interesting. At a science camp, you'll get to conduct amazing experiments. At circus camp, you'll learn tricks and acrobatics. At leadership camp, you can develop your leadership abilities through teamwork games. There is a special type of camp for every interest.

(4) Summer camp can also be a chance to experience really cool places. Many summer camps are located in a special place, such as in the forest, beside a lake, or in a big city. As a student in the camp, you'll be able to live in this unique place for a while. You might get to explore a new area or city, and you'll come home from camp with new experiences.

(5) Summer camp can be a life-changing experience for students. Spending part of your summer at a camp will help you meet new people, learn about your favorite subject in an interesting way, and possibly experience a new place. There is a summer camp for everyone, so don't spend your summer on the couch at home!

6. What is the author's thesis in this essay?
   a. Summer camp is a chance to experience really cool places.
   b. Summer camp can enrich a student's life.
   c. There is a summer camp for everyone.
   d. For some students, summer camp is scary.

7. What type of essay is this?
   a. persuasive
   b. informative
   c. expository
   d. narrative

8. According to the author, what is one *effect* of going to summer camp?
   a. making good use of your summer
   b. relaxing
   c. losing your friends
   d. learning new things in unusual ways

9. Which word best describes the tone of this essay?
   a. hopeful
   b. dull
   c. enthusiastic
   d. pushy

10. Who is the intended audience for this essay?
   a. other students
   b. the school principal
   c. the writer's parents
   d. the summer camp director

Exercise 3

Recycle!

(1) It's not only right to recycle, it's our duty. In nature, everything is recycled. A dead animal, for example, is food for many levels in the food chain; it even feeds organisms in the soil. Nothing is wasted. But humans have created things like plastic that can't be broken down by nature. In other words, we've created permanent litter. Our trash kills animals and pollutes water and soil, and if we continue to let it pile up, we may eventually have a trash mess that's out of control. If nature can't reuse it, we must recycle it. We've made a mess, and we should clean it up—because nature can't.

(2) Recycling is also the right thing to do for another reason. The earth is rich in resources, but its supply of materials is not endless. We use up our resources much faster than the earth is able to replenish them. For example, each year we cut down approximately four million acres of timber. But it takes an average of 25 years for replacement trees to mature. Like a dog who "bites the hand that feeds him," we are foolish to use Earth's resources recklessly. Recycling can help us reduce the risk of using up our natural resources.

(3) In most cities, it's fairly simple to recycle. Collect your recyclables at home, and then find out what kind of recycling system is available in the area. If your city uses a commingling system, just put all your recyclable materials together in a bin. The recyclables will be sorted at the collection center. If your city program wants them to be separated, organize your recyclables by material: glass, plastic, paper, and metals. With just a few minutes of extra organizing at home, we can do our part to keep reusable materials out of the landfills.

11. What is the implied main idea of the first paragraph?
   a. Humans are creating permanent litter.
   b. Natural resources are limited.
   c. Recycling protects our limited natural resources.
   d. We use four million acres of timber each year.

12. Which of the following statements from the text represents a *fact*?
   a. We've created permanent litter.
   b. The recyclables will be sorted at the collection center.
   c. We've made a mess, and we should clean it up.
   d. In most cities, it's fairly simple to recycle.

13. In the third paragraph, what does *commingling system* likely mean?
   a. The recyclables are all mingled together.
   b. The recyclables are divided by material.
   c. Recyclable materials are removed from regular trash.
   d. No recycling is available.

14. What is the organizing principle in this text?
   a. cause and effect
   b. order of importance
   c. comparison and contrast
   d. chronological

15. Reread this sentence from the second paragraph:

   > Like a dog that "bites the hand that feeds him," we are foolish to use Earth's resources recklessly.

   What literary device is used in this sentence?
   a. metaphor
   b. alliteration
   c. simile
   d. personification

Answers

Exercise 1

1. c. The second paragraph introduces the letter's main idea, and the next two paragraphs describe in detail the exciting things that have happened to Maya. One paragraph is about the zoo (choice **a**), but that's not broad enough to be the main idea. Maya might miss her friend Shinto (choice **b**), but she doesn't emphasize that idea, nor does she mention visiting Shinto's school (choice **d**). If you missed this question, please refer back to Lesson 2.

2. b. This is a very common homophone error. *Too*, *to*, and *two* are easily confused or mistyped, so read your work carefully to check for this kind of simple mistake. If you missed this question, please refer back to Lesson 30.

3. b. The day on which Maya visited the zoo is not relevant to the main idea, and it doesn't lead to any further descriptions. The fact that Maya's family didn't go on a trip (choice **a**) leads to a description of what she *did* do on Spring Break. The mention of her mother's favorite animal (choice **c**) leads to a question about gazelles near Shinto's home. And choice **d** expresses Maya's excitement about an upcoming event she has been describing. If you missed this question, please refer back to Lesson 29.

4. d. Maya describes the two events that have happened to her in chronological order. If you missed this question, please refer back to Lesson 7.

5. c. The casual, relaxed tone suggests that Maya is writing to one of her peers, rather than a teacher (choice **a**). She mentions previous letters between her and Shinto, so Shinto can't be a new friend (choice **d**). Paragraph 3 mentions Japan as Shinto's home, so Shinto must be a Japanese friend, not an American friend (choice **b**). If you missed this question, please refer back to Lesson 18.

Exercise 2

6. b. The thesis appears at the end of the first paragraph to introduce the main idea that ties together the whole essay. The idea that summer camp is a chance to experience cool places (choice **a**) is one of the supporting details. The other options are smaller ideas within the essay but not large enough to be the main idea. If you missed this question, please refer back to Lessons 17 and 28.

7. a. This essay does present some information about summer camps, but its main purpose is to convince the reader to join a summer camp. The essay is not narrative because it does not include the writer's personal experiences or reflections on summer camp. If you missed this question, please refer back to Lessons 18 and 28.

8. d. Each of the three supporting paragraphs explains one effect: meeting new friends, learning in unusual ways, and experiencing a new place. Making good use of your summer (choice **a**) is a possible *cause* or motive for joining a summer camp. Choices **b** and **c** are not effects described in the text. If you missed this question, please refer back to Lesson 9.

9. c. The writer is enthusiastic, but not vaguely hopeful (choice **a**), dull (choice **b**), or overly pushy (choice **d**). If you missed this question, please refer back to Lesson 14.

10. a. The thesis of the essay and the conclusion paragraph suggest that the reader should also spend the summer at a camp. Thus, the intended audience must be other students, rather than adults. If you missed this question, please refer back to Lesson 29.

Exercise 3

11. c. The emphasis in this paragraph is on the role of recycling to protect natural resources. Choice **b** is too limited because it ignores recycling. Choice **a** is the main idea of paragraph 1, and choice **d** is a supporting detail, not a main idea. If you missed this question, please refer back to Lesson 17.

12. b. This persuasive essay uses a combination of facts and opinions, so it can be difficult to separate them. But choices **a**, **c**, and **d** are all statements that could be argued against, so they are opinions. If you missed this question, please refer back to Lesson 4.

13. a. The context tells you that the recyclables can all be mixed together and will be separated at the recycling center. However, the text explains that the recyclables first need to be separated from your regular trash (choice **c**). If you missed this question, please refer back to Lesson 3.

14. b. The writer has organized her ideas by order of importance, from most to least important. The strongest opinions appear in paragraph 1, with supporting facts in paragraph 2, and related information in the final paragraph. The writer starts with strong emotional statements to capture the reader's attention and get the reader emotionally involved with the topic. If you missed this question, please refer back to Lesson 7.

15. c. The sentence contains a comparison, so it must be a metaphor or simile, but it uses the word *like*, so it must be a simile. If you missed this question, please refer back to Lesson 15.

Congratulations!
You've finished 31 lessons, and your reading and writing skills should be much better now. But these skills are like muscles: If you don't use them, you might lose them. Practice what you've learned in this book. Read, read, read! Find some authors that you enjoy. (There's a list of suggested authors and books in the Appendix.) Pay attention to how your favorite authors write, and practice your own writing skills. And reward yourself for a job well done!

POSTTEST

Congratulations! You've finished all of the lessons in this book and have dramatically improved your reading comprehension skills. This posttest will give you a chance to measure your new reading and writing abilities.

The questions on this test are different from the pretest, but the format is the same. Take the test, using as much time as you need. Then grade yourself and compare your score with your pretest score. If you have a much better score, congratulations—you've significantly improved your reading and writing skills. If your score is only a little better, there are probably some lessons you should review. Is there a pattern to the types of questions you got wrong? Do they all seem to deal with the same reading or writing strategies? Did you remember to read every passage actively? Did you revise your writing?

For the multiple choice questions, there's an answer sheet to use on the next page, or you can simply circle the correct answers. If you don't own this book, write the numbers 1 through 40 on a piece of paper and record your answers there. For the composition section, write in the space given, on your own piece of paper, or type up your answer. When you finish, check your answers against the key on page 288. The key tells you which lesson covers the skills tested in each question.

Good luck!

1. ⓐ ⓑ ⓒ ⓓ
2. ⓐ ⓑ ⓒ ⓓ
3. ⓐ ⓑ ⓒ ⓓ
4. ⓐ ⓑ ⓒ ⓓ
5. ⓐ ⓑ ⓒ ⓓ
6. ⓐ ⓑ ⓒ ⓓ
7. ⓐ ⓑ ⓒ ⓓ
8. ⓐ ⓑ ⓒ ⓓ
9. ⓐ ⓑ ⓒ ⓓ
10. ⓐ ⓑ ⓒ ⓓ
11. ⓐ ⓑ ⓒ ⓓ
12. ⓐ ⓑ ⓒ ⓓ
13. ⓐ ⓑ ⓒ ⓓ
14. ⓐ ⓑ ⓒ ⓓ

15. ⓐ ⓑ ⓒ ⓓ
16. ⓐ ⓑ ⓒ ⓓ
17. ⓐ ⓑ ⓒ ⓓ
18. ⓐ ⓑ ⓒ ⓓ
19. ⓐ ⓑ ⓒ ⓓ
20. ⓐ ⓑ ⓒ ⓓ
21. ⓐ ⓑ ⓒ ⓓ
22. ⓐ ⓑ ⓒ ⓓ
23. ⓐ ⓑ ⓒ ⓓ
24. ⓐ ⓑ ⓒ ⓓ
25. ⓐ ⓑ ⓒ ⓓ
26. ⓐ ⓑ ⓒ ⓓ
27. ⓐ ⓑ ⓒ ⓓ
28. ⓐ ⓑ ⓒ ⓓ

29. ⓐ ⓑ ⓒ ⓓ
30. ⓐ ⓑ ⓒ ⓓ
31. ⓐ ⓑ ⓒ ⓓ
32. ⓐ ⓑ ⓒ ⓓ
33. ⓐ ⓑ ⓒ ⓓ
34. ⓐ ⓑ ⓒ ⓓ
35. ⓐ ⓑ ⓒ ⓓ
36. ⓐ ⓑ ⓒ ⓓ
37. ⓐ ⓑ ⓒ ⓓ
38. ⓐ ⓑ ⓒ ⓓ
39. ⓐ ⓑ ⓒ ⓓ
40. ⓐ ⓑ ⓒ ⓓ

Directions: Read each of the following passages carefully and actively and answer the questions that follow each passage. Take as much time as you need for this test. Then use the answer key at the end of the test to check your answers.

Improved Literacy

Over the past 40 years, worldwide illiteracy rates have consistently declined. The main reason for this decline is the sharp increase in the literacy rates of young women, which is the result of campaigns to increase educational opportunities for girls. For example, between 1970 and 1990, the literacy rate among women in the United Arab Emirates increased from 7% to 76%.

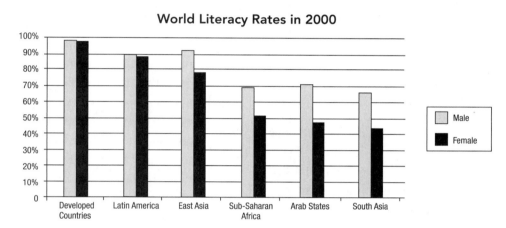

World Literacy Rates in 2000

Source: Data taken from UNESCO Institute for Statistics

1. What is the author's purpose in writing this passage?
   a. to inform the reader
   b. to entertain the reader
   c. to tell a personal narrative
   d. to persuade the reader

2. According to the passage, which of the following is directly responsible for the sharp increase in literacy rates for young women?
   a. the United Arab Emirates
   b. increased funding for education
   c. a drop in illiteracy rates worldwide
   d. campaigns to increase educational opportunities for girls

3. According to the graph, what was the approximate literacy rate for women in East Asia in 2000?
   a. 43%
   b. 48%
   c. 78%
   d. 92%

You will need to know the following words as you read the next story:

pumice: a type of lava that is very light in weight
stalactites: icicle-shaped formations on a cave's ceiling

The Ape Caves

(1) Mount St. Helens erupted with the force of a nuclear explosion on May 18, 1980. Volcanic ash shot 14 miles into the air and fell over the entire Pacific Northwest, from Eugene, Oregon, to Seattle, Washington, and beyond.

(2) I could have safely watched the cataclysm a mere four miles away, from the entrance to the Ape Caves in what is now Mount St. Helens National Volcanic Monument, but the force of the blast would have made the top of the mountain simply disappear.

(3) In fact, the explosion sent ash in the opposite direction from the caves, and later eruptions lightly dusted the cave area with pumice. At that point, I might have sought refuge in the underground Ape Caves, or lava tube. At nearly two-and-a-half miles long, this is the longest such tube in the Western Hemisphere.

(4) The Ape Caves were formed about 2,000 years ago, but they were not discovered until 1951. Early explorations of the caves were made by a local Boy Scout troop, who named themselves the "Mount St. Helens Apes."

(5) Standing in that same location recently, I felt the wind whistle past me, into the cool depths of the cave. My hiking group had chosen to hike the lower part of the Ape Caves first. Most casual visitors prefer this section. It has a downward slope with a sandy floor. Its highlight is the "meatball," a huge, round ball of lava wedged ten feet above the cave floor. Beyond it, the cave ends in a low series of crawlways.

(6) As we descended 40 feet below ground by stairs, the change of environment was striking—from the warmth, greenery, and birdcalls above, to the cool, dark silence below. Sound seemed to be swallowed up by the volcanic walls, and the temperature dropped to a cool and damp 42°. The darkness was so jet black that the beams of our flashlights seemed weak and outmatched by the inescapable inkiness.

(7) Old lava flows had left a variety of markings in the passage. Large gas bubbles had popped at the surface of the molten flows, leaving circular rings, frozen ripples, and deep gutters in the hardened lava on the floor. This made walking unusually challenging. On the ceiling, which rose as high as 20 feet in places, small stalactites pointed their mineral deposits down at us from above.

(8) There's a rumor that a local jogger has carefully paced out the Lower Cave and, in doing so, has developed a mental map that allows him to run the route without the aid of a lantern or flashlight. How disturbing it would be for a few cave explorers like us to hear quickly advancing footsteps and then see a jogger appear out of nowhere, run past, and then disappear once more.

(9) After lunch, we elected to try the Upper Cave. This cave is twice the length of the Lower Cave and a much more challenging climb—not a good choice for the timid or unskilled underground adventurer. In the Upper Cave, when our conversation ceased, only the drip, drip, drip of seeping water and our breathing could be heard. Our flashlights soon became an obstacle. There were spots where we needed both hands for climbing over the increasingly large and jagged rockfalls. Where were some miners' helmets when we needed them?

(10) We met two other groups that had turned back after encountering a nine-foot wall of stone in a narrow passageway. The daunting, smooth stone face rose before us. It had once been a dramatic lava waterfall. Refusing to turn back, we boosted one person up over the top.

This person got to the next level and then turned to assist the rest of us. Dirty, scraped, and unstoppable, we pressed on.

(11) Just about then, my flashlight went dead. (The guidebook had suggested that we carry three sources of light per person but that had seemed overly cautious.) I found myself fervently wishing for an old-fashioned lantern, or even a book of matches. Our passage slowed to a crawl as we picked our way carefully through the gloom, relying on the beams of our companions' flashlights, anxious not to suffer a fall or twisted ankle.

(12) Fortunately, we were near the exit, close to the end of the Upper Cave. Our tired party had readied itself to climb the ladder into the blinding light when we thought we heard hurried footsteps rushing toward us. Perhaps it was just cave anxiety, but we flew up the rungs in an orderly panic.

(13) Looking back down into dimness, we saw a man walk past in brisk, measured strides, keeping track of something on his digital watch. He wore a sweat suit and carried a tiny flashlight. Looking up, he gave us a quick nod and was quickly swallowed by the dark. We looked up then, too, and blinked in wonder at the dazzling south view of Mount St. Helens.

4. Read the first two paragraphs of the passage again. Then think about this sentence from the second paragraph.

> I could have safely watched the cataclysm a mere four miles away, from the entrance to the Ape Caves in what is now Mount St. Helens National Volcanic Monument.

As it is used in this article, what does the word *cataclysm* mean?
a. a creative and dramatic performance
b. a sudden, violent change in the earth
c. a new discovery about the earth
d. an exploration of new territory

5. The author probably wrote this article to
a. encourage people to explore the Ape Caves.
b. inform people about volcanoes.
c. inform people about the Ape Caves.
d. persuade people to visit Mount St. Helens.

6. Which event in the story represents the rising action?
a. Boy Scouts explored the Ape Caves.
b. The author's group eats lunch.
c. The author's group climbs over a wall of rock.
d. The author sees the gorgeous view of Mount St. Helens.

7. The author suggests that the Upper Cave is best explored by someone who
a. is young and quick.
b. has had previous experience as a jogger.
c. has had previous experience as a rock climber.
d. has patience and confidence.

8. Based on the article, which of the following statements about the Ape Caves is false?
a. They were explored by a Boy Scout troop.
b. They were formed about 2,000 years ago.
c. They were discovered about 50 years ago.
d. They were buried by the 1980 eruption of Mount St. Helens.

9. Which of the following sentences from the passage expresses an opinion?
a. Mount St. Helens erupted with the force of a nuclear explosion on May 18, 1980.
b. At nearly two-and-a-half miles long, this is the longest such tube in the Western Hemisphere.
c. This cave is twice the length of the Lower Cave and a much more challenging climb— not a good choice for the timid or unskilled underground adventurer.
d. On the ceiling, which rose as high as 20 feet in places, small stalactites pointed their mineral deposits down at us from above.

10. The style of this passage is best described as
  a. distant and matter-of-fact, providing only essential information to readers.
  b. very detailed, using description to create a picture of what it's like inside the cave.
  c. full of short, choppy sentences that create a sense of excitement.
  d. dry and repetitive, with little variation in sentence structure.

Treating Burns

(1) There are three different kinds of burns: first degree, second degree, and third degree. Each type of burn requires a different type of medical treatment.

(2) The least serious burn is the first-degree burn. This burn causes the skin to turn red but does not cause blistering. A mild sunburn is a good example of a first-degree burn, and, like a mild sunburn, first-degree burns generally do not require medical treatment other than a gentle cooling of the burned skin with ice or cold tap water.

(3) Second-degree burns, however, do cause blistering of the skin and should be treated immediately. These burns should be immersed in warm water and then wrapped in a sterile dressing or bandage. (Do not apply butter or grease to these burns. Despite the old wives' tale, butter does not help burns heal and actually increases the chances of infection.) If a second-degree burn covers a large part of the body, then the victim should be taken to the hospital immediately for medical care.

(4) Third-degree burns are those that char the skin and turn it black or burn so deeply that the skin shows white. These burns usually result from direct contact with flames and have a great chance of becoming infected. All third-degree burn victims should receive immediate hospital care. Burns should not be immersed in water, and charred clothing should not be removed from the victim as it may also remove the skin. If possible, a sterile dressing or bandage should be applied to burns before the victim is transported to the hospital.

11. The main idea of this passage is best expressed in which sentence?
  a. Third-degree burns are very serious.
  b. There are three different kinds of burns.
  c. Some burns require medical treatment.
  d. Each type of burn requires a different type of treatment.

12. This passage uses which of the following patterns of organization?
  a. cause and effect, comparison and contrast, and order of importance
  b. cause and effect, chronology, and order of importance
  c. comparison and contrast only
  d. cause and effect and comparison and contrast only

13. A mild sunburn should be treated by
  a. removing charred clothing.
  b. immersing it in warm water and wrapping it in a sterile bandage.
  c. getting immediate medical attention.
  d. gently cooling the burned skin with cool water.

14. This passage uses the third-person point of view because
  a. the author wants to create a personal and friendly tone.
  b. the author wants to present important information objectively.
  c. the author wants to put readers in his or her shoes.
  d. the author does not have a specific audience.

Sylvia

(1) For perhaps the tenth time since the clock struck two, Sylvia crosses to the front-facing window of her apartment, pulls back the blue curtain, and looks down at the street. People hurry along the sidewalk. Although she watches for several long moments, she sees no one enter her building.

(2) She walks back to the center of the high-ceilinged living room, where she stands frowning and twisting a silver bracelet around and around on her wrist. She is an attractive young woman with a narrow, delicate face and light brown hair held back by a barrette. She is restless now, because she is being kept waiting. It is nearly two-thirty, and a woman named Lola Parrish was to come at two o'clock to look at the apartment.

(3) She considers leaving a note and going out. The woman is late, and besides, Sylvia is certain that Lola Parrish will not be a suitable person with whom to share the apartment. On the phone she had sounded too old.

(4) However, the moment for saying the apartment was no longer available slipped past, and Sylvia found herself agreeing to the two o'clock appointment. If she leaves now, as she has a perfect right to do, she can avoid the awkwardness of turning the woman away.

(5) Looking past the blue curtain, however, she sees the sky is not clear but veiled by a white haze, and the air is still. She knows that the haze, the stillness, and the heat are conditions that often precede a summer thunderstorm—one of the electrical storms that have terrified her since she was a child. If a storm comes, she wants to be at home in her own place.

(6) She walks back to the center of the room, aware now that the idea of sharing the apartment, which was never appealing, has actually begun to alarm her. Still, she knows she will have to become accustomed to the notion, because her savings are nearly <u>exhausted</u>. She has a low-paying job, and, although she has considered seeking another (perhaps something connected with music—in her childhood she had played the flute and people had said she was gifted), she finds she has no energy to do that.

(7) Besides, although her job pays poorly, it suits her. She is a typist in a natural history museum with an office on the top floor. The man for whom she works allows Sylvia to have the office to herself, and from the big window to her left, she can look out on a peaceful, park setting.

15. Which of the following adjectives best describes Sylvia's mood as depicted in the story?
  a. anxious
  b. angry
  c. meditative
  d. serene

16. Based on the tone of the passage and the description of Sylvia at this moment, which of the following is the most likely reason Sylvia's job suits her?
  a. Her office is tastefully decorated.
  b. She likes her employer at the museum.
  c. She is musical and enjoys listening to the birds sing.
  d. She is able to work alone in a space that feels open.

17. When Sylvia looks out her apartment window, the weather appears
  a. gloomy.
  b. ominous.
  c. springlike.
  d. inviting.

18. Based on the story, which of the following would most likely describe Sylvia's behavior in relationship to other people?
  a. distant
  b. overbearing
  c. dependent
  d. malicious

19. Which of the following images is most appropriate for describing Sylvia's state of mind as she waits for Lola?
  a. a child eagerly digging for buried treasure
  b. a dog joyfully rolling on its back in fresh, green grass
  c. a rat trapped in a maze
  d. a forest fire

20. The word *exhausted*, underlined in paragraph 5, most nearly means
  a. tired.
  b. weakened.
  c. spent.
  d. sick.

21. The description of Sylvia's physical appearance in paragraph 2 might be said to foreshadow the rest of the story because
  a. silver jewelry suggests wealth and self-confidence.
  b. her youth and attractiveness make her perfect.
  c. her delicate appearance reflects her shy, reserved personality.
  d. the frown indicated tragic plot developments.

22. What is the best word to describe Sylvia in paragraph 3?
  a. timid
  b. curious
  c. irritated
  d. sad

On Top of the World

(1) For over a hundred years, the highest mountains in South America have lured climbers from all over the world. But until 1908, Peru's Mount Huascaran resisted the efforts of all those who attempted to climb to its summit. One mountaineer, Annie Smith Peck, vowed to overcome the obstacles to be the first to the top of Mount Huascaran. In order to succeed, she would have to organize expeditions, deal with reluctant companions, survive bad weather, and climb steep cliffs of ice and rock.

A Love of the Mountains
(2) Annie Smith Peck was born in the United States in 1850. Although she didn't start mountain climbing until she was in her thirties, it soon became clear that she had found her life's work. She started by climbing mountains in North America and Europe. Even as she began setting records, Peck was always searching for the next great challenge. At that time, mountain climbing was not considered appropriate for women, so Peck's activities made her notorious.

The Beginning of the Quest
(3) Peck traveled to Bolivia in 1903 to make an attempt to reach the summit of Mount Sorata. This was her first trip to South America and also the beginning of her lifelong interest in the continent. Her first try at Sorata failed, and in 1904, when a second expedition also failed, she turned her eyes to Mount Huascaran. Huascaran had three features that made it irresistible to Peck: It was a tall peak, no one had yet climbed it, and it was in South America.

Again and Again
(4) Annie Peck mounted four expeditions and made five attempts before she finally conquered Mount Huascaran. All her failed attempts fell short because of bad weather and trouble with other members of the climbing team. Between expeditions, Peck returned to the United States

to raise money. She received help from many scientific organizations, including the Museum of Natural History, which even lent her the snowsuit worn by Admiral Peary on his trip to the North Pole. Still, Peck struggled at least as much to raise money as she did to climb her beloved mountains.

Success at Last
(5) In 1908, Peck scraped together the funds for yet another expedition to Mount Huascaran. This time, she hired two Swiss guides to assist her with the climb. On their first trip up the mountain's slopes, one of the guides became ill, and the entire team was forced to turn back even though they were very close to the top. Being so close to success was very frustrating. Peck could not even prove how close they had come because she had accidentally brought the wrong kind of film and was not able to photograph the climb.

(6) The team rested for a few days, and the guide recovered. On August 28th, they set off again. The climb was extremely difficult. Steps had to be hacked one by one into the steep ice. Snow bridges and crevasses had to be carefully crossed. The weather was so cold that everyone suffered from frostbite. When Peck and her two guides were a short distance from the top, they stopped to determine the exact height of the mountain. One of the guides took advantage of Peck's distraction to climb the few remaining feet to the summit so that he could boast that he had been there before her. Although Peck was understandably angry, she focused on the triumph of achieving her goal. On September 2, 1908, Annie Peck finally stood at the top of Mt. Huascaran.

Life after Mount Huascaran
(7) Peck was 58 when she climbed Mt. Huascaran, but she wasn't done with mountain climbing. Several years later, she returned to Peru to climb Mount Coropuna. At the

summit, she left a banner that read *Votes for Women*. For the rest of her life, Peck lectured and wrote about women's rights, her expeditions, and life in South America.

23. As it is used in the first sentence of the passage, the word *lured* most nearly means
  a. trained.
  b. attracted.
  c. irritated.
  d. brought comfort to.

24. Which of these events happened first?
  a. Peck planted a banner reading *Votes for Women*.
  b. Peck borrowed Peary's snowsuit.
  c. Peck climbed to the top of Mount Huascaran.
  d. Peck hired two Swiss guides.

25. According to the passage, Peck wanted to reach the summit of Mount Huascaran because
  a. the government of Peru encouraged her to do it.
  b. the Swiss guides had dared her to do it.
  c. she was being paid to climb it.
  d. no one else had been able to do it.

26. Information in the passage suggests that on her expeditions to Mount Huascaran, Peck brought along
  a. binoculars.
  b. a camera.
  c. a flashlight.
  d. a map.

27. Based on information in the passage, the reader can conclude that Peck
  a. enjoyed raising money for her trips to South America.
  b. liked South America more than the United States.
  c. enjoyed taking risks and facing challenges.
  d. worked at the Museum of Natural History.

28. The passage suggests that several scientific organizations in the United States probably thought Peck
    a. was foolish.
    b. needed advice.
    c. deserved support.
    d. wanted attention.

29. Which of the following best summarizes this passage?
    a. Annie Peck was a mountain climber. She had climbed mountains on other continents, but the mountains of South America were taller.
    b. Annie Peck was a popular writer and speaker who climbed mountains in South America. She faced many challenges but overcame them all.
    c. Annie Peck raised money from many sources to finance her expeditions to Mount Huarascan. Her ascent of the mountain in Peru made her famous worldwide.
    d. Annie Peck showed much determination in becoming the first woman to climb Mount Huarascan, in Peru. Despite several setbacks, she finally achieved her goal in 1908.

30. The main purpose of the information under the *Success at Last* heading is to
    a. describe the obstacles that Peck faced before she reached her goal.
    b. show that Peck suffered permanent physical damage when she climbed Mount Huascaran.
    c. explain why Peck was angry with one of her Swiss guides.
    d. explain why the climb to the top of Mount Huascaran was so expensive.

31. As she is presented in the passage, Annie Peck can be described by all the following words EXCEPT
    a. timid.
    b. determined.
    c. purposeful.
    d. adventurous.

A Narrow Fellow in the Grass
by Emily Dickinson

  1   A narrow Fellow in the Grass
  2   Occasionally rides—
  3   You may have met him—did you not
  4   His notice sudden is—
  5   The grass divides as with a comb—
  6   A spotted shaft is seen—
  7   And then it closes at your feet
  8   And opens further on—
  9   He likes a Boggy Acre—
10   A floor too cool for corn—
11   Yet when a Boy, and Barefoot—
12   I more than once at Noon
13   Have passed, I thought, a Whip-lash
14   Unbraiding in the Sun
15   When, stooping to secure it
16   It wrinkled, and was gone
17   I know and they know me—
18   I feel for them a transport
19   Of cordiality—
20   But never met this Fellow
21   Attended, alone
22   Without a tighter breathing
23   And Zero at the Bone

32. Who or what is the "Fellow" in this poem?
    a. a whip-lash
    b. a snake
    c. a gust of wind
    d. a boy

33. The phrase "Nature's People" means
  a. nature lovers.
  b. children.
  c. animals.
  d. neighbors.

34. The speaker of this poem is most likely
  a. an adult man.
  b. an adult woman.
  c. a young boy.
  d. Emily Dickinson, the poet.

35. The phrase "Without a tighter breathing/And Zero at the Bone" suggests a feeling of
  a. cold.
  b. grief.
  c. awe.
  d. fright.

36. The setting of this poem is most likely
  a. a big city.
  b. a rural area.
  c. a desert.
  d. a snowy mountainside.

37. This poem is a good example of which of the following?
  a. logical appeals
  b. the first-person point of view
  c. chronological order
  d. a chain of cause and effect

38. Lines 17 through 19 suggest that the speaker of the poem
  a. dislikes all animals.
  b. works in a zoo.
  c. has lots of pets at home.
  d. gets along well with most animals.

39. "The grass divides as with a comb" (line 5) is an example of which of the following?
  a. simile
  b. metaphor
  c. alliteration
  d. personification

40. The speaker uses repetition of the *s* sound in lines 4 ("His notice sudden is") and 6 ("A spotted shaft is seen") to
  a. create a soft, soothing sound.
  b. suggest that he has a stutter.
  c. suggest the slithering, hissing sound of a snake.
  d. create a tongue twister for the reader.

Composition

Write an instructional text explaining how to play your favorite game or sport. Use second-person point of view, and write to an audience of your peers. Jot down some prewriting notes to help you prepare a focused, well-organized essay. Remember to reread, edit, and revise your essay, too.

You might also choose to include a drawing of the playing field or equipment. If you prepare an illustration, be sure to include a title and labels.

_____

_____

_____

_____

_____

_____

_____

_____

_____

_____

_____

_____

_____

_____

_____

_____

_____

_____

_____

Answers

If you missed any of the questions, you can find help with that kind of question in the lesson(s) shown to the right of the answer.

QUESTION	ANSWER	LESSON	QUESTION	ANSWER	LESSON
1	a	18	21	c	15, 17
2	d	1, 9	22	c	13, 14
3	c	24, 25	23	b	3
4	c	3	24	b	1, 7
5	d	18	25	d	1, 4
6	c	6	26	b	1, 19
7	c	1, 4	27	c	17
8	d	1, 13	28	c	1, 4
9	c	4	29	d	10
10	b	14	30	a	2, 17
11	d	2	31	a	1, 13
12	a	7, 8, 9	32	b	15
13	d	1, 4	33	c	15
14	b	12	34	a	12, 17
15	a	15, 20	35	d	14
16	d	15	36	b	6
17	b	14, 15	37	b	7, 9, 12, 18
18	a	17, 20	38	d	13, 17
19	c	14, 17	39	a	15
20	c	3	40	c	15

Composition

Answers will vary, but your paragraph should be well organized and focused. It should describe the materials needed for the game, the object of the game, and details on how to play. Here is one possible response:

Capture the Flag

To play capture the flag, you will need two flags and several players. First, choose a playing field. This could be outdoors or indoors, in a small space or a large park. The playing field is divided into two halves, one for each team. Each team hides a flag somewhere on their side of the field. The object of the game is to run into the enemy's territory, find and take their flag, and then bring it back to your own side. If you are tagged in enemy territory, though, you'll have to be in "jail" until someone from your own team tags you to set you free. The game is tricky because each team assigns players to guard the flag, the center line, and the jail!

APPENDIX: SUGGESTED READING FOR 8TH GRADERS ▶

Thist book wouldn't be complete without a list of great books and magazines to read. Studying reading comprehension and answering reading test questions is fine, but the best way to improve your reading ability is *to read*. Read every day, even if you read only for 15 minutes. What follows is a list of books, arranged by category, and a list of magazines. Read what you like, and if you find a favorite subject or author, stick with it. You will be on your way to reading success!

Autobiography

Angelou, Maya, *I Know Why the Caged Bird Sings* (Bantam, 1983)

Frank, Anne, *Anne Frank: The Diary of a Young Girl* (New York: Bantam, 1993)

Fulghum, Robert, *All I Really Need to Know I Learned in Kindergarten* (New York: Ballantine, 2004)

Wright, Richard, *Black Boy* (Harper Perennial, 1998)

Fiction

Achebe, Chinua, *Things Fall Apart* (Anchor, 1994)

Block, Francesca Lia, *Violet and Claire* (HarperCollins, 1998)

Blume, Judy, *Here's to You, Rachel Robinson* (Laurel Leaf, 1995)

Blume, Judy, *Tiger Eyes* (Laurel Leaf, 1982)

Bunting, Eve, *A Sudden Silence* (Fawcett, 1991)

Brooks, Bruce, *The Moves Make the Man* (Harper Trophy, 1996)

Christie, Agatha, *Murder on the Orient Express* (Harper, 1991)

Cisneros, Sandra, *The House on Mango Street* (Vintage, 1991)

Cormier, Robert, *The Chocolate War* (Laurel Leaf, 1991)

Cormier, Robert, *We All Fall Down* (Laurel Leaf, 1993)

Duncan, Lois, *Don't Look Behind You* (Laurel Leaf, 1990)

Gaiman, Neil, *The Graveyard Book* (HarperCollins, 2008)

Guest, Judith, *Ordinary People* (Penguin, 1993)

Hinton, S. E., *The Outsiders* (Puffin, 1997)

Kadohata, Cynthia, *Kira-Kira* (Aladdin, 2006)

Kerr, M. E. *Gentlehands* (HarperTrophy, 1989, 1990)

L'Engle, Madeleine, *The Arm of the Starfish* (Laurel Leaf, 1980)

L'Engle, Madeleine, *A Wrinkle in Time* (Yearling, 1973)

London, Jack, *The Call of the Wild* (Tor, 1990)

Markandaya, Kamala, *Nectar in a Sieve* (Penguin, 1998)

Mazer, Norma, *After the Rain* (Flare, 1997)

Myers, Walter, *Hoops* (Laurel Leaf, 1983)

Nixon, Joan Lowery, *The Kidnapping of Christina Lattimore* (Laurel Leaf, 1992)

O'Neal, Zibby, *The Language of Goldfish* (Puffin, 1990)

Paterson, Katherine, *Jacob Have I Loved* (HarperTrophy, 1990)

Pike, Christopher, *Bury Me Deep* (Archway, 1991)

Saroyan, William, *The Human Comedy* (Dell, 1991)

Voight, Cynthia, *Runner* (Fawcett, 1986)

Zusak, Markus, *The Book Thief* (Knopf Books for Young Readers, 2006)

Zindel, Paul, *The Pigman* (Bantam Starfire, 1983)

Science Fiction/Fantasy

Adams, Douglas, *Life, the Universe and Everything* (Ballantine, 1995)

Asimov, Isaac, *Robot Dreams* (Ace, 1994)

Bradbury, Ray, *Fahrenheit 451* (Ballantine, 1995)

Keyes, Daniel, *Flowers for Algernon* (Skylark, 1984)

Le Guin, Ursula, *A Wizard of Earthsea* (Bantam Spectra, 1984)

Lewis, C. S., *The Lion, the Witch and the Wardrobe* (HarperCollins, 2000)

Lowry, Lois, *The Giver* (Houghton Mifflin 1993)

McCaffrey, Anne, *Dragonsong* (Bantam Spectra, 1977)

McKinley, *The Blue Sword* (Ace, 1991)

Orwell, George, *Animal Farm* (Signet, 1996)

Pascal, Francine, *Hanging Out with Cici* (Pocket, 1978)

Peck, Richard, *Remembering the Good Times* (Laurel Leaf, 1986)

Rowling, J. K., *Harry Potter* series (Thorndike, 2007)

Tolkien, J. R. R., *The Hobbit, Lord of the Rings* (Houghton Mifflin, 2002)

Verne, Jules, *Twenty Thousand Leagues Under the Sea* (Dodo, 2007)

Yep, Lawrence, *Child of the Owl* (HarperTrophy, 1990)

Nonfiction

Bridges, Ruby, *Through My Eyes* (Scholastic, 1999)

Burns, Loree Griffin, *Tracking Trash: Flotsam, Jetsam, and the Science of Ocean Motion* by (Houghton Mifflin, 2007)

Crowe, Chris, *Getting Away with Murder* (Dial, 2003)

Cummins, Julie, *Tomboy of the Air* (HarperCollins, 2001)

Davis, Sampson, Jenkins, George, Hunt, Ramack, and Sharon Draper, *We Beat the Street: How a Friendship Pact Led to Success* (Puffin, 2006)

Filipovic, Zlata, *Zlata's Diary: A Child's Life in Wartime Sarajevo* (Penguin, 2006)

Fleischman, John, *Phineas Gage: A Gruesome but True Story About Brain Science* (Sandpiper, 2004)

Friedel, David, and Linda Schele, *A Forest of Kings: The Untold Story of the Ancient Maya* (Harper Perennial, 1992)

Harding, Samuel B., *The Story of the Middle Ages* (Yesterday's Classics, 2006)

Hersey, John, *Hiroshima* (Vintage, 1989)

Heyerdahl, Thor, *Kon-Tiki: Across the Pacific in a Raft* (Pocket, 1990)

Hoose, Phillip, *The Race to Save the Lord God Bird* (Farrar, Straus, and Giroux, 2004)

Krakauer, Jon, *Into the Wild* (Villard, 1996)

Lansing, Alfred, *Endurance: Shackleton's Incredible Voyage* (Basic Books, 1999)

Lekuton, Joseph Lemasolai, and Herman Viola, *Facing the Lion: Growing Up Maasai on the African Savanna* (National Geographic Children's Books, 2005)

Levine, Ellen, *Darkness over Denmark: The Danish Resistance and the Rescue of the Jews* (Holiday House, 2002)

Ma, Adeline Yen, *Chinese Cinderella: The True Story of an Unwanted Daughter* (Laurel Leaf, 2001)

Nelson, Kadir, *We Are the Ship: The Story of the Negro Baseball League* (Hyperion, 2008)

Nelson, Pete, *Left for Dead: A Young Man's Search for Justice for the USS Indianapolis* (Delacorte Books for Young Readers, 2003)

Paulsen, Gary, *My Life in Dog Years* (Yearling, 1999)

Schlosser, Eric, *Chew On This: Everything You Don't Want to Know About Fast Food* (Sandpiper, 2007)

Stanley, Diane, *Michelangelo* (HarperCollins, 2003)

Sterling, Dorothy, *Freedom Train: The Story of Harriet Tubman* (Scholastic, 1987)

Thimmesh, Catherine, *Team Moon: How 400,000 People Landed Apollo 11 on the Moon* (Houghton Mifflin, 2006)

Utley, Robert, *The Lance and the Shield* (Ballantine, 1994)

Warren, Andrea, *Surviving Hitler: A Boy in the Nazi Death Camps* (HarperCollins, 2002)

Magazines

Boys' Life

This is a great general interest magazine for boys. Read about a wide variety of topics.

Creative Kids

Appropriately named, this magazine is meant to encourage your creativity.

Cricket

This is a general interest magazine with stories, recipes, science articles, and games.

Dig

Want to be an archaeologist? *Dig* is a perfect magazine for you. Mummies, dinosaurs, and ancient civilizations fill its pages.

Girls' Life

This magazine has plenty of advice, stories, celebrity interviews, and other topics of interest to girls.

National Geographic World

With great articles about wildlife and world cultures, this award-winning magazine is perfect for pleasure reading.

Sports Illustrated for Kids

Are you a sports fan? Check out this magazine and read all about your favorite teams, players, and sports events!

Scientific American

An in-depth magazine covering scientific developments, research, and literary science writing.

Teen Voices

A great magazine written by and for teen girls that focuses on real-life topics.

Time for Kids

From the editors of *Time* comes this current events magazine filled with great articles, photos, and maps.

Young Money

Show me the money! This magazine is a great introduction to saving, investing, and learning about the economy.

ADDITIONAL ONLINE PRACTICE ▶

Whether you need help building basic skills or preparing for an exam, visit the LearningExpress Practice Center! Using the code below, you'll be able to access additional online practice. This online practice will also provide you with:

Immediate Scoring
Detailed answer explanations
Personalized recommendations for further practice and study

Log in to the LearningExpress Practice Center by using the URL: **www.learnatest.com/practice**

This is your Access Code: **9483**

Follow the steps online to redeem your access code. After you've used your access code to register with the site, you will be prompted to create a username and password. For easy reference, record them here:

Username: _____ **Password:** _____

With your username and password, you can log in and access your additional practice materials. If you have any questions or problems, please contact LearningExpress customer service at 1-800-295-9556 ext. 2, or e-mail us at **customerservice@learningexpressllc.com**.